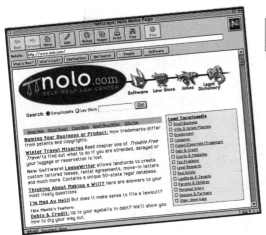

4TH EDITION

FOR SALE BY OWNER

IN CALIFORNIA

BY GEORGE DEVINE
CALIFORNIA REAL ESTATE BROKER

EDITED BY MARCIA STEWART & ROBIN LEONARD
ILLUSTRATED BY LINDA ALLISON

NOLO PRESS  BERKELEY

YOUR RESPONSIBILITY WHEN USING A SELF-HELP LAW BOOK

We've done our best to give you useful and accurate information in this book. But laws and procedures change frequently and are subject to differing interpretations. If you want legal advice backed by a guarantee, see a lawyer. If you use this book, it's your responsibility to make sure that the facts and general advice contained in it are applicable to your situation.

KEEPING UP TO DATE

To keep its books up to date, Nolo Press issues new printings and new editions periodically. New printings reflect minor legal changes and technical corrections. New editions contain major legal changes, major text additions or major reorganizations. To find out if a later printing or edition of any Nolo book is available, call Nolo Press at 510-549-1976 or check our Website at www.nolo.com.

To stay current, follow the "Update" service at our Website at www.nolo.com. In another effort to help you use Nolo's latest materials, we offer a 25% discount off the purchase of the new edition of your Nolo book when you turn in the cover of an earlier edition. (See the "Recycle Offer" in the back of the book.) This book was last revised in: APRIL 1999.

FOURTH EDITION	April 1999
EDITORS	Marcia Stewart & Robin Leonard
ILLUSTRATIONS	Linda Allison
BOOK AND COVER DESIGN	Stephanie Harolde & Toni Ihara
INDEX	Thérèse Shere
PRINTING	Custom Printing Company
PROOFREADING	Karyn S. DiCastri

Devine, George, 1941-
    For sale by owner in California / by George Devine. -- 4th ed.
       p. cm.
    Includes index.
    ISBN 0-87337-474-6
    1. House selling--California. 2. Real property--California.
  3. Real estate business--California. I. Title.
  HD266.C2D48   1998
  333.33'83'09794--dc21   98-17306
                                       CIP

For information on bulk purchases or corporate premium sales, please contact the Special Sales Department. For academic sales or textbook adoptions, ask for Academic Sales. Call 800-955-4775 or write to Nolo Press, Inc., 950 Parker Street, Berkeley, CA 94710.

ACKNOWLEDGEMENTS

This edition of *For Sale by Owner* resulted from the support of many readers who bought the various printings of the first three editions and from many friends and colleagues who offered valuable reactions and suggestions, especially Daniel F. McHugh, Esq., L. Ann Wieseltier, C.P.A., E.A., the staff of Old Republic Title Company in San Francisco, and the co-authors of Nolo's book *How to Buy a House in California*: real estate agent Ira Serkes and Nolo's editor-in-chief Ralph "Jake" Warner.

Many others at Nolo Press had a hand in the work, particularly Marcia Stewart and Robin Leonard in the subsequent editions and Mary Randolph, Jackie Mancuso, Carol Pladsen, Keija Kimura, Toni Ihara, Stephanie Harolde, Julie Christiansen and Steve Elias in the first edition..

On a regular basis, the project was kept going by the encouragement and empathy of my wife, Joanne; my son, George; and my daughter, Annemarie; in addition to my cat, appropriately named FSBO; her predecessors, Kitty and Morris; and my many good friends and colleagues at the University of San Francisco.

TABLE OF CONTENTS

Appendix

Index

INTRODUCTION

Who can sell your house in California? *You* can!

Without a real estate broker?

Sure. And you can save many thousands of dollars if you do. And even if you hire professional help, you can still save thousands by doing most of the work yourself.

Yes, there are a number of procedures to follow and rules to learn, but if you're already something of a "do-it-yourselfer," you won't find selling your own house difficult. Of course, any involved task involves locating and paying close attention to good, tight step-by-step instructions. That's where this book comes in.

We provide practical, easy-to-use forms and the legal, financial and real estate knowledge needed to sell your house yourself. The book covers the major steps involved in selling a single family residence in California, specifically:

- determining an advantageous time to sell
- meeting all legal and tax requirements of selling a house
- accurately pricing your house
- getting the word out that your house is for sale
- preparing your house for sale and making all necessary disclosures
- evaluating who can afford to buy your house
- negotiating offers and making counteroffers
- signing a legally valid sales contract
- completing the escrow process, which transfers title of the house and sales proceeds

- juggling the sale of one house and the purchase of another, if necessary
- evaluating creative financing options such as seller financing with a second mortgage note or a lease-option agreement.

Most people will have little problem handling the entire house sale transaction without a real estate agent—assuming you are willing to master a reasonable amount of detail. But deciding to sell on your own does not mean that you need to do everything yourself.

You may need or want a real estate agent's help for some tasks—such as advertising your house in the local Multiple Listing Service, reviewing the contract paperwork or helping you through the escrow process. Fortunately, you are not limited to hiring an agent at full commission—typically 6% of the selling price, or $12,000 on a $200,000 house. You can hire an agent by the hour or negotiate a lower commission for limited services.

The book is arranged in rough chronological order of subjects important to sellers—beginning with determining the best time to sell and ending with transferring title to your property. But, please read (or at least skim) the entire book before you begin the process of selling your house. The reason is simple: To successfully sell your own house, you have to master and apply, in logical order, a lot of information. But you also need a good overview of the whole process.

Note on selling a condominium or co-op. This book primarily covers selling single-family detached homes. If you want to sell a condominium or co-op unit, or if your house is part of a subdivision with a homeowners' association, special legal requirements apply. For example, condominium sellers must provide buyers with documents disclosing financial and organizational information about the condominium development. I alert you to these rules in the appropriate chapters and tell you when you may need some additional legal help.

ICONS USED IN THIS BOOK

The caution icon warns you of potential problems.

This icon refers you to helpful books or other resources for further information.

This icon lets you know of important time limits.

When you see this icon, you may be able to skip some material that isn't revelant to your situation.

This icon suggests that you may need the assistance of an attorney or other professional.

Chapter 1

WHEN IS THE BEST TIME TO SELL YOUR HOUSE?

Before running to put your house on the market, let me suggest that you take the time to research the pros and cons of selling your house right now. You may conclude that now isn't the right time and that you'd be better off delaying your house sale, at least for a little while. You will rarely hear a real estate agent say this, of course, because brokers earn their commissions only when a house changes hands. Just the same, if brokers spoke frankly, most would tell you that too many people sell their homes for too little money because they sell at the wrong time or are in too much of a hurry.

A. Plan the Timing of Your Sale

Put bluntly, there are times when it's unwise to put a house on the real estate market. Why? Because sometimes the market is flat and getting a fair price is extremely difficult. I've seen hundreds of houses sell for considerably less than they would have had they been sold a year or two earlier or later. Indeed, in recent years, with fast changes in interest rates and consumer confidence, a few months one way or the other can mean a difference of thousands of dollars in the price of a house.

My point is simple. When it comes to selling your house, you are in the driver's seat, if you really want to be. By planning properly, you can choose a good time to sell, set a fair price and wait until you get it. Unfortunately, the reverse is also true: If you don't take the time to really understand how the real estate market works, you can lose a bundle.

B. Why Sell Your House?

People have many reasons for wanting to sell their house:

Job change. You can't—or don't want to—commute to your new job from your old house.

Personal status or lifestyle change. You get married or divorced, move in with someone (or someone moves in with you), you have a new child, your daughter leaves for college, your spouse dies, your health argues against continuing to live in a house with stairs or in a city with very cold weather, or you've always wanted to try living in Hawaii.

Investment or lifestyle upgrade. You're selling your existing home to move up to a nicer one. Your old house isn't that bad, but now you can afford something you like more—because it's bigger, closer to work, in a better neighborhood or school district; has a pool; is a better investment; or provides something else that's important to you.

Financial needs. You can't afford the mortgage payments. This doesn't necessarily mean you're headed for foreclosure or bankruptcy, but it does mean that an unreasonable share of your income is going towards housing payments, and you have other priorities—like paying your other bills and having cash to spare, taking trips or helping your children go through college or buy homes of their own. You'd like to live in a place that costs you less per month, or where the cash you take out of selling a more expensive one can make a real difference in the quality of your life.

SHOULD YOU SELL NOW OR WAIT?

When to Sell Now	When to Wait
You need to sell your house for financial reasons—you can't afford the mortgage payments and hope to sell your house and move into a less expensive residence before an actual foreclosure.	You're financially strapped but your lender is willing to work out a reasonable payment schedule and you anticipate getting back on your feet soon.
You're buying a new house and can't afford to own two homes at once.	You're buying a new home and can arrange "bridge" financing that allows you to wait on selling your home until you get a good price. (See Section D2, below.)
The real estate market is about to peak in prices and you can make a larger profit by selling now than by waiting.	The market is sluggish but is likely to rebound with vigor in a year or two—for example, interest rates are going down or the neighborhood value is expected to increase with a new shopping center.
You must move as soon as possible—or example, your new job is too far to commute—and you are sure you won't return to the same location. Or an imperative health concern requires a move.	You don't have to move immediately, or you are not sure if a new location will work out, and the market favors buyers.

While some reasons are more urgent than others, many situations clearly fit into "the sale can wait if it needs to" category. This doesn't mean your family isn't cramped since the new baby was born or that it might be better for your health or pocketbook to move. But it does mean that selling your house next week, or even next month, isn't essential if by doing so you are not likely to get the best price. Also, remember that it's often unwise to make major moves or decisions within at least a year or so of a serious emotional shock—for example, a sudden death in the family, divorce or job loss—providing the move can possibly be avoided or deferred.

Another way to think about time pressure when it comes to selling a house is to follow one of the basic axioms of the real estate business: A seller who is under abnormal pressure to act almost always accepts too little. If all considerations are equal, here's some advice on whether to sell your house now or wait.

C. The Best and Worst Times to Sell a House

Below are several situations that can help you determine the best and worst times to sell your house. You may think most of this is obvious, but I urge you to slow down and think it through. Large numbers of otherwise intelligent people make serious errors when it comes to timing the sale of their houses.

1. When mortgage interest rates are low, the pool of potential buyers goes up. This is especially true because many people have been priced out of the market in the past because of high interest rates and have been anxiously awaiting their drop. Thus, even a relatively small decrease in interest rates may mean a huge increase in the number of people who qualify to buy your house. (See Chapter 8 for more on qualifying a buyer.)

2. When the economic climate of your region is healthy, a lot of people feel confident about the future and the pool of potential buyers widens. As we approach the 21st century, investment continues to be strong in California, particularly coming from Asia and the eastern United States. In a regional economic slump, on the other hand, it's often best to hold on to your home until conditions improve. Especially in California, no downturn ever seems to last very long.

3. At times when your area is considered especially attractive for any number of reasons, the pool of buyers widens and prices go up. If considerably more people are looking to buy than are looking to sell in a particular geographic area—for example, if a major local employer moves in—this is considered a "hot" or seller's market. Prices tend to rise (often quickly) and buyers must bid competitively. For example, San Diego was "discovered" in the early 1990s, and many people wanting to move to Los Angeles, but finding it too costly, have moved south to a less expensive area.

In contrast, a "cold" or buyer's market is one where prices are dropping; there are many houses for sale and few buyers. Sellers must frequently court buyers by lowering prices and offering innovative financing packages that often include the seller taking back a second mortgage. (See Chapter 8.) In a "lukewarm" housing market prices are relatively stable.

The popularity of geographic areas, cities and neighborhoods can change quickly for all sorts of reasons. For example, Sacramento and a number of other cities in California's Central Valley and foothills are far more popular now than they were just a few years ago, but less of a bargain—due to rising prices—than they once were. On the downside, the housing markets in Silicon Valley and in oil-producing areas such as Kern County have turned soft. And of course, significant changes in the desirability of particular areas can and do happen at the neighborhood level. Recently, for example, a number of older neighborhoods in cities, such as San Francisco, Los

Angeles, Berkeley, Stockton, Sacramento, San Diego, Oakland and San Jose have become very desirable, and home prices have increased, sometimes dramatically. This is especially true of single-family homes of wood-frame construction that are on rocky soil and have survived well in California's recent earthquakes. On the other hand, since the 1991 East Bay fire, buyers have been wary of homes in the Oakland and Berkeley hills unless they are sure reasonable fire safety measures have been taken.

My point is that you should do some strategic thinking of your own. There are many ways that your area might become more desirable: The large, loud and filthy refinery nearby is about to close; new restaurants and retailers are moving in; public transportation systems are improving dramatically. Check your local planning department for other upcoming changes. If you conclude that better times are just around the corner in your area or neighborhood, hold off your house sale if you can.

4. Certain times of the year are better than others. At the times of the year when most people are apt to make a move, prices usually increase, sometimes significantly. Two generalizations apply:

- Spring and summer are traditionally good times to sell. House prices usually jump in the spring, absent some major external factor such as a recession. Families with children are anxious to buy so they can move during summer vacation, before the new school year.

- From mid-November through mid-January, the market is slow and the pool of people wanting to move begins to shrink. Most people don't think about buying a house during the holiday season.

Remember that the trick to selling anything, from donuts to jewelry to a single-family house, is to market your property when most folks are apt to buy. There can easily be good reasons for anyone to pay top dollar for your house at any time of year, especially if economic conditions are favorable and interest rates are low.

WILL CALIFORNIA HOME PRICES CONTINUE TO RISE?

California has historically been a seller's market, due to a relatively strong economy, high immigration and slow-growth and environmental concerns that limit new house construction in many areas. In the short term, however, no one can guarantee that any particular area will be a seller's market. Local factors, such as the 1991 East Bay hills fire, the 1989 Loma Prieta earthquake, the 1994 Northridge earthquake and the continuing threat of drought can make California houses hard to sell in some communities. Also, in times when interest rates are relatively high, or just after house prices have already gone up extremely fast, a short-term buyer's market may exist. In the early part of the 21st century, this may continue to be the case in many developed coastal areas before another round of buyer pressure reverses it.

Even if house prices flatten or fall for a couple of years, they're likely to go back up. Here's why:

Population growth. California adds several hundred thousand people each year through a combination of reproduction and immigration, yet has restrictive land-use policies—for example, local slow-growth ordinances. As a result, a supply-demand imbalance will necessarily tend to increase some sale prices over the years.

Return on investment. Even allowing for "down times," single-family homes in California have given their long-term owners, on average, a return of about 10% a year on their equity over the last two decades. This is a strong incentive to invest in a home as compared with other potential uses of money.

Pent-up demand. As people continue to desire the benefits of home ownership, and to save their money, the time comes when they feel they can't wait any longer to make a home purchase, even if the house they buy is not as nice, as big or as well-situated as the eventual "home of their dreams." All it takes, usually, is one factor like a lowering of interest rates or a salary raise to translate intention into action.

Household formations. This is sociological jargon for the fact that the size of California families is projected to decline in the next two decades; there will be fewer people living under each roof, but more "household units" needed. More homes, especially smaller ones, (including condos and co-ops) will be required.

D. Selling One House and Buying Another

If you plan to sell your home and buy another, questions of timing inevitably arise. Is it better to sell your old house before buying a new one? Or should you focus primarily on buying, even if it means that you may have to sell your present house quickly to close on the new one?

➡ *If you're not buying another house, you can skip this section. Also, homeowners looking to sell who can afford to own two houses at once (even if for just a short period), don't need to worry about perfectly timing their purchase and sale transactions, and can go on to Section E.*

If you sell first, you'll be under time pressure to find another house quickly. This is stressful, and rarely results in your finding a truly good new house at a reasonable price. Even if you do find a great house, you're likely to overpay in an anxious effort not to lose out to another purchaser.

On the other hand, buying a new house first and then scrambling to sell your old one is no fun either—especially if you're trading up substantially and need to sell your old house for top dollar to make the down payment on the new one. Selling a house fast and getting the best possible price are normally mutually exclusive concepts. Too often, you're under time constraints to close on the new house, and will accept a lower than optimum price on your old house in order to make a quick sale.

Here are some constructive steps to minimize the psychological and financial downsides of selling one house while buying another.

1. Check the Housing Market Carefully

Before you put your house on the market or commit to buying a new one, carefully investigate the selling prices of houses in the areas where you'll be selling and buying. It's essential that you have a realistic idea of how much you'll get for your house, and how much you'll pay for the one you buy, as part of developing a strategy to sell high and buy low. (See Chapter 5 for more information on accurately pricing a house.)

If, after investigating prices, you decide to go ahead and buy a new house, you next must focus on whether the market is "hot" (favors sellers) or "cold" (favors buyers). Judging the relative temperature of the market is important to buyers and sellers, and is crucial for people who are both. Your dual position lets you adopt a strategy of protecting yourself in your weaker role while letting your stronger role take care of itself.

a. Strategies in a Seller's Market

If sellers have the advantage in the communities where you both now own and plan to buy, it follows that selling your current house will likely be easier than buying a new one. Thus, you want to compete aggressively in purchasing a new house, while insisting on maximum flexibility as to the date you move out of your present house.

You can guarantee yourself this leeway by stipulating that the sale of your current house be contingent upon your finding and closing on a new one. When a buyer makes an offer on your house, include a provision spelling this out in your written counteroffer. Although few buyers will agree to an open-ended period, some will be so anxious to buy your house that they'll agree to delay the closing until you close on a new house or until a certain number of days pass, whichever comes first. (See Chapters 9 and 10 for more on offers and counteroffers.)

b. Strategies in a Buyer's Market

In a buyer's market, where sellers outnumber buyers who can afford to purchase houses, you're in a stronger position as a buyer than as a seller. Consider protecting yourself by making your offer to buy a new house contingent upon your selling your current one. A seller having a hard time finding a buyer is likely to accept this contingency, even though it means waiting for you to find a buyer.

NOLO'S BOOK FOR HOME BUYERS

Nolo Press publishes *How to Buy a House in California,* by Ralph Warner, Ira Serkes and George Devine. That book contains practical, up-to-date information about the financial realities, legal rules and real estate customs of buying a house in California. It covers homebuying from start to finish, including defining your home needs and budget, finding a house, working with a real estate agent, arranging financing, making an offer, negotiating, going through escrow and dealing with potential problems. Sample contracts for all aspects of homebuying are included.

How to Buy a House in California is available in most bookstores. Or, to order it directly from Nolo Press with a credit card, call 510-549-1976 or 800-992-6656 (outside the 510 area code) or visit Nolo's website at www.nolo.com. To order by check, see the order form at the back of this book.

2. Bridge Financing: How to Own Two Houses Briefly

Unfortunately, no matter how carefully you time things, you may not perfectly dovetail the sale of one house with the purchase of another. You may own no houses, in which case you'll have money in the bank and will need a temporary place to live, or you may own two houses at once. The following suggestions should help you pull this off:

Raise as much money as possible to put toward the down payment on a new house. Most people have some money saved to combine with the profit from the sale of an existing house to make the down payment on the new one. If your savings, without the sale, put the second house within reach, maximize your cash by charging living expenses, getting an advance from your employer or selling personal possessions you no longer need. Although the interest on credit cards is high, you'll be able to pay bills off promptly when your existing house sells. If you raise a good amount of money this way, consider combining it with the next option.

Borrow down payment money from family or friends.
Point out that you need help for only a short period
and offer a competitive interest rate. Keep in mind
that it's easier to borrow short-term money than to
borrow a large sum for 20 or 30 years. If, for example, your parents have money put aside for
retirement or your sister is saving to take a year off
from work, either may be willing to tap savings to
help you for the short time it will take to buy one
house and sell another.

If you follow this approach, give the lender a
promissory note, secured by a second mortgage
(deed of trust) on your new house. This arrangement
can often mean no monthly payments are due until
your first house sells and thus no negative effect on
your debt-to-income ratio. (See Chapter 8, Section D,
for more on second mortgages.)

Get a bridge loan from a financial institution. If you
have no other choice, you can normally borrow
money from a financial institution to "bridge" the
period between when you close on your new house
and when you get your money from the sale of your
old one. This simply amounts to getting a short-term
home equity loan on your existing house, using it
toward the down payment and closing costs on your
new house and repaying it when your first house
sells.

We say "no other choice" because bridge loans
can be very expensive. Interest rates are generally a
couple of percentage points above the prime rate,
and the loan lasts only a month or so. Lenders often
charge a host of up-front points or fees for credit
checks, appraisals, loan originations and physical
inspections. These charges can total up to 5% to 15%
of the amount borrowed. On $50,000, that's $2,500
to $7,500. This wouldn't be unreasonable if you
needed the money for a long time and spread the
cost over many years. It's very expensive, however, if
you need money for only a few months.

E. Benefits of Timing Your House Sale

Here are a few examples of how timing the sale of
your house can increase or decrease your profit.

1. Jon and Penny Timed a Job-Related Sale to Their Benefit

Jon was transferred by his company to Eureka in the
middle of November. His new job was a thousand
miles away from his current job in San Diego. Jon
and his wife Penny realized that houses often sell for
less in the winter and thought that because the
economy was stagnant, interest rates were likely to
fall in the spring. They guessed that their house
might go for $15,000 to $20,000 more in May or
June and they also didn't want their kids' schooling
interrupted. Accordingly, Jon and Penny decided to
try to put off the sale as long as possible. Fortunately,
when Jon explained the problem, his employer was
willing to help, including putting him up in a com-
pany-owned condominium in Eureka for very reasonable rent, and agreeing to pay for his airfare to
visit his family in San Diego on alternate weekends.
This not only allowed Jon and Penny time to pick out
a home in Eureka, but also let them wait until March
to put their existing home on the market. When their
house sold in April, with a June closing, Jon and
Penny got a very good price. Although not everyone
has an employer as cooperative as Jon's, your boss
may be willing to help take some pressure off you.

WHAT TO LOOK FOR WHEN SHOPPING FOR A BRIDGE LOAN

- The lender from whom you obtain your financing for your new house may offer you a less expensive home equity bridge loan than other lenders. Ask about this possibility before committing to a long-term mortgage.

- When applying for a bridge loan, ask the lender to waive inspection and appraisal of your existing house and to not charge points. If the equity in your existing house is much larger than the bridge you need, the lender may be willing.

- If you purchased or refinanced your existing house only a few years ago, find your paperwork. Some lenders will accept a recent appraisal, physical inspection or title report in lieu of charging you for new ones. Many, though, consider the information out-of-date if it's more than six months old.

- If you don't know whether you'll need a home equity bridge loan until the last minute, see if you qualify for a stand-by personal line of credit. Although interest rates are higher than on a bridge loan (and interest paid is non-deductible), up-front costs are minimal.

- Consider working with an experienced loan broker—a person who specializes in matching house buyers and appropriate mortgage lenders. If your situation is complex, be ready to pay for the service.

2. Ann Minimized the Financial Trauma of Sudden Widowhood

Ann was widowed suddenly. Her first impulse was to sell the home she and her husband had lived in for many years. "I had to get away from the memories," she said. Ann talked to a good personal counselor and learned that it is usually a mistake to make a major decision like the sale of a house within so short a time of such a shock. Her counselor even showed her one of several studies indicating that human beings' decision making abilities seem to be short-circuited by grief and shock for at least a year—often two. Nonetheless, Ann felt that living in her house was too much to bear. After checking with her tax advisor concerning the timing of her transaction, Ann rented her home to a friend's son and lived elsewhere for several months. Then, when she was ready to cope with business details, she sold the house and got at least $20,000 more than she would have had she sold immediately after her husband's death.

3. Fred Saved $50,000 by Waiting Patiently

When Fred purchased a larger house and sold his old one, he realized immediately that he wasn't under time pressure to sell. Accordingly, the first thing he did was work out his finances so that he had enough money to close on the new house without selling the old one immediately. This involved arranging a short-term loan from a friend. When Fred did find the house he wanted to buy, it was priced fairly, but at least $30,000 more than he could afford.

When Fred got friendly with the seller, he learned that she was extremely anxious to sell quickly so as to avoid losing a deal to purchase her custom-built dream house. As it was just after Christmas and houses weren't selling, Fred decided to make what he thought was a ridiculously low offer. As soon as the seller saw that he had the money and that his offer was not contingent on selling another house, she accepted. Fred held on to his old house for three months and priced it $15,000 more than was suggested to him, which was at least $20,000 over the current market. He figured that since he wasn't in a hurry, why not test the market for a while and hope that a little spring sunshine would cause a general price increase? The happy result was that Fred's house sold for his asking price at his first open house.

In short, by planning ahead, Fred estimated that he made about $50,000 more than he would have had he not used timing to his advantage.

4. Paul's Impatience Cost Him Thousands of Dollars

Paul wanted to move to a bigger, more expensive house. He had a nonassumable loan at a low interest rate on his existing house. Unfortunately at the time Paul wanted to move, interest rates were exceedingly high. This meant relatively few people could afford to buy his home, even though it was a desirable one. Paul couldn't afford to lend the money to a buyer through a second mortgage, because he needed as much cash as possible in order to buy the new house. Although Paul was warned to be cautious, he was impatient and committed himself to buying the new house, putting down a substantial nonrefundable deposit. When his existing house wouldn't sell at a decent price, Paul became desperate. He sold his house to a buyer who could pay cash even though the offer was for 15% less than a conservative appraiser had told Paul the property was worth. If Paul had continued to live in his house until the market improved, he could surely have sold for at least $10,000 more. ■

Chapter 2

LEGAL REQUIREMENTS OF SELLING YOUR OWN HOUSE

You can legally sell your own California house without a real estate broker or attorney. As long as you and all other owners are at least 18 years old and sane, you can do it yourself. You must, however, be aware of the legal rules that govern real estate transfers in California, such as who must sign the papers, who can conduct the actual sale transaction and what to do if and when encumbrances arise which slow down the transfer of ownership. This chapter covers these legal requirements—most importantly, California's community property and joint ownership laws. Chapter 7 covers the seller's responsibilities to disclose all material facts about the property. Chapter 11 covers the specific legal tasks involved in closing escrow or transferring ownership.

A. Property Sales Rules

Title, documented legal ownership, is shown by a deed recorded at the County Recorder's Office.

Most people who own and sell real estate in California hold title to their house in one of the following ways:

- as a single man or single woman
- as a married couple or as community property
- as joint tenants or tenants in common.

This section explains how to transfer property for these types of legal ownership. It also describes a few circumstances—specifically partnerships, conservators, guardians and trustees—which are complicated enough to require expert help.

1. Single Homeowners

If you are unmarried and have sole title to your home—that is, the deed to the property is in your name alone—with no joint tenants, co-tenants or partners, you can sell the house yourself.

2. Married Homeowners: Community Property Rules

If you are married, you must usually have the consent of your spouse to sell your home—even if you are no longer living with your spouse, but have not yet divorced. Under California's community property laws, both spouses usually have an ownership interest in a house and therefore both must consent in writing to any sale. (Family Code § 1102.)

Community property ownership of real property is often reflected on the deed by the words "as community property" after the names of the owners. Sometimes, however, spouses take title together as "tenants in common" or "joint tenants" (see Section 3), and occasionally title to real property owned by a married couple is in one spouse's name alone. No matter what the deed says, the real property of the great majority of married couples is a community property asset. Except in unusual situations, if income earned during marriage pays for part of the down payment, the mortgage, insurance, taxes or home improvements, at least a portion of the house is community property. Deciding whether real property is separate or community can be tricky, however. A house which starts out as separate property may easily become a mix of separate and community.

Of course, there are married homeowners who own their home as their separate property. You may have owned the house prior to a marriage or received it by gift or inheritance during the marriage, and have used no community property money to pay for property taxes, insurance, mortgage payments or improvements.

Nevertheless, escrow companies and financial institutions always require the signatures of both spouses when a house is sold by a married couple. They do it to protect themselves, as they can't verify a sole ownership status short of having the seller obtain a court order establishing it. A non-owner spouse may give consent to the sale by signing a sales contract, escrow instructions or a quitclaim deed that gives complete ownership to the other spouse. (Sales contracts and escrow are covered in Chapters 9 and 11.)

Using a Quitclaim Deed

A quitclaim deed is appropriate when the non-owner spouse wants to remove himself or herself from the sales transaction completely.

The person who signs a quitclaim deed releases all claims to ownership, as of the date the deed is issued. It says, in effect, "I'm not saying for sure that I have any claim on the property, but whatever claim I do have I will now quit!"

Example: *Sue and Peter were recently married and plan to move into a new house. They first need to sell Peter's house, which he owns outright as part of a divorce settlement from his previous marriage. Sue executes and records a quitclaim deed, giving Peter any interest she might have in the house. When that's done, the public record will show escrow companies, title insurance companies, financial institutions and potential buyers that Sue has no interest in the house.*

See The Deeds Book, *by Mary Randolph (Nolo Press) for more information on deeds, as well as tax and planning aspects of property transfers.*

A sample completed quitclaim deed is below; a blank form is in the Appendix.

Recording requested by

    Peter Hammond
    3942 Wale Lane
    Rosamond, CA 98309

and when recorded mail this deed
and tax statements to:

    same as above

For recorder's use

QUITCLAIM DEED

☐ This transfer is exempt from the documentary transfer tax.

☒ The documentary transfer tax is $ _330_ and is computed on

    ☐ the full value of the interest or property conveyed.

    ☒ the full value less the value of liens or encumbrances remaining thereon at the time of sale.

The property is located in ☐ an unincorporated area.

                          ☒ the city of _Rosamond, CA_ .

For a valuable consideration, receipt of which is hereby acknowledged,

    Susan Hammond

hereby quitclaim(s) to

    Peter Hammond

the following real property in the City of _____ Rosamond _____ ,
County of ___ Kern _____ , California:

    Lot 357 as shown on the map entitled "Map of Green Acres Subdivision No.
    2, Kern County, California," recorded January 15, 1976, in Volume 3 of
    Maps, at page 89, Kern County Records.

Date: _March 1, 1999_   ___Susan Hammond_____

                                       _____

                                       _____

                                       _____

State of California

County of Kern   } ss.

On _March 4, 1999_ , _Susan Hammond_____ , known to me or proved by satisfactory evidence
to be the person(s) whose name(s) is/are subscribed above, personally appeared before me, a Notary
Public for California, and acknowledged that __she__ executed this deed.

    [SEAL]   *Sandra Barker*

                                      Signature of Notary

As shown on the sample quitclaim deed above, the owner spouse's name and address go in the upper left hand corner. Then you must indicate the documentary transfer tax, a tax you must pay for transferring real estate. The rate varies by locality, but $1.10 per $1,000 is the lowest. The tax is based on the value of the property less any debts against the property. When no money changes hands (as would be the case when a non-owner spouse signs a quitclaim deed to make selling the house easier for his spouse), the county may not charge the tax. Your local title company or county tax assessor's office can give you information on this.

The deed must include a legal description of the property. This can be copied from your original deed or obtained from a friendly title company hoping to get escrow business from you.

Finally, the non-owner spouse must sign the deed before a notary public.

 What if your spouse won't consent to your plan to sell the house? See a lawyer; this book won't help you until that problem is resolved.

3. Joint Tenants and Tenants in Common

In addition to the community property of married couples, there are two other common ways by which joint owners of real estate—whether married or unmarried—can hold title. These are joint tenancy and tenancy in common.

Joint tenancy. If you take title to real property as joint tenants, all owners share property ownership equally (two owners each own 50%; three owners all own 33⅓%; four owners all own 25%, and so on), with a right of survivorship. When one joint tenant

dies, her share automatically goes to the surviving title holder(s).

Tenancy in common. If you take title as tenants in common, the owners have equal or unequal undivided interests in property, without the right of survivorship. When one tenant in common dies, the other(s) do(es) not automatically own her share; the share of the deceased person passes to the person named in her will or living trust, or by intestate succession (the laws that govern who gets your property if you die and fail to specify).

For the purpose of selling property, it doesn't make much difference whether title to a house is held by joint tenants or tenants in common. If you want to sell jointly owned property, you need the signatures of all joint owners and any spouses. If one or more owners won't sign, you are limited to selling your share only, not the whole property. The mechanics of selling only a portion of a home depend on how the property is owned, and are always more complicated than selling the entire property. The details are not covered in this book.

4. Partnership

A partnership is a business owned by two or more people. There are two basic kinds of partnerships. The first, a general partnership, is a legal agreement by which all partners participate in the business and have equal and full liability for the partnership's debts. The second, a limited partnership, is primarily an investment device, with at least one general or managing partner with unlimited liability for debts and one or more limited partners who act as passive investors. Limited partners are not liable for partnership debts in excess of the amount they have invested in the partnership.

Partnerships, whether limited or general, normally are ruled by statutory law and written partnership agreements. Many partnership agreements require that detailed procedures be followed before real estate is sold. For example, many agreements specify a date or a number of years following the purchase in which the sale will take place. Furthermore, the agreement is likely to give any non-selling partner(s) the first right to purchase the share of the departing partner, at an agreed-upon price or at its currently appraised value.

Because of the many possible partnership agreement provisions that can affect the sale of real property, I do not specifically attempt to show you how to sell partnership property. The practical steps of marketing a piece of real estate outlined in this book, however, are the same whether or not the property is owned by a partnership. They work well for people owning property in general partnerships as long as all partners agree to sell to a third party. The advice also holds well for limited partnerships, assuming the managing partner has the authority to sell the property.

For more information on partnership law and written partnership agreements, see The Partnership Book, *by Denis Clifford and Ralph Warner (Nolo Press).*

5. Conservators, Guardians and Trustees

If you're a conservator, guardian or trustee for somebody who can't act for himself because he is insane, legally incompetent or a minor, or if you are an executor of an estate of someone who is deceased, you must strictly follow specific provisions of California law before selling real estate. I do not cover sales by people in these groups.

For details on conservatorships and guardianships, see The Conservatorship Book, *by Lisa Goldoftas and Carolyn Farren, and* The Guardianship Book, *by Lisa Goldoftas and David Brown. For information on executing the estate of someone who has died, see* How to Probate an Estate, *by Julia Nissley. All three books are published by Nolo Press.*

B. Encumbrances That May Impede Sale of Your House

Generally speaking, an encumbrance is something that slows down or impedes motion. Since we say, in a real estate transaction, that title to a house passes or moves from one party to another, an encumbrance on title is anything that slows down, impedes or blocks this passage or movement. For example, if you still owe on your mortgage, your home is encumbered for the amount outstanding. Similarly, if someone has sued you, obtained a judgment against you and properly recorded a judgment lien in the county where your property is located, title to that property is encumbered by the lien.

1. Deeds of Trust and Other Monetary Encumbrances

Most people owe money on their houses in the form of a mortgage or deed of trust. There is no problem dealing with this type of encumbrance as long as the sales price is more than enough to cover the total amount owed—or you come up with the difference from another source.

If you are selling your home to try to avoid foreclosure, a short sale may be your only option. For more information, see Stop Foreclosure Now in California, *by Lloyd Segal (Nolo Press). You might owe taxes on the difference, however, so be sure to discuss this with your tax advisor in advance. And even if the offer price you get is less than you owe on your mortgage, your lender may allow a short sale—that is, let the sale proceed for the amount of the offer and waive the difference. You'll also have to pay off any second mortgage or home equity loan or line of credit.*

Other monetary encumbrances include:

Property taxes and unpaid special assessment district bond liens (for locally elected expenditures like an airport, school or air-pollution control district).

Liens filed by home contractors (called mechanic's liens). California law allows any licensed contractor who furnishes labor or materials to your home to record (at the county recorder's office) a mechanic's lien against your property if you do not pay.

Income taxes. If you've failed to pay federal or state income taxes, the IRS or Franchise Tax Board may record a Notice of Tax Lien with the county recorder's office.

Judgment liens. If you are sued, and the other party obtains a money judgment against you, she may record a judgment lien against the title to your property. Even prior to judgment in a lawsuit, a lien may be placed against your real property by means of a writ of attachment. This document makes your property security for an eventual judgment lien that will be placed on your property if you lose the lawsuit. A judgment lien is, technically, a general lien against all your property in any county in California in which it is recorded; an attachment makes a specific piece of property security for such a lien. Sometimes a notice of a pending lawsuit (*lis pendens*) is filed against the record of a particular piece of property. Generally speaking, property with *lis pendens* on it cannot be sold, unless the court agrees to lift the *lis pendens*—which it may do if the seller posts a bond sufficient to ensure eventual payment of any judgment. If a *lis pendens* notice has been filed against your property, you will need to consult an attorney before selling.

In general, monetary encumbrances are paid off out of the sales proceeds of your home. Alternatively, the buyer may be willing to take them over, as long as you reduce the purchase price accordingly. Either arrangement can be made by the escrow company.

2. Non-Monetary Encumbrances

Non-monetary encumbrances are often far more troublesome if they severely restrict the use of the property, and may even require an attorney's assistance to resolve. Here are some of the more common non-monetary encumbrances:

Easement. An easement is the legal right of one person to use part of another person's property for a particular purpose—for example, a neighbor who uses a path on your property to gain access to his property. If your neighbor uses your property for five consecutive years or more without your permission, and you haven't tried to stop him during this period, he may have gained a right to keep using your property. To be legally certain, an easement must be recorded in public records or be obvious upon inspection. Easements are part and parcel of the land they affect and remain when the property changes hands.

Adverse possession. We used to refer to this as squatters' rights. To oversimplify, if someone occupies your property (lives there, collects rent on it, fences or posts it, or the like) without your permission for five consecutive years, in a reasonably obvious fashion, and pays property taxes on it for each of the five years, he owns it. As you might guess, this seldom happens these days.

Encroachment. This occurs when someone builds on your property, that is, crosses your property line.

Trespass. This does not constitute an encumbrance. I mention it here because if left unchallenged for long enough, a trespasser who makes unauthorized use of your property can occupy it and claim some form of easement or legal ownership, depending on the circumstances.

For a detailed discussion of easements and trespassing, see Neighbor Law, *by Cora Jordan (Nolo Press).*

How can you be sure that no encumbrances on your property exist other than the ones you know about? As part of the escrow process (see Chapter 11), a title company will do this for you. If you're unsure how you have title to your house, whether or not all your taxes are paid or if anyone has sued you, you can check for encumbrances yourself.

Start by looking at your deed. If you don't have a copy, go to the recorder's office in the county where your property is located. You can find this office by looking in the County Government section of your phone book. At the recorder's office, look up your name in the "Grantee Index," which will lead you to the recorded deed that originally transferred title to you. In addition, the public record for your property will indicate:

- whether any judgment liens, mechanic's liens, tax liens or other liens have been posted against your property

- how you hold title—whether in your name alone, as a tenant in common, joint tenant, or whatever.

Next, look up your name again in the "Trustor" or "Mortgagor" index. Here you will find a record of any mortgage or trust deed liens against the title to your property. If you wish, you can request a copy (at a nominal fee) of any of these recorded documents.

For more information about checking and interpreting escrow records, see the excellent book All About Escrow, *by Sandy Gadow (Escrow Publishers).*

C. Dealing With Brokers and Other Third Parties

The fact that you decide to sell your own house doesn't mean that you should never deal with a real estate broker. Chapter 4 explains several approaches to getting professional help at a very reasonable cost, far less than the usual 5%–8% real estate commission you are undoubtedly trying to avoid. Some of these approaches are so cost-effective that you may decide to combine doing a lot of your own work with paying for some professional help. For this reason, let's briefly examine California laws as to who can and cannot sell your house for you.

Basically, you don't need a real estate license to sell your own real property, or to buy real property for yourself. With a few exceptions, however, state law requires that anyone who acts as your agent or broker when you buy or sell real property in California must have an active real estate broker's license or a salesperson's license placed under the license of an active supervising broker.

If you pay someone who does not have a real estate license or does not conform to one of the legal exceptions described below to act for you as a real estate agent, you can be fined up to $100. Your non-licensed agent can be fined up to $10,000 and

sentenced to six months in county jail if prosecuted and convicted of violating this law. (Business and Professions Code §§ 10138, 10139.) Who would be likely to discover such an illegal arrangement and turn you over to the district attorney? Most likely, a distressed real estate agent who spots an unlicensed "agent" cutting into her licensed activities. Since there are so many people licensed to sell real estate in California (one to every 40 adults or so), it's best to assume that many such vigilant individuals exist and are ready to holler.

1. Power of Attorney

One exception to the brokerage license requirement involves people who have been entrusted with a power of attorney to carry out a particular real estate transaction by the owner(s), and who receive no compensation for doing so. You can legally give a trusted friend or relative a power of attorney to sign papers or otherwise act on your behalf to sell a house for a variety of reasons. For example, if you are unexpectedly called out of town on business when your sale is about to close, you can give your mate a power of attorney to sign documents on your behalf. In addition, when someone handles a house sale for

an ill family member or friend, she often uses a power of attorney.

Perhaps you and your sister want to sell the home of your ill father. Assuming Dad really does want assistance with the transaction and is willing to entrust the details to you, he should sign a durable power of attorney authorizing you to sell his home for him. Once a power of attorney is signed, you should be able to sell the house yourself without problems.

The real estate license requirement is also considered unnecessary or waived in the following exceptional situations. It's unlikely any of these will affect you, but in the interest of thoroughness, keep reading.

2. Attorney at Law Acting As Such

A member of the State Bar of California who does not have a real estate license may legally act as a real estate agent in a transaction, although she must charge a fee, not a commission. Because the lines of demarcation in the long-standing turf battle between the real estate industry and the legal profession are blurred, however, many attorneys who regularly handle real estate transactions get a broker's license, and members of the bar are allowed to sit for the broker's license exam without completing the usual statutory educational requirements.

3. Court Order

If the court orders you to act for another in a real estate matter, that's all the license you need, period. An example is a person named as conservator for an incompetent. Again, unless you're fairly experienced in this area, you will probably need the help of an attorney.

4. Power of Sale Under a Trust Deed

The trustee—not the borrower or lender, but a third party stakeholder under a trust deed provision in a real estate loan—may sell the property which equitably belongs to the borrower, not the trustee, without a real estate license if the borrower defaults. Individuals (as distinct from corporations) seldom are named as trustees. Again, see a lawyer if this affects you.

D. Legal Prohibitions When Selling Your Own House

When selling your own property, be aware of several legal prohibitions. Among the things you can't do are:

- State or imply that you have a real estate license or a membership or affiliation with a real estate firm. When you put up your property for sale, don't call yourself a real estate agent if you're not. Frankly, you have no incentive to do this anyway. If you're a private party selling your own property, advertising that fact makes your home more, not less, attractive for most prospective purchasers.

- Engage in any practice which violates state, federal or local laws prohibiting discrimination in the sale or rental of real property. It is illegal to conduct a discriminatory advertising campaign (see Chapter 6, Section A3) or to refuse to sell or rent to someone on the basis of a group characteristic such as race, ethnic background, religion, sex, marital status, age, family status or disability.

- Engage in certain real estate paper transactions. If you're selling or buying trust deeds or mortgage notes on a regular basis, your activities are limited by law. Such actions are far beyond the scope of this book; if you wish to deal with real estate paper as a business, consult an attorney. Good books on this subject are Real Estate Law and the Reference Book issued by the California Department of Real Estate (P.O. Box 187006, Sacramento, CA 95818-7006; 916-227-0945). ■

Chapter 3

TAX CONSIDERATIONS WHEN SELLING A HOUSE

Y ou need to be aware of important tax considerations when you sell your house. Here is a summary of the basics for both federal and California taxes.

![warning icon] *Before reading this chapter, pay particular attention to this warning. The narratives and illustrations given here are intended to cover most taxpaying homeowners, based on the most current tax advice available. No single part of this book, however, requires more frequent revision and invites more reader questions than the information on taxes. To be sure that what you read here is still correct and applies to your situation, consult a tax attorney or accountant. Also, see "More Information: Tax Rules and Publications," below.*

MORE INFORMATION: TAX RULES AND PUBLICATIONS

This chapter provides an overview of the tax consequences of selling your home. The best way to prepare for the real thing is to read the appropriate IRS publications:

- Publication 523, *Selling Your Home*, and
- Publication 521, *Moving Expenses*.

You should also study the form and instructions for IRS Schedule D, for the reporting of capital gain.

IRS forms and publications are available free-of-charge by calling 800-829-1040 or by checking the IRS Website at www.irs.ustreas.gov.

In addition, be sure to review corresponding California rules and procedures, which essentially follow those of the IRS. Contact the Franchise Tax Board at 800-338-0505 or check their Website at www.ftb.ca.gov.

You should consult your tax specialist as to how real estate tax regulations apply in your specific case, especially if you are taking depreciation deductions for a home office or if you are expecting huge gains from selling your home (more than can be excluded from tax under the law).

A. Calculate Your Gain

Your principal residence is a capital asset. If you sell your home at a profit, you will be taxed on the gain that exceeds $250,000 (single person) or $500,000 (married couple). If any portion of your home is used for a trade or business, that portion of the profit will be subject to capital gains, regardless of the amount.

If you sell your home for less than you paid for it, you will have a capital loss. You will receive no tax benefit from that loss—unless part of the property is used for a trade or business (in which case, you should consult your accountant).

Most likely, you will be selling your home at a gain. If your profit is below the $250,000 (single) or $500,000 (married couple) amounts and you meet specified requirements (discussed below), you are exempt from reporting your home sale to the IRS. If your profit exceeds these amounts, you are required to report the sale, using IRS Schedule D, the tax form which records sales of capital assets of all kinds.

To anticipate how much of your house sale profits will be taxable after you've taken all the deductions allowed by the IRS, you will need to calculate four items:

1. Adjusted Cost Basis
2. Amount Realized from the Sale
3. Gain or Profit
4. Taxable Gain

This section shows you how to calculate these four items.

1. Figure Your Adjusted Cost Basis

To figure your profit (gain) made on the sale of your house, start with how much you paid for it. That figure is called the cost basis.

You arrive at the adjusted cost basis by adding the cost of any capital improvements, and unamortized loan points and loan costs from the house purchase or refinance, to the cost basis. At the risk of oversimplifying slightly, capital improvements are additions to your property that increase its value, that you cannot remove and that have a useful life of more than one year. For example, a swimming pool, carport or new kitchen is a capital improvement. Less obvious examples include upgrades to components of the property, such as replacing galvanized pipe with copper, putting in new insulation or installing circuit breakers to replace a fuse box.

These costs are not fix-up or repair costs, such as painting or fixing a broken pipe. You will need to go through your files to find receipts to document the improvements made to your house.

Here is a quick checklist of common improvements:

- adding walks, sewer lines, septic tanks, lamp posts, retaining walls, fences, gates
- aluminum siding
- appliances, such as washer and dryer, dishwasher, garbage disposal, refrigerator
- built-in furniture or bookcase
- carpeting, linoleum or other flooring
- constructing or improving driveways, gutters, drain pipes, dry walls
- landscaping
- new furnace, heating system, air conditioning, plumbing
- new shower, bathtub
- permanent storm windows, storm doors
- replacing a roof
- restoring a run-down house
- room addition, including patio, deck, porch, garage
- swimming pool, tennis court, sauna, hot tub.

Example: *Joe and Trudy purchased a house in 1973 for $171,000 and added a new bathroom at the cost of $9,000 in 1986. Their adjusted cost basis is $180,000.*

Original purchase price	*$171,000*
Capital improvements	*+ 9,000*
Adjusted cost basis	*$180,000*

Sometimes it's hard to decide whether a particular expenditure qualifies as a capital improvement. In doubtful cases, check with a tax expert or the Taxpayer Assistance Service of the IRS. Or, if you're in the do-it-yourself spirit, consult the *U.S. Master Tax Guide* published by Commerce Clearing House (Chicago, Ill.), available in most libraries.

The basis also adjusts automatically under certain laws. For example, when one spouse dies and leaves a community property house to the other, the basis for federal tax purposes of the entire property (the one-half community property shares of both the deceased and surviving spouse) is increased from the original purchase price to its fair market value as of the date of the deceased spouse's death.

2. Figure the Amount Realized

The second step in figuring out the tax you owe is to figure the amount realized from the sale. The amount realized is the sales price minus selling expenses.

Selling expenses include broker's and attorney's fees and transfer taxes.

To continue our example, let's say Joe and Trudy sell their house for $479,000 and have costs of sale of $227. Their amount realized is $478,773.

Selling price of house	*$479,000*
Documentary transfer tax	*– 197*
Document fees	*– 30*
Amount realized	*$478,773*

3. Figure the Gain

To calculate the profit on the sale of their house, Joe and Trudy must subtract the adjusted cost basis (Section A1, above) from the amount realized (Section A2, above).

Amount realized	$478,773
Adjusted cost basis	− 180,000
Gain	$298,773

4. Calculate Taxable Gain

Once you figure out the gain, or your profit on the sale of your home, you need to determine how much of this is taxable. Calculate taxable gain by subtracting all applicable capital gain exclusions. As a result of the Taxpayer Relief Act of 1997, you can exclude up to $250,000 of capital gain on the sale of your home, tax-free, as an individual, and twice that amount (yes, half a million dollars) if you are filing jointly as a married couple. This exclusion applies regardless of your age and regardless of whether you (or your spouse or even your spouse's former spouse) have ever used this exemption before. This is a substantial liberalization and simplification of federal income tax laws.

To claim the whole capital gain exclusion, certain tests apply, notably: You must have owned and used your home as your principal residence for a total of at least two of the five years prior to the sale of the home.

You can use this exemption an unlimited number of times, but no more than once every two years.

Assuming Joe and Trudy (example above) met these tests, their entire gain of $298,773 would be tax deductible, since it is less than the $500,000 allowed for a married couple.

Do the ages of the homesellers make a difference? Under the new tax laws, no. And if you realize a capital gain greater than the exempt amount of $500,000 for a married couple, can you roll it over into the purchase of a new primary residence? Again, the answer is no under the new tax rules. But for most homeowners, changes in the new tax law are positive, rather than negative.

B. Time Your Sale

You must report your taxable capital gain, if any, in the tax year in which the escrow closes and you get your money from the house sale. Unless you've filed with the IRS to use a different fiscal year, the tax year begins January 1 and ends December 31. If you expect to owe a lot in taxes, you may be looking for ways to reduce your capital gain and cut your tax bill. One option is to choose the most financially advantageous date for the close of your home sale.

For some sellers, it may be possible to arrange for your sale to close escrow in a tax year when you expect to receive less total income from investments, salary and other sources—for example, if you're taking an early retirement or a job leave. If you also plan to sell a house which has appreciated dramatically, it would be advantageous to arrange the closing of the house sale in the same year you expect reduced income. If at all possible, try to avoid closing escrow in a year when you're earning a peak income or when you expect to return to lucrative employment.

When it comes to timing the sale of your home, you'll also want to consider any tax deductions that may be lost as a result of the transaction. If you're selling a home and not buying another, you'll lose the homeowner deductions that you've grown accustomed to. There is little doubt that this type of change will affect your finances—the question is how much. You could, of course, earn some income by investing your sale proceeds, but unless the investments are tax-free municipal bonds or a similar financial instrument, you will need to declare any earned interest as taxable income. This could result in a double whammy if you also lose your deductions for mortgage interest and real estate tax that you had as a homeowner. In this case, you may wish to time the closing of your house sale to take place late in the tax year in order to take full advantage of homeowner deductions—while you can still claim them. In addition, you may want to consider selling in a year when you have a low taxable income.

CALIFORNIA PROPERTY TAX RELIEF

As a result of the California initiative of the mid-1970s, Proposition 13, property taxes are assessed on the value as of March 1, 1975, or the date of any later transfer, except in transfers within a family.

For people who've owned homes for many years, their values are comparatively low. When they sell that house and purchase another, however, they pay property taxes on the price of the house being bought, which is likely to be higher than the one being sold.

To help older and disabled people deal with this, California law lets owners over age 55 (only one spouse of a married couple need qualify) or owners who are severely or permanently disabled and who sell one house and purchase another within two years in the same county to transfer their old tax assessment rate to the new house. Transferring the tax assessment inter-county is possible if you are moving to a country which participates in the statewide transfer system. The county tax assessor in each California county can tell you whether or not your county participates in the system.

To qualify, the new house cannot cost more than the amount the first house sold for if the purchase precedes the sale. If the sale is within one year of the purchase, the cost of the new house cannot exceed 105% of the cost of sale or 110% if two years after. (Revenue and Tax Code § 69.5.) Check with your county tax assessor to see if the law applies when you contemplate your transaction.

C. Installment Sales

In general, you don't pay taxes on income until you receive it. One way to avoid a large tax bill is to string out the profit over a number of years, using an installment sale. You will want to consult a knowledgeable tax accountant before proceeding with an installment sale.

Depending on your taxable income, stringing out the gain over several years may reduce the total net tax by keeping you in lower tax brackets. Remember, though, that when you finance a sale through installments, you must charge interest on the unpaid balance, and this interest is considered taxable income. Even if you don't charge interest, as might be the case if you sell to a family member, the IRS will impute interest at what it considers the going rate. This is changed from time to time, but is usually slightly less than the interest rate banks charge for a fixed rate long-term mortgage. (Internal Revenue code § 453.)

Rental Property Note: There are few advantages to selling rental property in an installment sale. If you want to sell rental property in installments, see a tax attorney or tax accountant first.

D. Short Sales

As mentioned in Chapter 2, if you're in financial distress and need to sell your house, you may not get any offers that cover the amount you owe your lender. In such a situation, your lender may be willing to let you sell for the amount of the offer you do get and waive the difference. This is called a short sale and increasing numbers of lenders prefer it to foreclosing.

Unfortunately, however, it's not always a gift from the heavens. Tax laws require that you declare the amount waived by the lender as income—and pay tax on it—unless you discharge it in bankruptcy or prove you were insolvent. (Internal Revenue Code § 108.) Make sure you have a clear understanding of your potential tax liability before agreeing to a short sale.

Short sales, foreclosures and other options for selling property during a financial crisis are covered in Stop Foreclosure Now in California, *by Lloyd Segal (Nolo Press).*

E. Keeping Track of Tax Deductions When Selling a House

There are many expenses associated with home ownership that affect your tax situation. Some are deductible in the year when paid. Others affect the calculation of capital gain at the time of sale. In the following section is a checklist showing different categories of expenses.

1. Tax Deductible Moving Expenses

Some expenses involved in selling a home and/or buying another are deductible when they are part of a job-related move that meets certain qualifications under IRS regulations. (See IRS Form 3903 and IRS Publications 521 and 523.) These expenses are listed below; a tear-out copy is in the Appendix.

Helpful information on moving and moving expenses is in Steiner's Complete How to Move Handbook, *by Clyde and Shari Steiner (Dell Publishing). The Steiners also provide information online at http://www.movedoc.com.*

2. Other Tax Deductions

Specifically, the following expenses will help keep down your tax bill.

Improvements. These do not result in any direct tax deduction at the time the expense is incurred, but they add to the original purchase price, thus increasing the cost basis of your home. Because many improvements take place over a multi-year period of home ownership, keep your records all the years you own your home. Also hold on to them for at least three years after you sell your house, in the unlikely event you are audited.

Costs of sale. These result in a reduction of the sales price (adjusted sales price) for the tax year in which you sell your house. Again, keep your records at least three years after you sell.

TAX DEDUCTIBLE MOVING EXPENSES

Direct moving expenses	
Airline/train/boat/bus tickets	$
Car use	$
Gas and oil for car	$
Car or truck rental	$
Gas and oil for truck	$
Professional mover's fee	$
Lodging during trip	$
Storing possessions before moving into new home	$
Costs of selling home (when paid by seller)	
Real estate commissions or hourly fees	$
Advertising	$
Documentary transfer tax	$
Appraisal fees	$
Escrow fees	$
Title fees	$
Points (as in FHA or VA transactions)	$
This book, when used to help sell home	$
Costs of buying home (when paid by buyer; not deductible presently, but add to basis)	
Real estate commissions or fees	$
Documentary transfer tax	$
Appraisal fees	$
Attorneys and/or accountant's fees	$
Escrow fees	$
Title fees	$
Costs of financing home purchase: points (deductible by buyer in year paid by buyer)	
Loan points not fully deducted on prior tax returns	$

a. Calculating Cost Basis of the House You're Buying

$ _____   Total original purchase price

$ _____   Loan application and appraisal fees paid when you purchased the house. Do not include points; points are considered interest and are deducted in the tax year when they are paid.

$ _____   Accountant and attorney's fees paid to assist you with the purchase of the house, including the part of your fee paid to an accountant for the purpose of preparing your tax return for the year in question that pertains to the real estate transaction

$ _____   Fees paid to real estate agents directly by you as the buyer (buyer's broker fees and hourly consultation fees) to help you with the purchase

$ _____   Title and escrow fees you paid when you bought your house

$ _____   Recording and notary fees you paid when you bought your house

$ _____   Capital improvements

Allowed costs. You can deduct only money you actually paid for labor and materials. You can't deduct any money toward the value of your labor or the labor of friends or relatives who worked on your house without being paid.

b. Calculating Adjusted Sales Price of the House You're Selling

$ _____   Documentary transfer tax you paid when you sold the house

$ _____   Commission you paid to any real estate broker(s)

$ _____   Fees you paid to attorney or accountant for help when you sold the house

$ _____   Loan repayment fees you paid to your lender when you sold the house

$ _____   Any notary and/or recording fees you paid when you sold the house

$ _____   Any title and escrow fees you paid when you sold the house (common in Southern California and counties near and north of Sacramento)

$ _____   Any advertising expense you paid in attempting to sell the house (includes printing, postage and the like)

$ _____   Purchase price of this book and other materials (such as a calculator) you incurred to help sell the house

c. Ongoing Tax-Deductible Expenses

These do not affect the basis at the time of purchase or gain at the time of sale; nevertheless, you should keep track of them and deduct them each year.

$ _____ Total home purchase or home equity mortgage interest (not principal)—up to limits set in the Internal Revenue Code— paid to lender(s). (Banks and savings and loan associations must give you a record of this at the end of each tax year, on IRS Form 1098. You can also get information from private lenders, specifying how much interest and how much principal was paid in the prior tax year. If you have any questions as to how much of what you pay each year is deductible and how it affects your tax situation, check with your accountant.)

$ _____ Real estate tax paid to the county; your cancelled check is usually your receipt, unless you ask the tax collector for an additional receipt. ■

How to Work With Real Estate Agents

Yᴏ ou undoubtedly want to sell your house yourself in order to save money on real estate commissions. If you follow the instructions in this book, there's no reason why you can't sell your house without a real estate agent—and get a good price and handle the paperwork correctly.

In some situations, however, you may need or want some assistance from a broker or agent. This doesn't mean that your only option is to hire an agent to list, show and sell your house, and then to pay that person the typical 5%–8% commission. Some agents charge by the hour, lower their commissions or can be hired for limited services. All of these arrangements are described in this chapter.

A. Services Offered by Real Estate Agents

If you decide to work with a real estate agent, you will want to achieve the maximum results for the minimum amount of money. Real estate agents will tell you that the only thing they have to sell is their time. Your goal then is to define your needs in advance and use a broker to help you meet those needs.

For example, you will waste money if you hire a broker who does nothing more than hold open your house and show it by appointment. He'll want the highest commission possible, but will have done the least amount of work. On the other hand, if you hire someone to help you at crucial times—to set the price (Chapter 5), to see if the buyer will qualify for a loan (Chapter 8) or to help you through escrow (Chapter 11)—you will have made the most of your relationship with a real estate professional.

REAL ESTATE PEOPLE DEFINED

Before getting help from someone in the California real estate business, you need to know who you're dealing with.

Salesperson. This is one of the foot soldiers of the real estate business who shows houses, holds open houses and does most of the other nitty-gritty tasks inherent in selling real estate. A salesperson must pass a state licensing examination and must be supervised by a licensed real estate broker. Most are completely dependent on commission income; they receive no other compensation from the broker they work for.

Salespersons are frequently called agents, although that term is generally used to describe anyone working for a seller or buyer. In addition, the term agent is often used to describe anyone who holds a real estate license, whether that person is a broker or a salesperson.

Broker. He may legally represent either the seller or buyer in the sale or purchase of real property. While brokers (except some buyer's brokers, see below) almost always receive compensation from sellers, they owe a legal duty of utmost care, integrity, honesty and loyalty (called a fiduciary duty) to whomever they have agreed in writing to represent (seller and/or buyer). A broker can legally supervise one or more salespersons, and must have two years of full-time experience as a real estate agent or salesperson, complete 24 units of college-level real estate courses and pass a more difficult state-licensing exam.

Buyer's Agent. She helps the buyer find a house and owes a legal duty of trust to the buyer, but may be paid a commission by the seller. Sometimes she is hired and paid directly by the buyer. This relationship requires a written contract.

Dual Agent. A dual agent is usually paid by the seller but, at least in legal theory, represents both buyer and seller. This legal arrangement must be confirmed in writing by the buyer, seller and agent.

Listing Agent. She is simply a broker (or salesperson who works for a broker) who lists the seller's house

for sale and markets it for the seller. Unless there is a specific Dual Agency Agreement, a listing agent presumably represents only the seller.

Real Estate Agent or Real Estate Professional. A term occasionally used to include both a real estate broker and a real estate salesperson.

Realtor. He is a real estate broker or salesperson who belongs to the National Association of Realtors, a private trade group. He will then also belong to the corresponding state association (California Association of Realtors) and a local Association or Board of Realtors.

Seller's Agent. He helps a buyer find a house, but is paid by (and owes a legal duty to represent) the seller. This legal relationship must be confirmed in writing by the buyer, seller and real estate professional.

Selling Agent. This is a general—but confusing—term for an agent who locates a buyer. Depending on the written agreement the parties sign, she can be either the buyer's legal agent, the seller's legal agent or a dual agent.

Sub-Agent (or Cooperating Agent). This is a general term for the broker or salesperson, in an office different from that of the listing agent, who helps a buyer find a house. Unless all parties agree in writing that he exclusively represents the buyer, or is a dual agent, he is legally a sub-agent of the seller's broker (the person the seller retains to list the house), and owes a legal duty of trust to the seller, not the buyer. He is paid a commission by the seller. Put slightly differently, although a sub-agent may work with the buyer and never even meet the seller, his legal duty as the seller's sub-agent is to the seller who pays his commission, not to the buyer.

California law requires that the nature of any agreement involving a salesperson or broker to buy or sell residential real estate of four-units or fewer be in writing. (Civil Code § 2079.14.) A standard real estate agency disclosure form is below.

DISCLOSURE REGARDING REAL ESTATE AGENCY RELATIONSHIPS

CALIFORNIA
ASSOCIATION
OF REALTORS®

**DISCLOSURE REGARDING
REAL ESTATE AGENCY RELATIONSHIPS**
(As required by the Civil Code)

When you enter into a discussion with a real estate agent regarding a real estate transaction, you should from the outset understand what type of agency relationship or representation you wish to have with the agent in the transaction.

SELLER'S AGENT

A Seller's agent under a listing agreement with the Seller acts as the agent for the Seller only. A Seller's agent or a subagent of that agent has the following affirmative obligations:
To the Seller:
A Fiduciary duty of utmost care, integrity, honesty, and loyalty in dealings with the Seller.
To the Buyer and the Seller:
(a) Diligent exercise of reasonable skill and care in performance of the agent's duties.
(b) A duty of honest and fair dealing and good faith.
(c) A duty to disclose all facts known to the agent materially affecting the value or desirability of the property that are not known to, or within the diligent attention and observation of, the parties.

An agent is not obligated to reveal to either party any confidential information obtained from the other party that does not involve the affirmative duties set forth above.

BUYER'S AGENT

A selling agent can, with a Buyer's consent, agree to act as agent for the Buyer only. In these situations, the agent is not the Seller's agent, even if by agreement the agent may receive compensation for services rendered, either in full or in part from the Seller. An agent acting only for a Buyer has the following affirmative obligations:
To the Buyer:
A fiduciary duty of utmost care, integrity, honesty and loyalty in dealings with the Buyer.
To the Buyer and the Seller:
(a) Diligent exercise of reasonable skill and care in performance of the agent's duties.
(b) A duty of honest and fair dealing and good faith.
(c) A duty to disclose all facts known to the agent materially affecting the value or desirability of the property that are not known to, or within the diligent attention and observation of, the parties.

An agent is not obligated to reveal to either party any confidential information obtained from the other party that does not involve the affirmative duties set forth above.

AGENT REPRESENTING BOTH SELLER & BUYER

A real estate agent, either acting directly or through one or more associate licensees, can legally be the agent of both the Seller and the Buyer in a transaction, but only with the knowledge and consent of both the Seller and the Buyer.

In a dual agency situation, the agent has the following affirmative obligations to both the Seller and the Buyer:
(a) A fiduciary duty of utmost care, integrity, honest and loyalty in the dealings with either Seller or the Buyer.
(b) Other duties to the Seller and the Buyer as stated above in their respective sections.

In representing both Seller and Buyer, the agent may not, without the express permission of the respective party, disclose to the other party that the Seller will accept a price less than the listing price or that the Buyer will pay a price greater than the price offered.

The above duties of the agent in a real estate transaction do not relieve a Seller or Buyer from the responsibility to protect his or her own interests. You should carefully read all agreements to assure that they adequately express your understanding of the transaction. A real estate agent is a person qualified to advise about real estate. If legal or tax advice is desired, consult a competent professional.

Throughout your real property transaction you may receive more than one disclosure form, depending upon the number of agents assisting in the transaction. The law requires each agent with whom you have more than a casual relationship to present you with this disclosure form. You should read its contents each time it is presented to you, considering the relationship between you and the real estate agent in your specific transaction.

This disclosure form includes the provisions of Sections 2079.13 to 2079.24, inclusive, of the Civil Code set forth on the reverse hereof. Read it carefully.

I/WE ACKNOWLEDGE RECEIPT OF A COPY OF THIS DISCLOSURE.

BUYER/SELLER _____ Date _____ Time _____ AM/PM

BUYER/SELLER _____ Date _____ Time _____ AM/PM

AGENT _____ By _____ Date _____
   (Please Print)   (Associate Licensee or Broker-Signature)

This Disclosure form must be provided in a listing, sale, exchange, installment land contract, or lease over one year, if the transaction involves one-to-four dwelling residential property, including a mobile home, as follows:
(a) From a Listing Agent to a Seller: Prior to entering into the listing.
(b) From an Agent selling a property he/she has listed to a Buyer: Prior to the Buyer's execution of the offer.
(c) From a Selling Agent to a Buyer: Prior to the Buyer's execution of the offer.
(d) From a Selling Agent (in a cooperating real estate firm) to a Seller: Prior to presentation of the offer to the Seller.

It is not necessary or required to confirm an agency relationship using a separate Confirmation form if the agency confirmation portion of the Real Estate Purchase Contract is properly completed in full. However, it is still necessary to use this Disclosure form.

Published and Distributed by:
REAL ESTATE BUSINESS SERVICES, INC.
a subsidiary of the CALIFORNIA ASSOCIATION OF REALTORS®
525 South Virgil Avenue, Los Angeles, California 90020

PRINT DATE

OFFICE USE ONLY
Reviewed by Broker
or Designee _____
Date _____

FORM AD-14 REVISED 10/95

The balance of this chapter describes what real estate agents can do, which will let you decide how much you want to do on your own and how much you want to farm out to an agent. Your decision will be based on several factors, including:

- your time
- whether or not you need to sell quickly
- whether you're in a buyer's or seller's market
- your negotiating skills, and
- how well you pay attention to details.

To help you make the decision, consider the following advantages of working with a real estate agent.

Access to the market through the Realtors' Multiple Listing Service (MLS) Book and allied computer services. The MLS book and computer services list most homes currently on the market. Because the vast majority of real estate agents participate in the MLS services, most agents will become aware of your house's availability, price and features. Your MLS listing can also indicate that you are looking for a cooperating agent who can earn a partial commission.

Business experience. An outstanding real estate salesperson will have successfully completed many transactions. Her experience in marketing houses, screening and qualifying buyers, and handling negotiations may be valuable in helping your house sale run smoothly. In addition, real estate agents are not emotionally involved in the sale of your home. Although they want to earn a commission, a good salesperson can honestly evaluate your asking price, whether you need to make repairs in advance, the house's presentation and other factors.

Knowledge of related professionals. A good real estate agent will be one source of referrals to title and escrow companies that you'll need in order to close on the sale. A competent agent can also recommend inspectors and contractors to help satisfy any inspection and repair contingencies in your house contract.

B. How California Real Estate Agents Are Paid

In California, it is illegal for brokers to establish statewide or regionwide commission rates. By common practice, however, most real estate brokers set their individual commissions at 5%–8% of the sales price of a house. That translates into $12,500 to $20,000 on a $250,000 home. For more expensive homes (over $300,000), sellers can sometimes negotiate a sliding scale for commission—for example, 6% of the first $200,000, 5% of the next $100,000, and 2.5% thereafter. On a $350,000 home, a sliding scale commission might total $18,250—$12,000 on the first $200,000, $5,000 on the next $100,000 and $1,250 on the last $50,000.

While California law requires that brokers tell prospective clients (sellers) that commissions are negotiable, most brokers (except those hired for limited purposes) won't represent you for less than 5%. Because most real estate transactions involve two brokers—the one producing the buyer and the one helping the seller—the commission is usually divided 50-50 between the two brokerage offices. (The individual salesperson gets a percentage—often 50%—of the brokerage office's share.) If both salespeople are in the same office, typically each salesperson gets a third of the commission and the office keeps a third. The type of contract you sign with an agent (see Section D) affects the commission you pay.

C. Standard Broker's Contract: Exclusive Listing

Usually, a broker asks a house seller to sign a listing agreement, called an Exclusive Authorization and Right to Sell. An exclusive listing obligates you to pay a commission (usually 6%–8%) if your house sells during a specified period of time—typically 90 days. Any real estate agent you deal with will have an ample supply of exclusive listing agreements, which will probably look like the form below.

EXCLUSIVE AUTHORIZATION AND RIGHT TO SELL, PAGE 1

CALIFORNIA ASSOCIATION OF REALTORS®

EXCLUSIVE AUTHORIZATION AND RIGHT TO SELL

1. **EXCLUSIVE RIGHT TO SELL:** _____ ("Seller") hereby employs and grants _____ ("Broker") the exclusive and irrevocable right, commencing on (date) _____ and expiring at 11:59 P.M. on (date) _____ ("Listing Period") to sell or exchange the real property in the City of _____, County of _____, California, described as: _____ ("Property").

2. **TERMS OF SALE:**
   A. **LIST PRICE:** The listing price shall be _____ ($_____).

   B. **PERSONAL PROPERTY:** The following items of personal property are included in the above price: _____

   C. **ADDITIONAL TERMS:** _____

3. **MULTIPLE LISTING SERVICE:** Information about this listing ☐ will, ☐ will not, be provided to a multiple listing service ("MLS") of Broker's selection and all terms of the transaction, including financing if applicable, will be provided to the MLS for publication, dissemination and use by persons and entities on terms approved by the MLS. Seller authorizes Broker to comply with all applicable MLS rules.

4. **TITLE:** Seller warrants that Seller and no other persons have title to the Property, except as follows: _____

5. **COMPENSATION TO BROKER:**
   Notice: The amount or rate of real estate commissions is not fixed by law. They are set by each Broker individually and may be negotiable between Seller and Broker.
   A. Seller agrees to pay to Broker as compensation for services irrespective of agency relationship(s), either ☐ _____ percent of the listing price (or, if a sales contract is entered into, of the sales price), or ☐ $ _____ as follows: AND
      1. If Broker, Seller, cooperating broker, or any other person, produces a buyer(s) who offers to purchase the Property on the above price and terms, or on any price and terms acceptable to Seller during the Listing Period, or any extension;
      2. If within _____ calendar days after expiration of the Listing Period or any extension, the Property is sold, conveyed, leased, or otherwise transferred to anyone with whom Broker or a cooperating broker has had negotiations, provided that Broker gives Seller, prior to or within **5 calendar days** after expiration of the Listing Period or any extension, a written notice with the name(s) of the prospective purchaser(s);
      3. If, without Broker's prior written consent, the Property is withdrawn from sale, conveyed, leased, rented, otherwise transferred, or made unmarketable by a voluntary act of Seller during the Listing Period, or any extension.
   B. If completion of the sale is prevented by a party to the transaction other than Seller, then compensation due under paragraph 5A shall be payable only if and when Seller collects damages by suit, settlement, or otherwise, and then in an amount equal to the lesser of one-half of the damages recovered or the above compensation, after first deducting title and escrow expenses and the expenses of collection, if any.
   C. In addition, Seller agrees to pay: _____
   D. Broker is authorized to cooperate with other brokers, and divide with other brokers the above compensation in any manner acceptable to Broker;
   E. Seller hereby irrevocably assigns to Broker the above compensation from Seller's funds and proceeds in escrow.
   F. Seller warrants that Seller has no obligation to pay compensation to any other broker regarding the transfer of the Property except: _____

      If the Property is sold to anyone listed above during the time Seller is obligated to compensate another broker: (a) Broker is not entitled to compensation under this Agreement and (b) Broker is not obligated to represent Seller with respect to such transaction.

6. **BROKER'S AND SELLER'S DUTIES:** Broker agrees to exercise reasonable effort and due diligence to achieve the purposes of this Agreement, and is authorized to advertise and market the Property in any medium selected by Broker. Seller agrees to consider offers presented by Broker, and to act in good faith toward accomplishing the sale of the Property. Seller further agrees, regardless of responsibility, to indemnify, defend and hold Broker harmless from all claims, disputes, litigation, judgments and attorney's fees arising from any incorrect information supplied by Seller, whether contained in any document, omitted therefrom, or otherwise, or from any material facts which Seller knows but fails to disclose.

7. **AGENCY RELATIONSHIPS:** Broker shall act as the agent for Seller in any resulting transaction. Depending upon the circumstances, it may be necessary or appropriate for Broker to act as an agent for both Seller and buyer, exchange party, or one or more additional parties ("Buyer"). Broker shall, as soon as practicable, disclose to Seller any election to act as a dual agent representing both Seller and Buyer. If a Buyer is procured directly by Broker or an associate licensee in Broker's firm, Seller hereby consents to Broker acting as a dual agent for Seller and such Buyer. In the event of an exchange, Seller hereby consents to Broker collecting compensation from additional parties for services rendered, provided there is disclosure to all parties of such agency and compensation. Seller understands that Broker may have or obtain listings on other properties, and that potential buyers may consider, make offers on, or purchase through Broker, property the same as or similar to Seller's Property. Seller consents to Broker's representation of sellers and buyers of other properties before, during, and after the expiration of this Agreement.

8. **DEPOSIT:** Broker is authorized to accept and hold on Seller's behalf a deposit to be applied toward the sales price.

Seller and Broker acknowledge receipt of copy of this page, which constitutes Page 1 of _____ Pages.
Seller's Initials (_____) (_____)   Broker's Initials (_____) (_____)

THIS FORM HAS BEEN APPROVED BY THE CALIFORNIA ASSOCIATION OF REALTORS® (C.A.R.). NO REPRESENTATION IS MADE AS TO THE LEGAL VALIDITY OR ADEQUACY OF ANY PROVISION IN ANY SPECIFIC TRANSACTION. A REAL ESTATE BROKER IS THE PERSON QUALIFIED TO ADVISE ON REAL ESTATE TRANSACTIONS. IF YOU DESIRE LEGAL OR TAX ADVICE, CONSULT AN APPROPRIATE PROFESSIONAL.

The copyright laws of the United States (Title 17 U.S. Code) forbid the unauthorized reproduction of this form, or any portion thereof, by photocopy machine or any other means, including facsimile or computerized formats. Copyright © 1998, CALIFORNIA ASSOCIATION OF REALTORS®, INC. ALL RIGHTS RESERVED.

Published and Distributed by:
REAL ESTATE BUSINESS SERVICES, INC.
a subsidiary of the CALIFORNIA ASSOCIATION OF REALTORS®
525 South Virgil Avenue, Los Angeles, California 90020
PRINT DATE

REVISED 10/97

OFFICE USE ONLY
Reviewed by Broker
or Designee _____
Date _____

EQUAL HOUSING OPPORTUNITY

EXCLUSIVE AUTHORIZATION AND RIGHT TO SELL (A-14 PAGE 1 OF 2)

EXCLUSIVE ATHORIZATION AND RIGHT TO SELL, PAGE 2

Property Address: _____

9. **LOCKBOX:**
   A. A lockbox is designed to hold a key to the Property to permit access to the Property by Broker, cooperating brokers, MLS participants, their authorized licensees and representatives, and accompanied prospective buyers.
   B. Broker, cooperating brokers, MLS and Associations/Boards of REALTORS® are **not** insurers against theft, loss, vandalism, or damage attributed to the use of a lockbox. Seller is advised to verify the existence of, or obtain, appropriate insurance through Seller's own insurance broker.
   C. (If checked:) ☐ Seller authorizes Broker to install a lockbox. If Seller does not occupy the Property, Seller shall be responsible for obtaining occupant(s)' written permission for use of a lockbox.
10. **SIGN:** (If checked:) ☐ Seller authorizes Broker to install a FOR SALE/SOLD sign on the Property.
11. **DISPUTE RESOLUTION:**
   A. **MEDIATION:** Seller and Broker agree to mediate any dispute or claim arising between them out of this Agreement, or any resulting transaction, before resorting to arbitration or court action, subject to paragraph 11C below. Mediation fees, if any, shall be divided equally among the parties involved. If any party commences an action based on a dispute or claim to which this paragraph applies, without first attempting to resolve the matter through mediation, then that party shall not be entitled to recover attorney's fees, even if they would otherwise be available to that party in any such action. THIS MEDIATION PROVISION APPLIES WHETHER OR NOT THE ARBITRATION PROVISION IS INITIALED.
   B. **ARBITRATION OF DISPUTES:** Seller and Broker agree that any dispute or claim in Law or equity arising between them regarding the obligation to pay compensation under this Agreement, which is not settled through mediation, shall be decided by neutral, binding arbitration, subject to paragraph 11C below. The arbitrator shall be a retired judge or justice, or an attorney with at least five years of residential real estate experience, unless the parties mutually agree to a different arbitrator, who shall render an award in accordance with substantive California Law. In all other respects, the arbitration shall be conducted in accordance with Title 9 of the California Code of Civil Procedure. Judgment upon the award of the arbitrator(s) may be entered in any court having jurisdiction. The parties shall have the right to discovery in accordance with Code of Civil Procedure §1283.05.

   "NOTICE: BY INITIALING IN THE SPACE BELOW YOU ARE AGREEING TO HAVE ANY DISPUTE ARISING OUT OF THE MATTERS INCLUDED IN THE 'ARBITRATION OF DISPUTES' PROVISION DECIDED BY NEUTRAL ARBITRATION AS PROVIDED BY CALIFORNIA LAW AND YOU ARE GIVING UP ANY RIGHTS YOU MIGHT POSSESS TO HAVE THE DISPUTE LITIGATED IN A COURT OR JURY TRIAL. BY INITIALING IN THE SPACE BELOW YOU ARE GIVING UP YOUR JUDICIAL RIGHTS TO DISCOVERY AND APPEAL, UNLESS THOSE RIGHTS ARE SPECIFICALLY INCLUDED IN THE 'ARBITRATION OF DISPUTES' PROVISION. IF YOU REFUSE TO SUBMIT TO ARBITRATION AFTER AGREEING TO THIS PROVISION, YOU MAY BE COMPELLED TO ARBITRATE UNDER THE AUTHORITY OF THE CALIFORNIA CODE OF CIVIL PROCEDURE. YOUR AGREEMENT TO THIS ARBITRATION PROVISION IS VOLUNTARY."

   "WE HAVE READ AND UNDERSTAND THE FOREGOING AND AGREE TO SUBMIT DISPUTES ARISING OUT OF THE MATTERS INCLUDED IN THE 'ARBITRATION OF DISPUTES' PROVISION TO NEUTRAL ARBITRATION."   Seller's Initials _____/_____   Broker's Initials _____/_____
   C. **EXCLUSIONS FROM MEDIATION AND ARBITRATION:** The following matters are excluded from Mediation and Arbitration hereunder: (a) A judicial or non-judicial foreclosure or other action or proceeding to enforce a deed of trust, mortgage, or installment land sale contract as defined in Civil Code §2985; (b) An unlawful detainer action; (c) The filing or enforcement of a mechanic's lien; (d) Any matter which is within the jurisdiction of a probate, small claims, or bankruptcy court; and (e) An action for bodily injury or wrongful death, or for latent or patent defects to which Code of Civil Procedure §337.1 or §337.15 applies. The filing of a court action to enable the recording of a notice of pending action, for order of attachment, receivership, injunction, or other provisional remedies, shall not constitute a violation of the mediation and arbitration provisions.
12. **EQUAL HOUSING OPPORTUNITY:** The Property is offered in compliance with federal, state, and local anti-discrimination laws.
13. **ATTORNEY'S FEES:** In any action, proceeding, or arbitration between Seller and Broker regarding the obligation to pay compensation under this Agreement, the prevailing Seller or Broker shall be entitled to reasonable attorney's fees and costs, except as provided in paragraph 11A.
14. **ADDITIONAL TERMS:** _____
_____
_____
15. **ENTIRE CONTRACT:** All prior discussions, negotiations, and agreements between the parties concerning the subject matter of this Agreement are superseded by this Agreement, which constitutes the entire contract and a complete and exclusive expression of their agreement, and may not be contradicted by evidence of any prior agreement or contemporaneous oral agreement. This Agreement and any supplement, addendum, or modification, including any photocopy or facsimile, may be executed in counterparts.

Seller warrants that Seller is the owner of the Property or has the authority to execute this contract. Seller acknowledges that Seller has read and understands this Agreement, and has received a copy.

Seller _____ Date _____   Seller _____ Date _____

Address _____   Address _____

City _____ State _____ Zip _____   City _____ State _____ Zip _____

Real Estate Broker (Firm) _____   By (Agent) _____ Date _____

Address _____   Telephone _____

City _____ State _____ Zip _____   Fax _____

This form is available for use by the entire real estate industry. It is not intended to identify the user as a REALTOR®. REALTOR® is a registered collective membership mark which may be used only by members of the NATIONAL ASSOCIATION OF REALTORS® who subscribe to its Code of Ethics.
PRINT DATE

Page 2 of _____ Pages.

REVISED 10/97

OFFICE USE ONLY
Reviewed by Broker or Designee _____
Date _____

EQUAL HOUSING OPPORTUNITY

EXCLUSIVE AUTHORIZATION AND RIGHT TO SELL (A-14 PAGE 2 OF 2)

An exclusive authorization listing obligates you to pay the full commission on the sales price, even if:

- you, not your broker, find the buyer

- your broker finds a buyer willing to pay the full price and to agree to all other terms but you change your mind and don't sell, or

- you accept an offer on somewhat different terms from those in the listing agreement—for example, the price is lower, you provide some financing or you pay for repairs.

If you have an exclusive authorization listing agreement, the only times you are not required to pay full commission are when you don't receive any offers at the full listing price or you don't voluntarily agree to sell at different terms.

This standard broker's contract is too restrictive and costly for FSBOs. The whole idea of "For Sale By Owner" is to avoid paying a full commission by doing some of the home-selling work yourself. Keep reading to learn about the alternatives to exclusive listings.

D. Modifying the Standard Contract and Commission

If you want to sell your own house with some help from a real estate agent, but consider a 5%–8% commission too high, here are two ways you can have your cake and eat it too.

- Find a broker who won't charge full commission unless there is a cooperating broker.

- Find an independent broker who will charge a lower commission.

1. Find a Broker Who Won't Charge Full Commission Without a Cooperating Broker

The Exclusive Authorization and Right to Sell contract contemplates that you will have one broker and the buyer will have another. The agreement, however, usually allows your broker to keep the entire commission even if he represents the buyer. In other words, if you list with ABC Realty and it produces a buyer, the firm keeps the whole 5%–8% commission.

Some brokers in California, however, won't charge the full 5%–8% commission if they don't have to split it with a cooperating broker from an outside office who produces a buyer. Instead, these brokers will try to find a buyer themselves, and then charge a commission of only 2.5%–4%. The obvious problem with this arrangement is that you have no guarantee that your broker will find a buyer. If he doesn't and the buyer comes with his own broker, you'll have to pay the entire commission.

2. Find an Independent Broker Who Will Charge a Lower Commission

Some independent brokers not associated with a large company or franchise will agree to a total commission in the 4%–5% range (allowing for half to go to a cooperating broker) if you sign an Exclusive Authorization and Right to Sell contract. On the down side, you still pay a pretty good-sized commission and brokers working for buyers will be less likely to show your house, because the commission is less. Also, some small independent brokers may provide less service than you need.

Many independents do a great job, however, so if you go this route be sure to check references (see Section G for advice on choosing an agent). See the box on page 4/11 for a listing of some of these agents.

E. Alternative Real Estate Contracts

Despite the attractions of the alternatives to the Exclusive Authorization and Right to Sell contract described in Section C, above, most FSBOs are usually better off with a completely different kind of arrangement.

The six approaches discussed below are listed from the most common to the least common. All substantially deviate from the Exclusive Authorization and Right to Sell contract and its alternatives, and therefore engender opposition from real estate traditionalists. Nevertheless, if you want to use one of these approaches, shop around until you find a broker who will agree to it. Don't get caught up with full service brokers and end up paying for services you don't need or use.

1. Exclusive Agency Agreement

An Exclusive Agency Agreement lets you sell your property while your broker also tries to sell it. If you sell your house yourself, you pay no commission. If the broker arranges a sale, he gets the commission. The arrangement potentially gives you the best of both worlds. You can pick and choose a variety of broker services, such as using the Multiple Listing Service. At the same time, if you find the buyer, you avoid paying a commission.

Unfortunately, there is a very good chance that you will end up paying a full commission. Because your broker can draw on the entire resources of the real estate business, chances are pretty good that either he or a cooperating broker will sell your house before you do. Moreover, many agents won't sign this kind of listing agreement because of the potential dispute over who brought in the buyer.

If you use an Exclusive Agency Agreement, you will want to make sure it sets up a system to clearly identify who brought in the purchaser. One way to avoid disputes is for you and the broker to periodi-cally give each other lists of the potential buyers who show an interest in the house.

2. Single Party Listing Agreement: Cooperating With a Broker

A broker may call you and say, "I have a qualified buyer for your property. Will you cooperate by paying me a commission?" If you say yes, the broker may ask you to sign a Single Party Listing Agreement. Before doing so, find out:

- the name of the interested purchaser (or be sure the contract includes a provision which will provide you with the potential buyer's name within 24 hours), and

- the commission the broker wants—most will ask for something between 2.5%–6%. You should be fairly aggressive about negotiating the lowest possible commission rate.

If the broker agrees to a commission at the low end of the range, seriously consider the offer, especially if the prospective buyer is willing to pay top dollar for your house. Brokers have been known to use this "I have a buyer" technique when they have a few potential buyers and are just trying to back-door you into giving them an exclusive listing. You hold the upper hand because if the broker doesn't agree to your terms, she gets nothing.

3. Low Commission Listing

Another way to save on the broker's commission is to hire your own broker and refuse to pay any commission to a cooperating (or buyer's) broker. You can pay your broker a low commission (2.5%–3.5%) to help you find a buyer and handle the necessary paper-work. If you go this route, you will have to widely publicize the availability of your house because your broker has no authority to work with another broker;

thus, the number of brokers who will show your house to potential buyers is greatly reduced.

It's quite possible that a broker working with a buyer will surface and ask for a commission directly from you—rather than from your broker—as compensation for presenting an offer. If it's an offer you can't refuse, seriously consider the proposal. You could wind up paying the cooperating broker almost as much as you would have paid had you signed an Exclusive Authorization and Right to Sell contract in the first place.

Paying the full commission isn't inevitable, however, as a growing number of brokers specifically represent buyers. Their job is to find a suitable house for a buyer and their commission is paid directly by that buyer. If you wait for this scenario—you pay your broker's commission and the buyer pays her broker—you'll probably sell your house eventually, but don't expect tremendous numbers of brokers working with buyers to knock on your door.

MONICA: HOW I SPLIT THE WORKLOAD AND THE FEE

I decided to sell my own house to save what seemed like an exorbitant real estate commission. After checking prices in my area, I estimated my Sacramento County house was worth between $180,000 and $200,000. To test the market, I asked for $190,000.

As soon as my listing appeared in the paper, real estate brokers called and asked if I would "cooperate." I didn't know what they meant. Finally, someone explained it to me—would I sell to a buyer they produced in exchange for a small commission? After some thought, I decided to pay a 2.5% commission if a broker brought me a full-price offer. It turned out to be a pretty good strategy. One broker found me a buyer and did all the paperwork for both the buyer and me. True, I ended up paying a commission of $4,750 but I got a great price for my house and did very little work to sell.

I also learned that brokers didn't resent my selling myself as soon as they learned that I would cooperate on full-price offers. At my first and only open house, at least a dozen real estate people brought potential buyers.

4. Flat Rate and Discount Agreements

Some real estate brokers offer a package of services for a set fee rather than a commission. The best known of these flat rate or discount brokers is Help-U-Sell, which has franchises throughout the U.S. Typically, brokers like Help-U-Sell assist sellers by providing for sale signs, sales leads, help with the offer and acceptance process and advice during escrow.

Many flat rate brokerage firms offer what I consider to be poor value for the money, by charging a fee of $4,000 or more—equivalent to a 2% commission on a $200,000 house. They frequently encourage sellers to "cooperate" with the broker who locates the buyer, thus causing the seller to incur an additional cost of half of a 5–6% full service commission. You might set out to save money only to end up paying as much as if you had signed up with any local broker—but with fewer services.

Another problem with flat rate brokers is that their advertised price usually covers only their no frills service, which may not include what you need, such as listing your house in the Multiple Listing Service or negotiating with buyers. Once you're signed up, the brokerage often pushes a more extensive and expensive combination of services. For this reason, scrutinize the list of services offered by any flat rate or discount broker with pencil and paper before signing up and be sure you know the cost of additional services.

5. "Permission to Show" Agreement

Under a "Permission to Show" agreement, all you agree to is to let the broker show your house to potential buyers. You don't agree to sign a listing. If the broker presents a buyer with an acceptable offer, you pay a commission. This oral agreement gives the broker no protection, but some brokers will agree to it nonetheless.

6. Open Listings: Non-Exclusive Authorization to Sell

This is like the exclusive agency arrangement described in Section E, above, but may be given to more than one broker at a time. You invite a number of brokers at once to help market your property, with the one who procures the buyer getting the commission. At the same time, you try to sell your house yourself so that you will owe no commission at all. This type of listing is less popular among brokers than is an exclusive agency because it provides little incentive for a broker to advertise or market the property for buyers who may be brought in by another broker.

As a general rule, however, open listings are accepted by multiple listing services and so some brokers will put your property into the MLS for a fee.

F.   Paying a Broker by the Hour

As the purchaser of a book on how to sell your own house, you probably prefer not to list your house with a broker at all. You may, however, want at least a little help from someone experienced in selling houses. It is not hard to do this. Many brokers provide advice for an hourly consultation fee to people who are handling their own sales. This sort of help usually ends up costing you far less than a typical commission.

Hourly fees vary widely, but $60 to $150 an hour is common and you can expect to spend from two to 100 hours, depending on the types of services you need. To help you decide what services to purchase, consult the following chart.

Selling a typical home involves about 80–100 hours of the time of the seller, the real estate agent or both. If your house sells for $200,000 and your agent is getting a 3% commission, your cost is $6,000. You can save substantially by doing some of the work yourself.

Before hiring a real estate broker by the hour, be clear on what services you want from the broker and what tasks you want to perform for yourself. This will help define your relationship with the broker and develop an estimate of the costs. If you're not sure, start with the bare minimum—that is, the broker looks over the contract and walks the deal through the escrow—and you do everything else. Then estimate the time and money involved in adding services to that basic foundation—for example, you ask the broker to conduct your negotiations with the buyer, to hold the house open a couple of times, to pay for advertisements and to take calls from ads.

Below is a sample contract to hire a broker by the hour; a blank tear-out copy is in the Appendix.

REAL ESTATE SERVICES YOU MIGHT PURCHASE BY THE HOUR

This chart illustrates different areas where help is often necessary and an estimate of hours you might need. It also indicates where you can turn in this book for more information and suggests some low-cost or free alternatives to real estate professionals.

Activity	Estimated total hours	Chapter	Alternatives
Giving tax advice	3-5	3	brokers can't help; see a tax attorney or tax accountant
Pricing your house	3-5	5	brokers often do this for free with the hope of getting a listing
Placing ads	2	6	
Posting signs	3	6	may be purchased at a sign shop
Holding open house	5 (per week)	7	
Showing house by appointment	2 (each time)	7	
Qualifying the buyer	2-10	8	loan brokers, who are paid by the buyers' lender, can do this
Meeting to receive buyer's offer	2-4	9	
Preparing counteroffer	3	9-10	
Presenting counteroffer	3	9-10	
Dealing with escrow or title company	2-10	11	many title or escrow company employees will help you
Dealing with inspectors	2-10	11	

G. Evaluating Real Estate Agents

When you look for a real estate agent, what qualifications and factors should you consider? Should the agent be affiliated with a nationally known firm? Should the agent work full-time? How many years of experience in real estate should the agent have? Should the agent belong to the Multiple Listing Service? What about the ethical reputation of the agent? Will you find it easy to work with the agent? Some of these questions are easier to answer than others. While you can always get rid of a salesperson you don't like, it's better to find someone good in the first place.

If you know a broker you like who has experience in selling homes, ask her if she will do work on a limited-service/limited-fee basis, or will work by the hour. If not, ask for referrals to someone who will. Also get recommendations from friends and relatives whose judgments you trust. If you don't know anyone to ask for a recommendation, call several real estate offices (look for those who have lots of SOLD signs on houses in your neighborhood) and talk to different salespeople who have sold comparable homes. Title companies may also give you good leads.

HOURLY BROKER FEE AGREEMENT

_____ ,

the seller(s) of the real property located at _____

_____ , in the City of

_____ , County of _____ , California, hereby engage

_____ , a licensed real estate broker in the State of California, to

advise them as to the mechanics involved in selling their own house, with the intention that the broker shall act as

needed as an advisor as to typical sales procedures, the preparation of routine forms, comparable sales prices,

information on available financing, and suggestions as to competent professionals, such as attorneys, accountants,

pest control inspectors, general contractors, etc., as needed.

Broker shall not receive a commission but shall be compensated at $_____ per hour, not to exceed a

total amount of $_____ , based on the broker's estimate that the advice required shall not call for more

than _____ hours of the broker's labor. Broker shall be paid as follows:

_____

_____

If the seller and broker agree that more of the broker's time is needed, an additional written contract will be

prepared.

It is understood that sellers are handling their own sale and are solely responsible for all decisions made and

paperwork prepared. In addition, it is expressly agreed that broker will not provide any legal direction or tax or

estate planning advice, and shall make no representation concerning the physical condition of the property or the

legal condition of title to any party. Broker expressly recommends that sellers seek the appropriate professional

advice offered by attorneys, tax accountants, pest control inspectors, and/or general contractors as needed.

Agreed this date of _____ , by:

_____

_____

Seller(s)

_____

Broker

_____

By

SPLITTING THE WORK LOAD WITH AN AGENT CAN BE PROFITABLE

Margaret, a recent retiree, owned a single-family home in San Francisco and was considering an eventual move to a condominium. She wanted to save money on a real estate commission by selling her home herself. But she wanted some help.

She didn't mind holding open houses and greeting people, but she wanted help in negotiating with anyone who made a serious purchase offer. She also wanted assistance in gearing up for her first open house. In addition, she knew she'd probably receive offers through real estate agents expecting compensation so she wanted these agents to know about her home through the Multiple Listing Service.

Margaret found a broker willing to take a reduced commission. He agreed to list her home in the MLS, and to help her with the first couple of open houses and appointment showings until she felt ready to go it alone. He also agreed to advertise the property in newspapers and put up a "for sale" sign. Finally, he agreed to handle the contract for her. He lowered his commission—normally 3% for full service (one-half of a full service commission)—to 2% because he would not be responsible for open houses and appointment showings. He pointed out that if another brokerage office brought in an acceptable offer, they would require motivation in the form of a 3% commission on the selling price. He also asked that Margaret agree to pay him his commission even if another broker or a buyer without a broker made an acceptable offer.

A prospective buyer—unaccompanied by an agent—fell in love with the house one Sunday afternoon when Margaret held it open. Her broker negotiated the price and the buyer signed Margaret's counteroffer. The house passed its inspections and the broker walked the deal through escrow. His commission was 2% of the $369,500 sale price—$7,390. Because the buyer had no broker, Margaret's broker's commission was the only one she paid. Had she listed with a "full-service" office, the commission would likely have been 6%—$22,170. Margaret saved $14,780, and had the benefit of professional assistance to the extent she felt it necessary.

In general, you'll probably find that independent brokers are usually the best candidates for limited service or a help-by-the-hour arrangement. Few brokers who work for large companies, including the franchises of nationally advertised groups, will work by the hour. No matter what explanation they give, the main reasons are that their overhead is too high to allow for abbreviated services; they make far more money earning commissions and they don't want to take on all the potential liability without proportional compensation.

Here are issues to consider when choosing a real estate agent:

- Find out what types of services the agent or realty firm can provide to market your home and explain what help you want and don't want.

- Compare hourly rates. You should be able to negotiate a lower "volume" rate the more hours you buy.

- Does the agent have specific experience selling homes and the type of services you need? For instance, if your home is in a subdivision tract, has the agent ever dealt with subdivision restrictions and community associations before?

- Does the agent work for an office that belongs to the local Board or Association of Realtors and which participates in the local Multiple Listing Service? If not, you won't be served well by this agent, because your property won't be exposed to the market properly.

- Get references from previous clients and find out the agent's track record—for example, how quickly did the agent sell similar homes and did the seller get full price?

Unfortunately, you'll find it virtually impossible to locate any information on complaints. Although some real estate offices belong to the local Better Business Bureau, BBBs usually have no information except publicly documented cases where a firm has committed a gross enough offense to be drummed out of the corps in the public square, in which case you wouldn't be dealing with them anyway.

A local Board of Realtors provides even less information, as its job is to serve members of the real estate industry and they won't risk getting sued for trading damaging information about its members. The Department of Real Estate has information on licenses that have been restricted, suspended or revoked, but will not reveal anything about pending complaints, which it treats as privileged.

H. Getting Rid of a Broker You Don't Like

Suppose your relationship with your real estate agent isn't working. Maybe he isn't advertising your house as promised or doesn't negotiate as hard as you'd like. Even if he simply doesn't return your phone calls promptly, you'll want to work with someone else.

Because tens of thousands of dollars are involved in a house sale, you should be very satisfied with your salesperson. If you're not, don't hesitate to switch. Here's how to legally end a relationship with a particular broker or salesperson:

1. If you've agreed to pay the broker on an hourly basis, pay for the hours you've used and notify the broker that you don't need his services anymore. For the sake of clarity this notification should be in writing.

2. If you've pre-committed to a set number of hours but haven't used them, see whether or not there is a practical use for the unused hours contracted for. If there isn't, pay only for what you've used. The broker may demand payment for the rest. If so, point out that she has a legal duty to try to earn other income in the remaining hours and to subtract that income from what you owe. (This is called mitigating damages.) You may eventually decide to make a small settlement, but don't be in a hurry or pay for time you haven't used.

And don't pay a large chunk of money to someone who has done nothing to earn it. If you refused to pay because you received no services, the broker must sue you to collect. Few brokers want it known publicly that they sued a seller because the broker didn't do his job. Also, before you're actually sued, you'll probably have a chance to settle the dispute for a smaller amount. If you do, get a release of all claims when you make your payment. (See Nolo's *101 Law Forms for Personal Use*, by Robin Leonard and Ralph Warner.)

3. If you've signed a listing agreement with a broker, which terminates at a specific future date, ask the broker to agree to terminate the contract early, simply on the ground that there is bad chemistry between you. If the broker refuses, remind her that she'll earn no commission at all unless the property sells for your full asking price within the contractual period, and that there will be no extension of the existing contract term.

Or, if you just can't abide the thought of keeping your property on the market—in even a limited capacity—with this broker, tell her you plan to submit the matter to arbitration. Virtually all listing contracts contain an arbitration clause in bold print. In addition, Associations and Boards of Realtors locally have arbitration committees; although their function is really to handle disputes between their own members, it might not hurt to tell the broker you plan to go to such a committee, if for no other reason than to induce the broker to give up the listing.

4. If you want to terminate an exclusive listing, the broker often fears that you have a buyer—or another broker—in the wings and want to end the first contract early to avoid the first agent's commission. As a protection against this possibility, many brokers will agree to release a homeowner from an exclusive listing on the condition that the seller neither sell nor re-list the property within 60–90 days unless the original broker is compensated. ■

Chapter 5

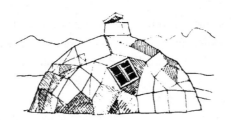

HOW MUCH SHOULD YOU ASK FOR YOUR HOUSE?

To decide how much to ask for your house, you must determine how much your property is actually worth on the market—called appraising a house's value. While no one can predict with precision how much a buyer will pay, real estate professionals use several realistic and reliable methods to arrive at a good estimate of what a house should sell for. This chapter shows you how to informally do your own appraisal, and how to hire a professional appraiser and evaluate any appraisals you receive. You're then shown how to pull together the appraisal information in order to come up with an asking price.

A. Determine Prices of Comparable Houses

Whether or not you hire a professional appraiser, you should understand that the most important factors used to determine a house's value are the sales prices of similar properties (comps). To get reliable data, real estate appraisers use the following sensible guidelines to distinguish comparable houses from others.

Look for recent sales. A comparable sale should have occurred within six months (the more recent, the better). In a market where prices fluctuate fairly fast, comps should be on sales within the last 30 to 60 days.

Look for nearby houses. A comparable sale should be within six blocks of your house. The six-block area should be shaved if the neighborhood changes significantly in a shorter radius—for example, if a major street, freeway or railroad clearly marks a border between two different residential areas.

Look for physically similar houses. A comparable sale should be for a house similar to yours. Look for houses of like age and location, and with similar numbers and types of rooms, square feet and yard size. This is relatively easy in developments where houses are uniform or near-uniform in size, age, construction and layout. In areas where houses were built one at a time and differ tremendously, however, comparisons must often be made among houses with more differences than similarities. A physically comparable house a few blocks away might be in a better school district, have a great view or be on a less busy street, which will raise the property's value.

The best comparable sales data are usually in a local association of realtors' comp book for the geographical area where you're selling. The comp book is sometimes bound in the back of the Realtors' Multiple Listing Book (described in Chapter 4), and lists the sales price of houses that sold recently. Real estate agents aren't supposed to show comp books to people not members of their association, but it's been known to happen. Also, this kind of information is now maintained on computer services by realtors. Of course, if you're working with a broker, you should ask for this sort of help in pricing your home. See Section C, below.

If you can't get access to the type of information an agent has in a comp book, ask a local title company for help. You can either provide them with the street addresses of recently sold properties and they'll give you the sales prices, or ask them to print out information on all sales on certain named streets. You can also get detailed information on specific property (a property profile). Property profiles are typically available for free if you've done business with the title company, or if it thinks you may do so in the future.

Comparable sales information is also available at the County Recorder's Office. You need to know the name of the buyer (grantee) or seller (grantor) of property you want information on. (If you don't know either, you can find out the owner's name at the County Assessor's Office.) You can then look up the deed in either the grantor (seller) or the grantee (buyer) index. (See Chapter 2, Section B.) When you find the deed, note the documentary transfer tax, located in the upper right-hand corner. The sales price is figured from that amount. The basic documentary transfer tax is $1.10 per $1,000 of price, except in cities and counties with local surtaxes.(Sometimes the tax is according to a sliding scale.) In San Francisco, for example, the tax is $5 per $1,000, and gradually rises for higher-priced properties, those $250,000 and more. A title company will often do this research for you for a small fee or even for free as part of providing a property profile.

Example: *You live in San Francisco, which has a documentary transfer tax rate of $5.00 for each $1,000 of the sale price, up to and including $250,000. The deed of a comparable house shows a documentary tax of $1,250. You thus know that the price was $250,000 by dividing $1,250 by $5.00 to get $250 and then multiplying $250 by $1,000.*

Keep in mind that the documentary tax does not necessarily reflect the full price paid by the buyer. If the buyer assumed loans held by the seller, this amount won't be included.

Example: *Skip sells his house for $150,000. Amanda, the buyer, assumed Skip's existing loan of $30,000. The deed shows a documentary transfer tax of $132, based on the following calculation: The property's value is considered $120,000—sales price of $150,000 less the assumed loan of $30,000. $1.10 times 120 is $132.*

COMPARABLE SALES PRICES AVAILABLE ONLINE

A few private companies now offer detailed comparable sales prices for many areas of California, based on information from County Recorder's Offices and property assessors. For information and fees, contact:

- DataQuick, 800-999-0152, www.dataquick.com (see the "Consumer Information Center"), and

- Experian, 888-397-3742, www.experian.com (see "Value a property" in the "Real Estate" area).

Consumer Reports also has a Home Price Service; for details, call 800-775-1212.

DOCUMENTARY TRANSFER TAX PORTION OF DEED SHOWING $1,250 TAX

Order No.
Escrow No. N-150900
Loan No.

WHEN RECORDED MAIL TO:

MR. AND MRS. GREGORY RANDOLPH
1635 Bradley Street
San Francisco, CA 94117

RECORDED AT REQUEST OF
FIRST AMERICAN TITLE CO. OF S.F
AT 8:00 AM 10/16/1986
D884872
City & County of San Francisco, California

SPACE ABOVE THIS LINE FOR RECORDER'S USE

MAIL TAX STATEMENTS TO:

same as above

DOCUMENTARY TRANSFER TAX $1,250**
XX Computed on the consideration or value of property conveyed; OR
...... Computed on the consideration or value less liens or encumbrances
remaining at time of sale.

_____ FIRST AMERICAN TITLE CO.
Signature of XXXXXXXX Agent determining tax – Firm Name

38/1707

GRANT DEED

FOR A VALUABLE CONSIDERATION, receipt of which is hereby acknowledged,
PETER M. MORIWAKI and LINDA T. MORIWAKI, husband and wife

An added bonus of checking with the County Recorder's Office for a house's documentary transfer tax is that you may wind up receiving help in making up your list of comparable sales. If you visit your recorder's office, tell the employee your exact purpose and be very friendly. You may receive extremely valuable help for no other reason than that you are a citizen, taxpayer and, at least as important, a voter, who needs help through the labyrinth of county records. A county employee may short-cut the whole deed-checking system by showing you a commercially published book that lists property transactions and sales prices. Such books—published under a trade name like REDI, Larwood or Realdex—are also in real estate broker's offices and title insurance company offices, but those offices won't show you the books unless they're convinced you'll do business with them.

A final way to get comparable sales data is to simply ask people who have recently sold their homes. Just remember to take their answers with a grain of salt—sellers commonly exaggerate what they received, or emphasize the sales price and fail to mention the cost of items they've agreed to repair.

Section F, below, explains how to determine the sale price of your house using a variety of comparable sales data.

B. Hire a Professional Appraiser

A real estate appraiser—not necessarily licensed as either an appraiser or a real estate agent—can give you a documented opinion as to your house's value. But no matter how experienced the appraiser is, her opinion is just that—an opinion. Only a buyer willing to put money in your pocket can tell you what your house is actually worth. And be aware that appraisals are often too high—appraisers are more likely to overstate the value of a house rather than to understate it. If you hire an appraiser, emphasize that you want a realistic estimate of what a reasonable buyer would pay for your property in its present condition.

For your purpose, you need a ballpark estimate of what your house is worth. You don't need photographs or detailed work sheets that normally accompany an appraisal presented in court or to the Internal Revenue Service. You do need an orally stated appraised value, or even better, a letter of appraisal giving the appraiser's opinion of the house's value and her reasons for arriving at that value.

Some appraisers—especially those licensed to perform written appraisals for lenders—provide slightly more detail in a check sheet or short form appraisal, in which the appraiser lists recent documented sales prices of comparable properties within a few blocks of your property. If you suspect that buyers seeking Veterans' Administration (VA) or Federal Housing Administration (FHA) funding will be interested in your house, be sure to get a check sheet or short form appraisal, which is required by those agencies. Even if your house is priced too high for VA or FHA funding, (see Chapter 8), a check sheet or short form appraisal can help you substantiate the property's value to a potential buyer during negotiations.

If your house has been inspected recently, be sure the appraiser has copies of any reports. In fact, you may want to have the house professionally inspected to help you set the asking price. If you don't, a subsequent inspection by a licensed contractor or pest control operator may find problems that will affect the ultimate sales price. If you're aware of the problems in advance, you can price your house accordingly. Even if you inspect your house before putting it on the market, don't be surprised if the buyer orders her own inspection reports. Buyers want to be sure they know what they're getting, and frequently make the house sale contingent on

satisfactory inspections (as discussed in Chapters 9 and 10).

In any event, you want your appraiser to be aware of all conditions—positive or negative—that would affect the value of your house. Without this information, an appraisal is only a guess. For example, a house appraised at $250,000 that later turns out to have serious foundation problems will probably sell for considerably less unless corrective work is done.

It's a good idea to ask your appraiser for suggestions on ways to maximize the sale price of your house. Appraisers are in business to recognize factors that increase or decrease a house's value, so it's not out of order to inquire. For example, you might ask if she feels your house could sell for $10,000 more if you spent $5,000 brightening up the kitchen or repainted the interior and exterior. If you're already paying for the appraiser's time and expertise, you may as well maximize the potential benefit to yourself.

You can find appraisers in your local telephone directory under Appraisers. An attorney who handles real estate matters may also be able to recommend a good appraiser, as may your bank or savings and loan. Also, your local association of realtors (check the telephone directory) can tell you about some of their members who appraise houses. Institutional lenders or, more likely, mortgage brokers might also be able to provide this sort of information. No matter how you find an appraiser, below are some basic issues to consider when selecting one.

Cost. Make sure you establish the appraiser's fee in advance. A basic appraisal of a medium-priced single-family home shouldn't cost more than $200–$300. You'll pay more for an appraisal of a luxury home or a house with a pool, outbuildings or other additional structures on the property.

Time required to prepare a written appraisal report.
An appraiser should not need more than three to four
hours to appraise a single-family home.

Method of appraisal. Most appraisers use the
comparable sales data approach described in Section
A, above. Get details on the range of time and the
geographic distance of houses sold included in the
appraiser's report. If an appraiser suggests a method
other than comparable sales data, find out why. Steer
away from any appraiser who suggests using a
replacement cost approach. This may work for
purchasing homeowners' insurance, but not for
selling your house.

Professional licenses or designations. A professional
appraiser must be licensed. In addition, several
professional appraiser associations establish standards of education and experience, and codes of
ethics. The two best known groups are the American
Institute of Real Estate Appraisers (AIREA) and the
Appraisal Section of the National Association of
Realtors (NAR). AIREA awards MAI (Member,
Appraisers' Institute) designations, which means the
holder is qualified to appraise all types of real
property. AIREA also gives RM (Residential Member)
designations, which is all that—or even more than—
you need.

Experience. Find out the amount and type of
experience an appraiser has, including hands-on
appraisals of homes in your specific area in recent
years, work for financial institutions and work for
government agencies, such as the Veterans' Administration or Federal Housing Administration. Ask for
and check references.

Affiliation with a real estate office. If the appraiser
could be a real estate agent seeking a possible listing
on your property, there may be a conflict of interest.
To avoid this, either choose another appraiser or
make it clear that this individual would not be a
candidate for any eventual listing of your property
with a real estate office.

SHOULD YOUR ASKING PRICE TAKE INTO CONSIDERATION FUTURE NEGOTIATIONS?

Chapter 10 covers the process of negotiating with a
potential buyer over such issues as contingencies,
inspections, financing and the like. The most important negotiation point with potential purchasers,
however, is over the price.

This raises questions about how best to negotiate.
For example, should you set a very high price and be
ready to come down, or a realistic price and stick to
it like a bulldog with a hambone? Should you throw
in appliances from the start and say you will pay for
termite work that needs to be done as the result of
physical inspections of the property, or should you
negotiate each of the points separately?

There is no one answer. Good negotiating
strategies reflect the personality of the negotiator. In
other words, if you hate bargaining, don't overprice
your home and plan to engage in a heavy-duty
bargaining session. You are almost sure to end up
hating the whole process and, as a result, are unlikely
to be successful at it.

You should decide your rock bottom sales price
and then adopt a strategy to get at least that much.
(See Chapter 10 for advice on negotiating strategies.)
If you are a small business person or someone else
who has daily experience in negotiating, doing this
will come easily to you. If you're the type of person
who dreads buying a new car because of the
haggling that's inevitably involved, why not pay a
broker for a few hours of time to help you adopt a
negotiating strategy and, as part of doing this, to
price your home? (See Chapter 4 for information on
hiring a broker by the hour.)

C. Ask a Broker for Help

Another way to determine what your house is fairly worth is to ask a real estate agent. Many agents offer a free comparative market analysis or property profile in the hope that you will list your house with them. This service is almost always offered at no cost and with no obligation on your part. Don't feel guilty about accepting free help even though you intend to sell your property yourself. You may end up hiring the broker to provide at least some help in one or more of the ways discussed in Chapter 4.

Brokers' opinions (free or not) should be in writing, using professionally accepted appraisal techniques. If the analysis isn't in writing, the broker can too easily change the estimate if the amount doesn't seem to meet with your approval. ("Well, maybe it is worth $259,000 instead of $229,000; lemme see....") This practice of telling homeowners what they want to hear is disparagingly referred to as "buying the listing" and happens with appalling frequency.

Even if you get an appraisal in writing, you can't be sure that the broker isn't trying to romance you by stating that your house is worth more than it really is. The best way to guard against this is to get several appraisals and to do your own cost comparisons. If any one appraisal is too high, it should be easy to spot.

D. Learn the Asking Prices of Houses for Sale

While actual sales prices of recently sold homes are the best source of information in pricing your home, asking prices of houses still on the market can also provide guidance. Despite the fact that asking prices don't tell you what a house will eventually sell for or even the house's appraised value, asking prices can give you some idea of the top of the range of market values in your area. As a general rule, asking prices are at least 10% over the market. This means, for instance, that a house asking $398,000 is probably worth only about $358,000, or even less if it has been on the market for more than a month.

To find out asking prices, do some window shopping in your neighborhood. Go to open houses, either on weekends when homes are shown to the public or on weekdays when local real estate agents have their tour day (often Tuesdays). Also, take note of how long a house has been on the market. Once you learn an asking price, don't confuse it with a selling price. Before saying (in a surprised tone) that "the house down the street is going for $388,000!" ask yourself if you actually mean that the house is *staying* around at that price because nobody will pay that much.

You can also learn something about an asking price by looking at real estate classified ads in newspapers. (Ads are covered in Chapter 6.) If an ad has run for a couple of months, the owner or agent has paid a lot for advertising without selling the property, which means the price is too high by a considerable amount. If the ad contains expressions like "motivated," "reduced," "owner will carry [financing]," "owner has bought" or "must sell," you know the owner is somewhat desperate, though not desperate enough to lower what is obviously an excessive asking price.

In general, keep in mind these two points:

- Even the lowest asking price in the bunch is above the house's market value or else the property would have sold already.

- The longer a property has been on the market, the more likely the asking price is at least 10% over the house's true value. If several houses have been on the market for more than a month or two in the same neighborhood, all sellers have unrealistic expectations. It could also mean, in extreme situations, that some condition has lowered values in the area generally—for example, a plant closing, toxic leakage or a sudden jump in interest rates.

E. Take the Temperature of the Local Housing Market

Knowing local conditions, comparable sale prices, asking prices of similar houses and the length of time similar houses have been on the market can help you determine how much to ask for your house. They tell you whether the market is hot (prices are going up), cold (prices are dropping) or lukewarm (prices are relatively stable). This is important information as the psychology of scarcity and abundance typically plays a major role in a house's selling price. A market perceived as hot (more buyers than sellers) feeds on itself and prices continue to rise. The opposite also tends to be true—falling prices triggered by an excess of houses tend to fall further, as sellers scramble to get the best prices they can.

In determining the temperature of your area, keep in mind these rules:

- If 25% or more of the houses sell within seven to ten days of being listed, the market is hot. (If 40% sell this quickly, the market is sizzling.)

- If more than half of the houses were on the market a month or more before selling, and most sold for less than their listing price, the market is cool.

- If the supply of houses on the market is steadily increasing, sales are slow, and prices of the houses in the neighborhood have decreased, the market is cold.

Reading the real estate sections of local papers for a month or more, visiting many houses and being aware of MLS computer services and comparable sales books are key ways to test the market. Another good long-term gauge of a market's temperature is current mortgage interest rates. As rates jump substantially (one percentage point or more), most housing markets begin to cool. Conversely, as rates drop, more people can afford houses and the market perks up. An exception occurs during times of unemployment, or underemployment, when consumer confidence is in the doldrums.

F. Price Your Own House

Let's suppose, now, that you are an extremely thorough person and have come up with a variety of appraisals as follows:

Professional appraiser you hire	$195,000
Real estate agent A	$205,000
Real estate agent B	$195,000
Real estate agent C	$198,000
Your own appraisal (from public records)	$190,000
Asking price of comparable home next door (interesting, but mostly irrelevant)	$229,000
What owner with a comparable house down the block says she got (not very relevant unless you really trust her)	$224,000

Given all the above data, at what price should you list your house for sale? If you're in a hurry to sell, keeping the price below $200,000 will probably move your house within a month in most markets, assuming the house is in good physical shape (see Section B, above, for information on finding out your house's condition before putting it on the market) and the average buyer can obtain financing. Given these appraisals, however, pricing the house under $200,000 probably means you will sell for too little. So you want to go above $200,000, but by how much? Because the comparable home next door has been on the market for two months at $229,000, you know you probably won't get that much without a long wait.

So pick a value somewhere in the middle—around $214,900. Of course, listing your house at a specific price doesn't mean you won't accept a lower one. Similarly, you can raise your asking price—especially if you've not listed with a broker—if you receive a number of offers at full price or more. Psychologically, however, most sellers find it harder to raise than to lower the asking price.

Remember that your asking price should not be too far out of line compared to similar properties, even if you think you must get a certain amount. If your price is unrealistic, even if a buyer makes an offer, she'll have a hard time getting financing if the lender's independent appraisal shows the price to be seriously inflated.

How local laws can affect your asking price. If you must comply with local laws requiring a house that changes hands to have energy-efficiency devices, smoke detectors or similar items (the most common local requirements are mentioned in Chapter 9), you need to consider how the cost of these items will affect your asking price. You can negotiate with a buyer to pay these costs, but it's usually easier to find out the total cost and add it to your asking price.

HOW ROBERTA AND SHIRLEY PRICED THEIR HOME

As part of selling their small two-story house, Roberta and Shirley checked their neighborhood to see what similar houses had sold for. Two identical houses in not as good shape had sold for $128,000 and $134,000 respectively, four and six months before. They then asked several real estate friends how they would price the house. The agents gave figures of $139,000 and $142,500.

Roberta and Shirley were a little disappointed to hear these low amounts, as they had done a lot of work on their kitchen and yard. They decided to wait for a few months to sell the house, as interest rates were dropping. Two months later, they put it on the market for $154,000. Interest rates had dropped dramatically and they quickly sold it for $152,000.

Why did they do so much better than the experts thought they would? The drop in interest rates was part of it; there were lots more potential buyers as a result, and prices went up. But in addition, Roberta and Shirley had worked hard for three years to get their house into perfect condition. Doing this had cost money, of course, but they looked at it as an investment. Some lookers didn't seem to care that the place was perfect, but a fair number (especially older people and dual-working couples) really did. They were willing to pay a little extra for a house that needed no work. ■

HOW TO TELL THE WORLD YOUR HOUSE IS FOR SALE

To sell your house for top dollar, you want to reach as many potential buyers as reasonably possible. Because for sale by owner homes won't appear in the inventory of real estate offices or the local multiple listing service, you'll have to do your own publicity. This chapter shows how, focusing on buying newspaper advertising, using for sale signs and effectively marketing your home through flyers.

A. Advertise—in the Classifieds

Many real estate ads placed by brokers engage in what I call "advertising overkill." Perhaps during an attack of insomnia you saw or heard real estate ads on late-night or early-morning TV or radio. Certainly you've seen good-sized display ads for expensive houses in exclusive magazines. This approach is not cost-effective, no matter how pricey the house is. Indeed, when big bucks are spent on advertising, usually the brokerage company, not the particular property, is being pushed. In addition, many ads deliberately omit the address of the property, to generate phone calls or walk-ins for the floor agent at the realty office, who can then show a variety of homes to her new client.

Your best bet is to advertise your house in the real estate classified section of local newspapers, which many potential buyers read. Classified sections offer bargain rates (compared to display ads in the rest of the newspaper) and cost less for private parties, as opposed to real estate agents, selling a house.

1. Decide Where to Advertise

You'll immediately notice a large price difference among ads in newspapers of small and large circulation. The more expensive rates of the larger papers reflect the fact that they reach many more people. Many sellers think it's better to pay the higher rates and advertise in the paper that the most people read. This is not necessarily so.

To illustrate this point, let's assume you have a house in Anaheim, where the major metropolitan paper is the *Los Angeles Times,* sold throughout Southern California. The *Anaheim Bulletin,* a community-based daily, is available locally and is mainly read by people inside its fairly narrow circulation area. Not surprisingly, the *Bulletin's* classified ad rates are considerably lower than those of the *Times.*

In which publication should you advertise an Anaheim home for sale? As with so many other things in life, it depends. If your house is valued at $300,000 or more, it's likely to appeal to executives transferring to Orange County from elsewhere in the United States. In this situation, the higher cost for advertising in the *Times,* or at least its Orange County edition, is justified.

But if your Anaheim home is worth $300,000 or less, it is not an executive-transfer candidate. It is more likely to be purchased by a first-time buyer who already lives in the area. Therefore, your ad will cost less, and may be more effective, if it appears in the *Anaheim Bulletin* rather than in the *Los Angeles Times* or its Orange County edition.

If your community has a weekly "shopper" or neighborhood paper, it may pay to advertise there. The rates are certainly low; about 10%–15% of what the metropolitan dailies charge. Such publications have a controlled circulation, meaning that they are typically delivered free door-to-door and sometimes in corner boxes, but in a very limited geographical area. Because of the small areas they cover, they are geared toward low-budget advertisers. I would suggest that you advertise in a local paper, but not exclusively. Try placing an ad there for one edition. If you don't get any offers during the first edition of the neighborhood paper, there's a good chance that everyone in the immediate vicinity knows your home is for sale and you need to tell your story to a wider readership. Then advertise in a paper with a greater circulation.

No matter what newspaper you choose, see if it has an "Open Home Guide" or "Open House" section. These sections are extremely effective for owners handling their own sales, and it perplexes me that not all newspapers have caught on to their value. An "Open Home Guide" consists of a specially boxed shopping list of classified ads for houses that are open—no appointment necessary—on a certain day (almost always Sunday and sometimes Saturday). The list is typically divided both geographically and by price, allowing readers to quickly zero in on homes in their price range and location of choice.

Otherwise, open house sections are the same as any other classified ad. They include the features of the house for sale, the address, phone number and an indication of whether it's for sale by owner or through a broker. You can include more detailed information on an answering machine tape or in a flier. (See Section D, below.)

A classified ad of two to three lines (often the minimum) in the Open Home section of a metropolitan daily is likely to cost about $30 to $40 each time you run it. In larger papers in cities like San Francisco, Los Angeles and San Diego, you may get a discount for running an ad on a weekend or an entire week, but you usually must prepay for the ad. Smaller papers (regional editions or small town papers) often charge about a quarter of what the big papers do—but the circulation is about a tenth to a third. But rates vary on all sizes of papers, so shop around.

If you're considering more than one paper, I'd suggest that you alternate your ads week by week. You can track the response pattern and decide where to advertise later. In a slow market, be cautious with your ad money so as to avoid spending oodles of dough buying expensive ads that nobody cares much

about anyway. In a hot market, consider running a media blitz to try to start a feeding frenzy.

2. Write a Good Classified Ad

Many real estate ads written by brokers are terrible. First, they use so much real estate lingo and abbreviations you need a Rosetta stone of real estatese to understand them. Second, because professionals often exaggerate the features of the house to please the seller, potential buyers are often very disappointed when they actually see the house behind the hype. To avoid both of these mistakes, your ad should be easy to understand (avoid abbreviations as much as possible), and should truthfully describe the important features of your home, such as its size, condition and location.

Here is a brief list of things your ad should mention:

- address, unless you want to encourage phone inquiries only, in which case you should at least list the neighborhood

- price

- for sale by owner

- number and type of rooms

- some indication of special charm—for example, patio, hot tub, big yard, fireplace or view

- facts about location, if desirable—for example, next to a park, near school or rapid transit

- financing facts, if noteworthy, such as owner will carry a loan

- dates and times of open house, and

- phone number for appointments.

Be sure that your ad doesn't exaggerate or play fast and loose with the truth. One function of your ad is to screen out people who won't be interested. If you describe a small tract home on a busy corner as if it is the first cousin to the Taj Mahal surrounded by

Yosemite National Park, you will waste a lot of people's time, including yours. At the same time, you want to lead with your strong suit. If there is a particular feature that distinguishes your home, be sure to emphasize it.

The list of items mentioned above is a suggestion to work from. You'll soon find, however, that you can't afford to publish all the information you consider important. Just keep in mind that you're trying to get people to come to see your home, not to buy it sight unseen through the newspaper. So, after highlighting your house's special feature, spend your advertising money on the items that people really must know: price, number of rooms, location, and how to see the home.

On the other hand, don't let frugality lead you into the pitfall of an ad which is so much shorthand it comes out gobbledegook.

A good way to prepare for ad-writing is to do some ad reading. Go through the open house ads in your local paper and circle the ones that get you interested in the homes they feature. Then try to emulate their approach. Chances are these ads will be brief, clear, contain essential information and perhaps show a touch of humor.

ADVERTISING YOUR HOUSE IN A HOT SELLER'S MARKET

In a super-heated seller's market, the demand for housing is intense and homes often sell for substantially more than their listed prices, even before a single open house has been held. This occurred, for example, in Santa Clara County's Silicon Valley and other parts of California beginning in early 1998, a time of rising employment and low interest rates.

To generate multiple offers in a hot seller's market, you may want to include in your flier or ad a statement that "Offers will be considered at 5 P.M. on [an appropriate date, probably a week or so in the future]." This doesn't guarantee multiple offers but does generate a sense of urgency on the part of home buyers. In that kind of atmosphere, you may find yourself choosing between several good offers and rejecting out of hand those which don't meet all your criteria—for example, prospective buyers who need to sell an existing home to buy yours or who aren't preapproved for financing.

If you don't receive any acceptable offers as of the date and time specified, you can revise your flyer or ad and set another deadline a week or two later, or you can simply drop the deadline altogether and accept offers whenever someone wants to submit one. As discussed in Chapter 9, Section B, to be binding, all real estate purchase offers must be both submitted and accepted in writing and must spell out specific terms.

GOOD ADS AND POOR ADS

GOOD AD:

All information spelled out completely and clearly.

BY OWNER, 950 PARKER, 3 BR, 2 BA, $175K

Hot tub, extra wide sunny fenced yard, Bay view, new kitchen.

Owner may carry 2nd for 10%. Call 549-1976 eves after 6 or leave message on tape.

POOR AD:

Information compressed by too many abbreviations.

3 BR, 2 BA, $175K, FSBO, 950 PARKER

Ht tb, x-wide yd, bay vu, OWC 2nd, 549-1976 after 6 or lv mess.

GOOD AD FOR FIXER UPPER:

Home seeks new owner with handy touch, at 950 Parker for only $129K. Old roof, old plumbing and wiring, old assumable loan. Owner will carry 2nd with good down payment. 3 BR, 2 BA, potential for expansion. 549-1976 for appointment.

3. Don't Discriminate

I am delighted to report that today virtually nobody advertises property for sale with a stated preference as to the age, race, color, sex, sexual orientation or religion of the buyer. That doing this is illegal needs no repetition from me. But even if you don't overtly discriminate in your ad, you could be accused of conducting a discriminatory ad campaign if the *way* you advertise ends up discriminating against certain groups. This might happen if your advertising excludes particular groups of people from even learning that your house is for sale—for example, if you list your house only in places where people of a particular group (racial, religious, ethnic, sexual) are likely to see it. Protect yourself from possible charges of discriminatory intent by placing an ad in a newspaper of general circulation in your county.

B. Advertise in Other Media

Newspapers aren't the only media in which to advertise. Below are a few other potential avenues.

FSBO publications. These tend to come and go, as it's not easy to finance their publication. But keep an eye out for them; ask bankers or title companies if they know of any.

FSBO phone shopping services. These operate like a multiple listing service hooked into an online data base, specifically for people selling their own homes.

Newsletters and publications such as those put out by women's or consumer groups and service organizations. Think creatively and concentrate on those with a real tie-in between the interests of the publication's readers and your property. For example, if your house is in a great school district, advertising in a local parents' magazine would be a great idea. If your land is zoned to allow the keeping of a horse, advertising in a local equine journal would make sense. If your house is a fixer-upper, you might advertise in a trade publication of local contractors. (But remember the cautions about discriminatory advertising in Section A3, above.)

Internet listings. See Section E, below.

C. Hang For Sale Signs

Good For Sale signs should be a major part of any campaign to sell a house. My experience suggests that they are as effective as classified advertisements in marketing residential property. For this reason, you want professional-looking signs indicating that you mean business. If you've taken care of your signs, it suggests that you've taken care of your home, and that you'll take care of the details in the transaction. You don't want potential buyers to think that you have a schlocky house because you have a schlocky sign.

1. Types of Signs

You will want to buy several ready-made, 18" x 24", flat "For Sale By Owner" signs. These should cost $10 at most, with an additional charge of $5 or so to add your telephone number in pre-cut vinyl letters. Red, blue or black letters on a white background are particularly easy to read.

You will also want to buy at least three A-boards, which stand up on their own. These are good for your front lawn and nearby intersections. I recommend ones with a chalkboard area to list your address. Each sandwich board will cost about $20; you add two of the one-sided ready-made exterior "For Sale by Owner" signs to each frame. The shop may do this for you with your order for free, or for a nominal charge.

All in all, you should figure on spending approximately $150 to buy reasonably durable and easy-to-read signs. Remember, signs can be treated as a cost of sale for tax purposes, provided the expense is incurred within 90 days of sale. (See Chapter 3, Section E.)

Obviously, your signs should be easy to read. Use thick chalk or adhesive pre-cut vinyl letters and make clear block letters on the chalkboard portion of your A-board signs. For signs on or in front of your house, you need only list the time and day of your open house, such as "2–4 PM SUN." For signs farther away from your house, include the street address. Don't clutter your sign by including the price or terms. The sign is meant to lead people to the property where they will find out the details.

If you want to show the house to prospective purchasers only during stated hours, prominently list the hours on the sign at your house, along with your phone number. Some people further try to protect their privacy by putting up for sale signs only during open house hours. Don't follow this approach—it obviously limits the effectiveness of your advertising campaign. If you put up signs only on weekends, no one who passes your house during the rest of the week will even know it's for sale. And if they don't know, they can't tell their friends. In my experience, people who leave signs up at all times, but indicate that the house is shown only during specific open house times or by appointment only, are not bothered to any substantial degree by people trying to see the house at other times.

To purchase signs for your house and A-boards for the neighborhood, check in the Yellow Pages under "Signs." You will likely find a number of local sign shops that sell everything you need. Shops that sell A-board signs will also have signs reading "For Sale By Owner" and "Open House" suitable for tacking on your house or placing in the yard. You should arrange to pick up the signs yourself, unless you want to incur additional shipping charges, which will cost almost as much as the signs themselves due to the size and weight of larger signs and A-boards. Small "For Sale" signs are commonly available at hardware and office supply stores.

What about custom-made signs? Before you go to the expense of ordering custom-made signs, ask yourself this: Do you want to sell the property or the sign? Remember, too, that sign shops sell custom-made signs only in minimum quantities—often ten or 12—with a hefty initial charge for art work. To sell just one house, it's not cost-effective.

2. Location of Signs

Where should signs be placed? In general, you should include the following locations.

- Use your flat ready-made signs around your house. At least one sign should be in the window of your house, on the side of the house, or in the yard, attached to a pole or a fence, where it's easy to see from both ends of the street. If you are on a corner, you will need at least two signs, at least one facing each street.

- On open house days, place an A-board with an arrow pointing to your house and listing the hours during which the home is open in the yard or on the sidewalk immediately in front of the house. You can also get an "Open House" sign and put it on a pole with your "For Sale By Owner" sign or in the window.

- Place A-boards at the two corners of your block. Usually it's best to put them on the same side of the street as your house unless for some reason they would be more noticeable to pedestrian or vehicle traffic on the other side. If you live in a semi-rural area without a conventional street grid, use your common sense to locate signs where the maximum number of passersby will spot them.

- Position A-boards showing your address at the nearest major intersection or street near your home, so that they can be seen by traffic in both directions. Never place signs more than one-third to one-half mile away—because once you're more than half a mile away, you're in a different neighborhood.

SELLING RENTED PROPERTY

If your house is currently being rented, discuss your sale plans with the tenants before you advertise. While you have a right to show the house for sale, your tenants are entitled to their privacy. You must give tenants reasonable notice of your intent to enter and show the house—24 hours written notice is presumed to be reasonable. (Civil Code § 1954.) Notice need not be in writing, but it's a good idea to give written notice and to keep a copy.

Try to get them to be at least somewhat cooperative, which is not always easy, as tenants who are about to lose their home are likely to be unhappy and may feel that you are intruding by showing the house to strangers. Limit the number of times you show the house in a given week, and make sure that your tenants agree to the evening and weekend times you want to show the house. You have the right to show the house only during normal business hours (customarily 9 A.M. to 5 P.M., Monday through Friday), after giving reasonable notice

Another way to get the tenant's cooperation is to reduce their rent somewhat during the time the house is being shown, in exchange for the inconvenience.

If you put up a sign advertising sale of the property, make sure it clearly warns against disturbing the occupant and includes a telephone number to call for information. A good compromise is a sign which says "Shown by Appointment Only" or "Do Not Disturb Occupant."

If, despite your best efforts to protect their privacy, your tenants are hostile, you will probably want to consider asking (or paying) them to leave. Whether you can legally do this depends on a number of factors, including whether the tenants have a lease or a month-to-month tenancy and whether the property is under a rent-control ordinance with a "just cause for eviction" requirement. Dealing with these issues is beyond the scope of this book. They are covered in the *Landlord's Law Book, Volume 1: Rights and Responsibilities* and *Volume 2: Evictions*, both by David Brown (Nolo Press).

Play off others' signs. You will observe that other open house showings in your neighborhood may begin as early as 1:00 or even noon. Great. Allow these signs to lead traffic into your neighborhood; don't duplicate them. In other words, you don't need a sign at a main intersection eight blocks away if there are already three signs listing houses within a few blocks of yours. What you do need are signs that lead traffic from the other open houses to yours. In this regard, it helps to wait until after 1:00 to put up your signs after you know where the others are.

Call your city planning board or local association of realtors for information on local ordinances and subdivision restrictions as to sign placement. For example, in some places it's illegal to place signs on pedestrian medians in the middle of wide streets. And obviously, law or no law, keep safety in mind. Avoid cluttering a corner with so many signs that pedestrians can't walk safely and motorists can't see your sign anyway.

D. Distribute Your Own Printed Property Fact Sheet

You will need to write a complete description of your house to pass out at your open house. So that it's not a last minute rush job, prepare it a few weeks ahead. To get ideas, visit open houses and see what other statements are like, noting the attractive features of the ones you like.

Your flyer should not only give the basic facts about your house, but should highlight all desirable features and let people know why you have enjoyed living there. Below are some of the items you should cover, in what I consider to be the order of importance:

- address (cross streets are helpful)
- number and types of rooms (bedrooms, baths, formal dining room, eat-in kitchen and the like)

- special features, such as deck, basement, attic, pool, new roof or carpet, air conditioning, fireplace or hot tub
- number of levels
- style of house—for example, California bungalow or ranch
- neighborhood information, such as school district or proximity to parks, shops and public transit
- financing terms, such as owner financing, down payment, assumable loans, if any (interest rate, payment amount, balloon payments), etc.
- "sex appeal"—a few items that make your house fun—for example, sunny yard, wonderful old tree or famous person used to live there
- yard (great garden, fenced in or other feature)
- age
- square feet of living area, excluding garage and attic
- garage, if any, and size (one- or two-car)
- lot size
- view and type (bay view, mountains, lake, woods)
- home warranties, if available
- zoning
- kitchen information, including any appliances that are included
- association fees or maintenance charges, if your home is in a subdivision
- price (this is not unimportant, but place it at the end so that potential buyers see all the "goodies" before seeing the price)
- when house will be shown—days of the week and hours, with appointments arranged at other times, and

- phone number for information and best times to call.

Your property description should be designed to achieve two goals:

- Attract people to arrange an appointment or come to your open houses.

- Provide the important facts to people who come to look at your house. This not only will save you answering the same questions over and over, it gives potential buyers something to take away with them for easy referral later. ("Was that a gas or electric range? And how much was the assumable first loan? I thought I'd written down the number of blocks to the elementary school, but….")

If you or a friend have an artistic flair, a sketch of the house or appropriate computer graphics can dress up your flier. If you're unartistic, call a local real estate office for recommendations of people who do line drawings of houses. You can also get suggestions for graphic assistance at a local copy center or desktop publishing business.

In addition, you can take a photo of your home, with good contrast, and add it to the top of your printed statement. Be sure your photo shows the full house, uncluttered by cars parked in the street, bikes or toys on the lawn and the like. Paste the photo (even a color one which will reproduce black-and-white) onto your original before copying. You will need to experiment with lighter-darker copier settings. If you really want a good-looking photograph on your flyer, have a black and white print made of your photo. A copy center can reproduce it sharply for a few dollars.

After you prepare your flyer following the samples presented below, have it copied on 8 ½" x 11" inch colored paper at a copy or printing shop. Experiment to see what color looks best and is easiest

to read. Assuming you make 300–500 copies, your flyers should cost less than a few cents each.

Distribute copies of your property fact sheet as widely as possible:

- Fact sheets should be given to friends, co-workers, neighbors and business associates such as your doctor, dentist, lawyer, insurance broker and anyone else you think might be interested. Include a brief cover letter asking for their help in getting the word out on your house. You might even consider holding a neighborhood open house, making it more like a party or social occasion.

- You can hire a high school student to distribute your fact sheet to homes in neighboring blocks.

- Flyers can be left in local stores such as laundromats, coffee shops, health clubs and delis, with the owners' permission.

- Send several copies of your fact sheet to relocation housing or personnel departments of local corporations and universities who often help their employees who are relocating to your area find housing. Include a brief cover letter with your fact sheet. Be sure to call first and get the name of the personnel director to give your letter a more personal touch.

- You can also mail fact sheets to people who call in response to your classified ad.

Think of it this way: If you distribute 200 flyers to people who then share each flyer with friends who are interested in moving, you have reached hundreds of potential buyers at a very low cost.

Below are five sample fact sheets. The first was used by a Nolo Press editor when he sold his house without a broker. The second, which I wrote, advertises luxury property. The third, written by another broker, gives detailed information on a subdivision home. The last two were written by enterprising FSBOs.

SAMPLE 1

House For Sale By Owner

1508 Rose Way
(corner of Main St., three blocks below Wegman Rd.)

Small, 2-story Salt Box style, in excellent condition
(a cheerful little house)

2 1/2 Bedrooms (the one-half is a small, but nicely
converted garage, in the house)

1 Bath with tub and shower (modern and cute)

1 Living room with fireplace and lots of light

1 Dining room
(small or cozy, depending on your point of view)

1 Kitchen (includes built-in/brand new gas stove top, wall
oven, dishwasher, new counter top, handmade, glass-
fronted cupboards, refrigerator)

1 Laundry room with washer and dryer

Amenities include deck, Japanese fish pond with four
friendly koi, picket fence, edible front yard (strawberries),
new shed for garden tools, bikes, etc., refinished wood
floors throughout house.

Other facts of interest include:

- Built in 1941 on concrete slab

- Efficient and relatively new forced air heating

- Walking distance to North Berkeley BART, Monterey
  Market area and Westbrae area (Toot Sweets,
  Brothers Bagels, etc.— important for Sunday
  morning)

- Four houses from Cedar Rose park with kiddie play
  area and tennis courts

- Two blocks from excellent elementary school; six
  blocks from middle school

Price: $151,900.

OPEN HOUSE on Sunday, February 16 and subsequent
Sundays 1:00 - 5:00 p.m. You can reach us at 555-1976
(day) or 555-0439 (evenings between 6:00 and 8:00 p.m.)

SAMPLE 2

For Sale By Owner

LUXURY HOME IN SAN FRANCISCO—142 Erewhon
Street

Only $422,900 buys this elegant 3 bedroom, 2 bath
home featuring cathedral ceilings, formal dining room,
separate breakfast room and attractive low maintenance
yard on a 33' x 100' lot.

Carpets and window coverings are included in this fine
home which offers such distinctive features as a window
seat in the living room, mahogany doors and trim in the
dining room, hardwood floors throughout the main floor,
including random plank flooring in the living and dining
area, and even a separate bathroom heater.

This pleasant residence features a 30-gallon Rudd Monel
water heater. The furnace, tar-and-gravel roof and
downspouts are only four years old, and the home's
interior has been painted within recent months. In
addition, a 110,000 BTU gravity furnace has been
installed four and a half years ago; all of these features
make for trouble-free living and "move-in" condition!

The garage accommodates two cars in tandem. Muni bus
#43 is at the corner, with easy access to a nearby Metro
station. A shopping center, including Tower Market, is a
few blocks away.

Qualified buyers should call 555-1312 for appointments
to see this home.

SAMPLE 3

For Sale By Owner

Residential Development in the Heights

Location: 45 Hadrian Court
                 Cross Street—Laguna

Abstract: Three bedrooms, two bathrooms, living room with fireplace, dining area, large kitchen, breakfast room, laundry room, large private patio, one car parking, storage.

Description: Constructed in 1962. The central location is convenient to schools, transportation, shops, and yet enjoys a quite wooded setting, located off of a central courtyard, and looks out to lush landscaping.

Price: $215,000

Expenses: Taxes will be based on Assessor's Office interpretation of Jarvis-Gann Law (Proposition 13); presently expected to be 1.15% of new sale price.

The property will be reassessed upon change of ownership. A supplemental tax bill will be received which may reflect an increase or decrease in taxes based on property value.

Maintenance: (Association Dues) $703/mo. which includes: professional management, taxes, insurance, water, garbage collection, window cleaning, repairs, maintenance. Blanket mortgage assessment is also included.

Contact: Call owners at 555-1899.

SAMPLE 4

SUNNYSIDE

Location: 477 Meurice Avenue (corner of Gennessee)

Description: Charmingly remodeled, detached, two bedrooms plus den, living room with fireplace and built-in bookshelves, dining room with built-in buffet, updated bath, updated eat-in country kitchen with dishwasher and disposal, hardwood floors, new carpet, updated wiring, mostly copper plumbing, newly painted in and out, large yard with fruit trees, full basement, bonus room (legality not warranted), and 1/4 bath down, garage and room for expansion.

Lot Size: Approximately 112.5' x 25' x 35' (irregular); built in 1923.

Price: $299,500

Contact: For Sale by Owner: Joseph Bruce, 555-2885.

SAMPLE 5

437 Castenada Avenue

$459,500

This formal architecturally designed **three bedroom+, two and one-half bath home** with a "Tandem Style" **garage** is located in **Forest Hill**, one of the premier residential areas of San Francisco. **Forest Hill** is only a short walk to one of two underground MUNI stations, West Portal shops, and public library.

This is one of the few homes in **Forest Hill** located on a **level street** that also offers a **great view** of Mt. Davidson, St. Francis Woods, San Bruno mountains, the Pacific Ocean, Zoo, Fort Funston, Olympic Golf Course, etc.

With **hardwood or tile floors** throughout, this lovely two-story home has a **sunken living room** with a **barrel ceiling** and wood-burning **fireplace**. Many doorways, walkways and windows are **arched**. There's a gracious **formal dining room** with a swinging door passage to an **updated**, bright and cheery **kitchen**, **breakfast room** and door to the backyard.

A **wide stairway** leads to the upstairs landing from which you can enter one of **three large bedrooms**. The main bathroom on this level has a tub in addition to a large tiled shower. There is a second tile and oak bathroom off the master bedroom.

A **bonus room** (formerly the maid's quarters), located in the basement, functions as a den or office. In the basement you'll also find a new water-heater and electric garage opener; a laundry area with heavy sinks; furnace/storage area and a third bathroom area next to a second walk-out door to a very private **rock patio** and backyard garden.

The front yard has **in-ground sprinklers** for both lawn and plants.

Plumbing and **electrical** systems have been updated.

Call for appointment 555-1652 daytimes or 555-2506 evenings until 9.

E. Marketing Your House on the Internet

Since the advent of the Internet and the World Wide Web in a great many business offices and homes, it is increasingly practical to expose a home for sale to househunters. Internet listings have the advantages of wide coverage and economy and allow you to show photos of your house.

One good way to do this, and to get information on the real estate market in general, is by accessing the International Real Estate Digest site at www.ired.com. This site is dedicated to the posting of independent real estate information on the World Wide Web. From this page you—and more importantly, potential buyers—can link to information on buyers, sellers and listings from throughout the United States and even beyond, including FSBOs. One good link is the Owners' Network at www.owners.com.

Other helpful sites are designed to serve FSBOs, including the following:

www.citybreeze.com/homes

www.fisbos.com

www.fsbo-net.com

www.fsboconnection.com

www.fsbofinder.com/index.sht

www.io.com/house/depos.html

www.openhouse-online.com

www.primenet.com/~fsbo/ca.html

These sites all vary by price and listings. Some, for example, will list your home for $9.95 a month; others charge $25 for a six-month period. Some have only a handful of lisitings, while others have hundreds. You will have to visit them all until you find the site or sites that fit your needs and your budget.

Finally, you can visit www.ca.living.net, a computerized multiple listing service sponsored by real estate agents and their associations. You can use it to get a sense of what is on the market. ■

Chapter 7

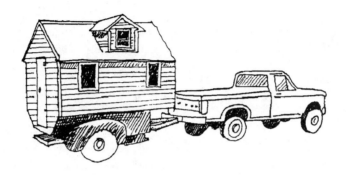

PREPARING YOUR HOUSE FOR SALE AND MAKING DISCLOSURES

Before showing your house to prospective buyers, make sure you've done the basic groundwork to advertise your property as described in Chapter 6.

- Place newspaper ads well in advance of open house dates. Check with newspapers for deadlines.

- Print and distribute your property fact sheet. Set aside at least one hundred copies to give prospective buyers who visit your home.

- Purchase For Sale signs, ready to place at predetermined locations.

But you need to do more preparation before putting out the welcome mat. You want to make sure your house is attractive to potential buyers, you need to prepare for open houses and you'll want to take steps to protect your property—and to protect yourself and your visitors from potential liability.

You also want to make sure you comply with all state and local disclosure requirements in selling your home—for example, regarding defects in the property and environmental hazards. This chapter explains these important legal obligations.

A. Handling Phone Calls

Your primary contact with prospective buyers will be over the telephone. People will see your For Sale signs or a newspaper ad and will call to ask questions. After all, it makes sense to rule out houses that are too large, too small or too expensive without having to go see them. Therefore, you must be prepared to treat each telephone call as a miniature business conference.

How to answer the phone. Answer the phone as you would ordinarily, but be prepared to give and receive information concerning your house. Keep the following material next to every telephone in the house so that you can keep notes and answer questions easily:

- copy of your property fact sheet
- a notebook or pad of paper
- a few sharpened pencils or working pens.

An organized, professional first impression is important—you certainly don't want to keep a potential buyer on hold while you hunt for a pen or paper.

Who should answer the phone. Don't let your children answer the phone, if at all possible, during the time your house is for sale. If children must answer the phone—for example, when you're not at home—make sure they ask politely for the callers' names and phone numbers and don't give out any information concerning the house ("my parents are asking $300,000 but they'll really take $275,000") or the family's selling needs ("my dad starts a new job in Peoria next month"). If you think it's cute to let your four-year old answer the phone, discontinue this practice while your house is on the market.

Leaving an answering machine message. When you're away from home, leave a message like the following on your answering machine or voice mail:

"You have reached 555-2001. We can't take your call right now, but please leave your name, telephone number and the time and date of your call, and we'll get back to you as soon as possible. If you're calling about the home for sale at 950 Parker Street, it has three bedrooms and two baths and the asking price is $300,000. It will be open every Sunday this month from two to four p.m. Now please wait for the tone and then leave any message you wish, including the best time to reach you."

What information to give over the phone. Keep in mind that most callers want to receive, not give, information. Many people want to know everything about the property, but are unwilling to give out even their names over the telephone! As a private party, you have a slight advantage over the professional agent, because people who call you shouldn't fear

being pestered by an aggressive salesperson if they give you their name. At any rate, you have a right to ask with whom you are speaking and to find out where you can call them back with further information if and when this is necessary.

Remember—you cannot sell a house over the phone. Therefore, you may want to volunteer only limited information, such as the asking price and number of rooms, plus a few other salient facts about your house—lot size, any assumable financing, view and the like. If the caller sounds very interested, offer to send or fax her a copy of your property fact sheet. You also want to let people know when they can see your house, either on an appointment basis or during an open house. Tell callers no more than that. Someone may call for dishonest purposes—for example, to find out when you're not home so they can burgle the place. Finally, you certainly don't want to start dickering over price or terms in a telephone conversation. Tell callers enough so they can decide whether or not they want to see the property and, if so, when.

Setting appointments to show the house. If a caller requests an appointment to see your house, be reasonable as to date and time but make sure the appointment is convenient for you. Try to show your home while there is still some daylight. If possible, get potential buyers to come during open house times. If that's not possible, try to "tandem" appointments. Having more than one person look at your house at the same time tends to heighten buyers' interest and improve your bargaining position. It also increases the chance that at least one of the prospects will show up.

Don't, however, cancel business commitments or important personal plans for an appointment to show your home. If you do, it's practically a slam-dunk cinch that the so-called buyer will stand you up, without so much as a by-your-leave, after you've given away theater tickets, called in sick at work, turned down an open appointment at your son's orthodontist or begged off on your daughter's school play. If you respect the commitments you're already made to your family and your job, you'll do about all you reasonably can to minimize the time you waste with the ever-popular "lookie-lous," but you'll still meet quite a few of them.

B. Making Your Home Attractive Before Showing It

Making your house look as nice as possible may seem obvious. Apparently it's not, because I've noticed that many sellers don't do much beyond vacuuming the living room rug and maybe cleaning the ring off the bathtub. With a little thought, you can surely do a lot better.

All the advertising in the world won't help if your house doesn't show well. And short of spending a lot of money to fix up your home, you can take several steps to make your house look as attractive as possible:

- Sweep the sidewalk, mow the lawn, prune the bushes, weed the garden and clear papers, debris, kids' toys and the like from the yard, front steps and porch. In general, make sure the house has curb appeal and looks good from the street.

- Clean the windows inside and out; make sure the paint (both exterior and interior) is not chipped or flaking.

- Be sure that the doorbell works.

- Clean, tidy up and make attractive all rooms and furnishings, floors, walls and ceilings—it's especially important that the bathroom and kitchen are spotless.

- Organize and make free from clutter all closets, cupboards and surfaces.

- Make sure that the basic appliances and fixtures work—get rid of leaky faucets and frayed cords.

- Leave window shades up about halfway and turn on a few lights, so there is sufficient—but not glaring—light.

- Make sure the house smells good—from an apple pie or cookies baking in the oven or from spaghetti sauce simmering on the stove. Keep some scented potpourri in an attractive container in the bathrooms. Hide the kitty litter box and eliminate any offensive odors—whether from animals, cigarette smoke, burnt food, strong perfume or pesticides.

- Put vases of flowers throughout the house—on the kitchen or dining room table, the fireplace mantel, coffee table in the living room and other locations.

- Pleasant (but unobtrusive) background music is a nice touch. Make sure there are no loud or irritating noises, such as heavy metal rock blaring from your teenager's stereo.

SHOULD YOU MAKE MAJOR REPAIRS?

It hardly pays to do considerable remodeling for purely aesthetic purposes. After all, you might spend a lot of money and time making the house look better to you, only to have the buyer completely redo it again. Except for obvious improvements such as a fresh coat of paint, it's typically counter-productive to redecorate. Some repair and remodeling jobs do deliver a good deal of bang for the buck, however, especially updating outmoded kitchens and bathrooms.

STEVE: FIRST IMPRESSIONS DO COUNT

Believe it or not, my wife Catherine and I almost bought a house in Novato in part because it had a variety of interesting reading material on the coffee table and bookshelf, including a Nolo Press book.

— Nolo Press Editor Steve Elias

JOANNE: LITTLE THINGS MEAN A LOT

Anything that you can do, relatively inexpensively, to make you feel pampered in your home will also help with buyers' fantasies. I bought roses, big plush towels, candlesticks and scented soap and bubbles for a shabby bathroom, along with an inexpensive opaque rose-colored shower curtain. Everyone commented that they loved the bathroom, despite the fact that it obviously needed work.

One successful real estate broker I know always recommends leaving magazines, books and record jackets where prospective purchasers can see them. If you do this, think about the person you expect to examine your house. In some neighborhoods you might display the *New York Times* or the *New Yorker;* in others areas, put out *Sports Illustrated* or *Sunset.* The idea, of course, is to encourage prospective purchasers to fantasize about how pleasant it will be to live in your house.

An experienced decorator or a friend with a good eye can tell you how to improve the look of your house without spending much money. For instance, a dining room light fixture on a standard switch has only two settings—off and on. But for about $10, you can buy a dimmer switch with installation instructions. A dimmer will give you soft lighting and enhance the atmosphere. Even if you can't install the dimmer yourself, a local electrician won't cost too much to do it. A more attractive house may mean an extra several thousand dollars in your pocket.

C. Preparing for a Safe Showing

Take a moment to think about how to protect prospective buyers from possible injury, and yourself from lawsuits. Walk through your home, checking for and dealing with everything that might cause injury, especially to someone who is not familiar with your house's layout. At some open houses, 50 or more people can show up at once, and a number of them are likely to be small, so think about safety for kids as well as adults. Here are a few things to check for:

- Slippery throw rugs—take them up
- Loose steps—fix them
- Slick areas, such as front steps—put down rubber mats
- Long electrical and phone cords—make sure they are out of the way
- Unsafe electrical wires and fixtures—replace them
- Potentially dangerous areas in yards—block them off
- Decks and pools—child-proof them
- Medicine, cleaning supplies or household chemicals that children could get into—lock them up
- Pets—put them in an enclosure, even if they have always been friendly; if they are likely to be noisy, arrange for them to take a brief vacation.

CONSIDER BUYING A HOME WARRANTY

If you're trying to sell your house, it may be worth your while—as a way to make your house more attractive—to purchase a home warranty. Typically, a warranty covers major housing systems (electrical, built-in appliances, heating, plumbing and the like) for one year. Most warranties cost $300–$400 and are renewable. If something goes wrong with any of the covered systems after escrow closes, the repairs are paid for—and the new buyer saves money.

According to the National Home Warranty Association (NHWA), on the average, homes that come with warranties sell 50%–60% faster and for a couple of thousand dollars more than homes that don't. Before buying, however, be sure you don't duplicate coverage. You don't need a warranty for the heating system, for example, if your furnace is just six months old and still covered by the manufacturer's three-year warranty.

SIGN-IN SHEET

WELCOME TO 950 PARKER STREET

Thank you for coming. Please take a fact sheet on our house and sign in before going through our home. Please print clearly.

Name	Address	Phone	How did you learn about this house?

D. Holding an Open House

Once you've taken the steps outlined in Sections A-C, you should be ready for your first open house. The following items can make it successful:

1. If your children are small, have them visit a friend or relative during open house times. Children are usually curious and want to be helpful. But they may be underfoot or demand attention when you're trying to conduct business with a potential buyer. In addition, children may blurt something out that you'd rather a prospective buyer not hear.

2. Anticipate buyers' questions and practical needs and have your answers ready. For example:

- Estimate the walking or driving time to the nearby commute train or bus, even if you don't use public transportation. Get fare rates and schedules and have them at the ready.

- Go through your home with a view toward its potential—for example, adding a room in the basement, remodeling the bathroom to add a stall shower, enclosing the porch, or whatever might strike a buyer's fancy—without representing the feasibility or cost of improvements.

3. Be on time. If your open house is scheduled to start at 2:00 p.m., have your A-frame For Sale signs in position by 1:45. Why? Because people will probably start arriving as soon as they see the first sign or as soon as the appointed hour strikes, whichever comes first. You don't want to keep your public waiting. One family member should be ready to open the door at 2:00 sharp while another takes

15 minutes to put out the signs. Fifteen minutes before the open house is scheduled to end, send one family member out to retrieve the signs.

4. Have a sign-in sheet ready to accompany your property fact sheets. Remember, you are exchanging facts with your visitors. If they have the right to enter your house and learn things about it, you have a right to know who they are. You also have a right to make follow-up calls to people who've seen your house to determine their reactions, likes, dislikes and possible interest. A sign-in sheet will also help you evaluate the effectiveness of your advertising.

A sample sign-in sheet is on the preceding page; a blank form is in the Appendix.

5. Be prepared to deal with "nosy nerds," or "nosy neighbors." These are not quite the same as "lookie-lous" who just go looking at houses for the fun of it when they have no intention of making a purchase. "Nosy nerds" only look at houses in their immediate neighborhood, in order to pat themselves on the back or console themselves concerning their own homes—even though they have no intention of selling in the near future. The only way to respond to these folks is to be polite but not waste much time on them. One way to defuse the "nosy nerd" bomb is to invite neighbors to your open house by means of a card which you can put in mailboxes of neighbors within a block or two of your house. Your invitation to neighbors could look something like this:

YOU'RE INVITED TO AN OPEN HOUSE

We've loved being your neighbors; we'll be moving soon. We're selling our home (asking $299,500) and will be holding it open this Sunday from 2–4 p.m. Why not drop by? Our home might be perfect for a friend or relative of yours!

John and Marcia Nolo, 950 Parker Street

---

6. Be prepared to talk with potential buyers. Here are a few tips:

- Talk about neutral subjects, such as family and neighborhood. Be pleasant, and do a lot of active listening, drawing the buyers out as to their needs and preferences—entertaining at home, which means maximizing the living-dining area; doing lots of cooking, which means a serviceable, bright and cheery kitchen and the like. These conversations can help you frame a subtle sales pitch geared toward the buyer's interests and practical needs—for example, if the potential buyer mentions that he took a recent bicycle trip, mention the nearby bike paths. If he says that bread is his favorite food, point out that three bakeries are in the area.

JASON: USING A SIGN-IN SHEET AS A MARKETING TOOL

At my first open house, I simply left out a blank pad of paper for people to sign in. I wasn't prepared for the 75 people who came by the first day, and neglected to ask most of them to sign in. I only got a few names and a handful of phone numbers. Next time around, I gave my sign-in sheet a lot more thought. First, I made a well-organized form with spaces for name, address and telephone number. I added a column for people to note how they heard about my open house. From this, I learned that more people came because of my ad in the local weekly, rather than the expensive ad in the daily newspaper. With this feedback, I changed my marketing strategy in subsequent weeks—and saved money on advertising.

- Don't volunteer personal information that may be used against you in negotiating a sales price or contract—for example, don't tell prospective buyers that you're incredibly anxious to sell because you're starting a new job out of state soon.

• Don't go overboard praising your house or its amenities—it may seem phony and be used against you when negotiating contract terms. At the same time, keep your disagreements about personal taste to yourself.

• Be cordial, but don't overwhelm prospective purchasers with energy or enthusiasm. Many people look at hundreds of homes; others check out houses as a hobby and don't ever really plan to buy one. If one person doesn't seem clearly interested, concentrate on someone who does.

• Learn to look at your house as if you were buying it, with a view toward:

✓ probable down payment, closing costs and monthly cost of ownership, including taxes, insurance and utility costs (see Chapters 8 and 11)

✓ neighborhood conveniences and services (school district, parks, shopping, transportation and the like)

✓ local zoning ordinances, including restrictions about adding on to a house.

• Listen carefully—you can learn a lot about questions and comments you hear over and over. For example, if prospective buyers seem intent on verifying reading scores or district boundaries of local schools, they obviously have or are planning to have children. Not only should you talk about the school district, but mention other child-related attractions, such as a nearby park or day care center, light traffic on the streets, other children in the neighborhood or whatever else.

• Above all, to sell your own house you must keep your sense of humor. Many buyers look at houses the way they look at used cars—they search for, and pounce on, every major and minor flaw. Apparently, they believe that emphasizing the negative will get the seller to accept a low offer. Often, however, this "exaggerate the flaws" approach does just the opposite because it makes the seller mad. Try not to take negative comments personally. Just remember, people who don't want to buy your house are not rejecting you. They probably want a larger yard or more bedrooms or just don't want an all-electric kitchen. Finally, don't take it to heart if the buyers don't fall in love with your home; remember, there's another buyer out there for your house, and the perfect match is yet to be made.

E. Protecting Your Property

The unhappy truth is that, while it's rare, there are times when prospective "buyers" are interested in seeing your home for just one reason: They want to "case the joint" so they can efficiently steal your possessions later. There is no way to completely prevent this, but you can and should take reasonable precautions every time your home is to be shown to strangers, be it individually or in larger numbers.

1. Don't display silver, china, expensive art or other valuable possessions—especially those which are easily stolen or accidentally broken.

2. Make sure items like credit cards, ATM-access cards, checkbooks and house keys are either on your person or under lock and key.

3. Don't discuss your personal schedule or lifestyle with strangers. Sometimes homeowners try to sell the neighborhood and, in doing so, make excessively revealing comments, like "It's so safe here we frequently leave the back door open during the day so the children don't need to carry a key!" or "It's only two blocks from church, and every day I can leave at just a quarter to twelve and be in my pew for Noon Mass."

4. Be sure people touring your home can enter and leave only through one door, except, of course, when you are escorting them through another, such as the door to the back yard or garage.

5. Escort and accompany prospective buyers. You needn't be at their side, but do keep them within sight at all times. This is obviously easier to do with one person who made an appointment than with 20 people at an open house. If you anticipate a house full of people, draft a few relatives or friends to help control traffic. If too many people show up at once, ask some of them to wait for the next "tour." Don't be afraid to structure the open house so that you feel comfortable.

6. Ask everyone who visits your home to sign a guest register, as described above. Obviously, an experienced thief will simply use a false name, but, even so, this sort of organized procedure may make some people think twice about victimizing you.

7. Consider hiring a private security guard. This costs money, but makes a lot of sense if you own a large luxury home full of valuable objects, and surely impresses prospective buyers with your seriousness of purpose as to the security of your property. And remember, security guards don't all have to look like "Rambo." Many companies provide guards in sportcoat-type outfits who blend in with the crowd.

KAREN: HOW I SOLD MY HOME AT THE SECOND OPEN HOUSE

After preparing our home for sale, it was easy to set a fair market price, because a home just like ours was on the market through a real estate service. They listed at $181,000. We asked $179,500. I discovered that our paper had a weekly feature called "Showcase of Homes." They sent out someone to take a photo of our home and I supplied charming copy. (It cost only $75.) Our ad announcing our open house ran in the weekend editions. I also created a spec sheet on our home that included a photo. The first open house weekend was dead. Two people showed (it had been raining). During the week I had a few calls and arranged for private showings. One couple seemed interested, and I invited them to come back for a second look during our second open house the coming weekend.

Early the morning of the second open house, I received a call from a local real estate agent who had a buyer from out of town who saw our ad. They wanted to come by before the open house. I told the agent I would work with her, and we'd discuss terms when they arrived. As the buyer looked in the back yard, the agent agreed to accept a 2% commission, which included handling all the paperwork. (The market has been in a real slump and anything was reasonable.) The buyer took photos to show her spouse and they left. A half hour later the agent came by with an offer $2,000 less than our asking price. The offer was good until 6 p.m. that day. Since our open house hadn't yet started, we declined to sign the offer, waiting to see if the other interested couple would arrive. We promised to get back to the agent afterwards.

Well, the agent told her buyer of the other interested party, and at 1 p.m., at the time our open house was to begin, she came back with her own counteroffer. She offered us full price! Little did she know that in our office we were making changes in the wording of her first offer and were ready to accept it!

MAGGIE: HONESTY IS THE BEST POLICY

I sold my house before the disclosure law went into effect. Nevertheless, I disclosed everything I could think of—even small things like rust spots on the gutters. In addition, I had copies of inspection reports available on the dining room table. When anyone seemed sincerely interested in the house, I asked him to read both my detailed disclosures and the inspection reports. A number of people remarked positively that they really appreciated this approach.

F. Obeying Anti-Discrimination Laws

Be courteous to everyone. If you refuse to show your property to or to entertain offers from anyone on the basis of their race, color, religion, sex, marital status, ancestry, national origin, physical handicap or other similarly arbitrary reason, you're in legal trouble. In other words, unless you have a good reason to believe a particular person is a bad credit risk, a thief or otherwise seriously undesirable—and you're prepared to defend that belief—you should show everyone your house and treat seriously any purchase offers.

G. Making All Disclosures

Sellers have specific legal obligations to disclose material facts about the property.

1. Real Estate Transfer Disclosure Statement

Sellers must, under California law, give buyers a statutory disclosure form, called a Real Estate Transfer Disclosure Statement. (Civil Code § 1102.) A copy is shown later in the chapter and a complete tear-out form is in the Appendix. Have copies available at your open house and provide a disclosure form to all prospective purchasers who express a se-

rious interest in your property. Anyone who signs a contract to purchase your house should acknowledge in writing that he has received your disclosure material. (See Clause 27 in Chapter 9.)

If you don't give a prospective purchaser a copy of the disclosure statement until she makes an offer, she has three days (five days if the statement was mailed, not personally delivered) to withdraw the offer. Obviously, this introduces considerable uncertainty into the transaction. If someone looks like a serious prospect, go ahead and give her the disclosure statement before she presents you with an offer.

You are responsible for disclosing only information within your personal knowledge—you don't have to hire professionals to answer the questions on the disclosure form. You must, however, fill out the form in good faith—that is, honestly. You must also take ordinary care in obtaining the information, which means that you are responsible for including information about the property that you know or, as a reasonable homeowner, should know.

Items you should disclose include:

- homeowners' association dues
- whether or not work done on the house was according to local building codes and with permits
- the presence of any neighborhood nuisances or noises which an occasional visitor (such as a prospective buyer) might not notice but which a homeowner would (such as a dog that barks every night or interference from a neighbor's ham radio that plays havoc with your TV reception)
- items included in the property, such as a burglar alarm or trash compactor
- any restrictions on the use of the property, such as zoning ordinances, planning restrictions and "covenants, conditions and restrictions" (CC&Rs); this information is available from local title companies.

DISCLOSE ENVIRONMENTAL HAZARDS

In addition to disclosing environmental hazards such as asbestos or lead-based paint on the Real Estate Transfer Disclosure Statement, you should provide prospective homebuyers a copy of *Environmental Hazards: A Guide for Homeowners and Buyers*. This booklet, published by the California Department of Real Estate and the Department of Health Services, is available from the California Association of Realtors (CAR), in Los Angeles. For price and order information, call CAR at 213-739-8227. You can obtain this booklet alone or with the *Homeowner's Guide to Earthquake Safety* or the other booklets on disclosures. Prices are nominal but vary depending on which booklets you order.

You should give a copy of this booklet only to people who are seriously interested in buying your home. Before signing a contract, make sure the prospective buyer signs the receipt inside the Environmental Hazards booklet, indicating that you gave them a copy. Keep the receipt for your records.

You must also make lead-related disclosures if you are selling a house built before 1978. Under the Residential Lead-Based Paint Hazard Reduction Act of 1992 (U.S. Code § 2852d), also known as Title X [Ten], sellers must:

- Provide buyers with any information on lead-based paint hazards from risk assessments or inspectors in your possession.

- Notify buyers of any known lead-based paint hazards.

- Give buyers a federally approved pamphlet on lead poisoning protection. "Protect Your Family from Lead in Your Home." (A tear-out copy is in the Appendix.)

- Complete a lead-based paint disclosure form. (A tear-out copy is in the Appendix.)

- Include certain warning language in the contract as well as signed statements from all parties that all requirements were completed (see Clause 27 in our contract in Chapter 9).

- Keep signed acknowledgments for three years, as proof of compliance.

- Give buyers a ten-day opportunity to test the house for lead.

The National Lead Information Clearinghouse has extensive information on lead hazards, prevention and disclosures. For more information, call the Clearinghouse at 800-424-LEAD or check its Website at www.epa.gov/lead/nlic.htm.

DISCLOSING DEATHS ON THE PROPERTY

California Civil Code § 1710.2 implies that the seller need not disclose that an owner had, or died from AIDS, but that the property owner or his agent should answer honestly any direct questions about the subject. In general, there is some disagreement in the California real estate industry as to whether it is required to disclose a death on the property. The case law on this subject, *Reed v. King*, 145 Cal.App.3d 261 (1983), states that a buyer has no grounds to sue a seller or agent who fails to disclose a death on the property more than three years before the sale. However, many prudent agents ask about, and disclose, deaths on property known to the seller even longer than three years prior. When no disclosure is made, it is likely that a disgruntled buyer who sues will lose. The court is likely to rule that an agent is not liable for nondisclosure of a death he did not know of, while the seller is not liable for nondisclosure of death he did not know would be important to the buyer. Given the cost of winning and defending a lawsuit, however, you are best off telling buyers about deaths on the property.

A few pages ahead is a copy of the California disclosure form (current as of this publication date). In completing the form, be as thorough as possible. Disclose anything and everything which you think would be of possible interest to the buyer. You can attach additional sheets or documents if necessary. You are responsible for making these disclosures whether or not you have—or the buyer has—a real estate agent. If any real estate agent gets involved in the transaction, she must make her own reasonably diligent inspection of the property and a written entry on the disclosure form.

If you don't know something asked for on the form and can't find out with a reasonable effort, you can make a reasonable approximation, as long as you indicate on the form that the information is an approximation based on the best information available to you. You need not pay for a bevy of professional inspectors to come check out your home. Any inspections you or a prospective buyer have done, however, are matters of your knowledge and must be disclosed, even if you believe the findings or estimated repair costs to be exaggerated.

If you carelessly or intentionally make an error or omission in the statement, the sale may still be valid, but you will be liable for any actual damages the buyer suffers, and one remedy sought by the buyer may be rescission of the sale.

The point is simple. Full disclosure of any property defects effectively protects you from any later claim or lawsuit by the buyer based on failure to disclose. This means you should go out of your way to tell people if the roof leaks, the water heater is old, the basement floods in heavy rains, the foundation is not sole-plated, dry rot is around the windows, the refrigerator is on its last legs or whatever else.

Don't be afraid that disclosing all problems with your house makes it harder to sell. Most buyers suspect that an older house will have some problems. Some buyers even get a bit paranoid, suspecting sellers of covering up all sorts of nasty defects that don't exist. A full and detailed disclosure of problems will go a long way towards convincing these people that, in fact, the house isn't in even worse shape, and will also weed out some problem buyers.

If you have any doubts about the condition of important features in your house, hire a contractor to walk through with you. If the contractor finds problems, disclose them to all potential buyers. To be completely thorough—and to answer any serious questions you have—you can hire a licensed general contractor to inspect the house and give you a report. It's also a good idea to do this before you set your asking price. You can use the report to complete your disclosure form and you can also give copies of the inspector's report to potential buyers.

If the buyer wants his own inspections after you've had the house checked out, do nothing to discourage him. On the contrary, let him feel satisfied by contracting and hiring one or more experts of his own choosing. This minimizes the chances of controversies and lawsuits in the future. Be ready to show copies of your inspections to the inspector hired by the prospective buyer. Also, be aware that some lenders will conduct their own inspections, particularly by a licensed pest control operator.

A thorough inspection—be it by your inspector or a prospective buyer's inspector—should cover the property from top to bottom. The inspector will examine the general conditions of the site, such as drainage, retaining walls, fences and driveways; the integrity of the structure and the foundation; the condition of the roof, exterior and interior paint, doors and windows, plumbing, electrical and heating systems.

HOME INSPECTION BOOKS

To get a good idea of what home inspectors look for and how they work, the following books can help—whether you're doing your own inspection or evaluating someone you hire to do it for you.

- *Inspecting a Home or Income Property,* by Jim J. Yuen (Ten Speed Press). Yuen is a long time California building inspector, and his book shows how to find dozens of hidden problems. No other book is as detailed on the construction problems a typical California house buyer is likely to encounter.

- *How to Inspect a House,* by George Hoffman (Addison-Wesley). This beautifully written book provides a very good overview of how to find major structural problems, such as a bad foundation, leaky roof or malfunctioning fireplace.

- *The Termite Report: A Guide for Homeowners and Home Buyers on Structural Pest Control,* by Donald V. Pearman (Pear Press). This is an excellent guide to discovering many hidden pest problems.

Accompany the inspector during the examination, so he can give you information about the maintenance and preservation of the house and answer any questions you may have. He should point out any problems that may need attention and tell you which are important and which are minor.

The final product of the inspection should be a detailed written report which you can keep for future reference. It should identify which items are in good condition, and which need repair or replacement. It should also give you information about earthquake protection, general safety measures, insulation and energy conservation. With all this information in hand, you will be more confident of the condition of your house. The cost for an average inspection and detailed written report should range from $300 to $500.

An oral report or walk-through by a contractor may suit your needs if you just want a general idea of your home's condition. It's certainly half to two-thirds of what you'd pay for a full written report. The only problems are that you don't have a record of what was discovered and the buyer can't sign a copy acknowledging your disclosure of the problems.

To find a good inspector for your home, use the same general principle that you would use in selecting an obstetrician, accountant, dentist or other professional—ask for recommendations from people you trust. Make sure the person doing the inspection is a licensed general contractor, or is licensed to perform specific tasks, such as electricity or plumbing, if your inspection covers that one area.

For referrals to local inspectors and information on home inspections, contact a professional association, such as the American Society of Housing Inspectors (ASHI), 800-743-2744, www.ashi.com, or the California Real Estate Inspection Association (CREIA), 800-848-7342, www.creia.com.

For information on pest control inspectors and termite reports, call the California Structural Pest Control Board phone at 800-737-8188 or check their Website at www.dca.ca.gov/pestboard.

DISCLOSURES FOR PROPERTIES WITH COMMON INTERESTS

The Real Estate Transfer Disclosure Statement asks you to indicate whether the property is subject to CC&Rs or a homeowners' association, or whether it has common areas. If you are selling property with common interests or common areas, in a planned unit development or subdivision, including condominium or co-op units, or with any association with the right to levy dues or assessments, you must provide as full a disclosure as possible. Be prepared to provide copies of by-laws, articles of incorporation, covenants, conditions and restrictions (CC&Rs), projected expenses, budgets, deferred maintenance and all other potentially pertinent documents. The California real estate landscape is littered with lawsuits over such matters. A standard title report generally does not disclose any of this material in detail, simply referring to CC&Rs. Also, state law requires sellers to inform buyers if the association is fighting a builder to make repairs and to provide a list of the association's demands. (Civil Code § 1368.)

DISCLOSURE OF MILITARY ORDNANCE

Sellers who know of any former federal or state ordnance locations (sites used for military training purposes which may contain potentially explosive munitions) within one mile of the property must provide written disclosure to the buyer as soon as practicable before transfer of title. (Civil Code § 1102.15.)

REAL ESTATE TRANSFER DISCLOSURE STATEMENT

(CALIFORNIA CIVIL CODE § 1102, ET SEQ.)

THIS DISCLOSURE STATEMENT CONCERNS THE REAL PROPERTY SITUATED IN THE CITY OF _____ ,
COUNTY OF _____ , **STATE OF CALIFORNIA, DESCRIBED AS** _____
_____ .
**THIS STATEMENT IS A DISCLOSURE OF THE CONDITION OF THE ABOVE DESCRIBED PROPERTY IN COMPLIANCE WITH
SECTION 1102 OF THE CIVIL CODE AS OF** _____ , **19**_____ . **IT IS NOT A WARRANTY OF ANY
KIND BY THE SELLER(S) OR ANY AGENT(S) REPRESENTING ANY PRINCIPAL(S) IN THIS TRANSACTION, AND IT IS NOT
A SUBSTITUTE FOR ANY INSPECTIONS OR WARRANTIES THE PRINCIPAL(S) MAY WISH TO OBTAIN.**

I

COORDINATION WITH OTHER DISCLOSURE FORMS

This Real Estate Transfer Disclosure Statement is made pursuant to Section 1102 of the Civil Code. Other statutes require disclosures, depending upon the details of the particular real estate transaction (for example: special study zone and purchase-money liens on residential property).

Substituted Disclosures: The following disclosures have or will be made in connection with this real estate transfer, and are intended to satisfy the disclosure obligations on this form, where the subject matter is the same:

☐ Inspection reports completed pursuant to the contract of sale or receipt for deposit.

☐ Additional inspection reports or disclosures:
_____ .

(List all substituted disclosure forms to be used in connection with this transaction.)

II

SELLER'S INFORMATION

The Seller discloses the following information with the knowledge that even though this is not a warranty, prospective Buyers may rely on this information in deciding whether and on what terms to purchase the subject property. Seller hereby authorizes any agent(s) representing any principal(s) in this transaction to provide a copy of this statement to any person or entity in connection with any actual or anticipated sale of the property.

**THE FOLLOWING ARE REPRESENTATIONS MADE BY THE SELLER(S) AND ARE NOT THE REPRESENTATIONS OF THE
AGENT(S), IF ANY. THIS INFORMATION IS A DISCLOSURE AND IT IS NOT INTENDED TO BE PART OF ANY CONTRACT
BETWEEN THE BUYER AND SELLER.**

Seller ☐ is ☐ is not occupying the property.

A. The subject property has the items checked below (read across):

☐ Range	☐ Oven	☐ Microwave
☐ Dishwasher	☐ Trash Compactor	☐ Garbage Disposal
☐ Washer/Dryer Hookups	☐ Rain Gutters	☐ Smoke Detector(s)
☐ Fire Alarm	☐ T.V. Antenna	☐ Satellite Dish
☐ Intercom	☐ Central Heating	☐ Central Air Conditioning
☐ Evaporator Cooler(s)	☐ Wall/Window Air Conditioning	☐ Sprinklers
☐ Public Sewer System	☐ Septic Tank	☐ Sump Pump

☐ Water Softener   ☐ Patio/Decking   ☐ Built-in Barbecue

☐ Sauna   ☐ Gazebo   ☐ Burglar Alarms

☐ Hot Tub ☐ Locking Safety Cover*   ☐ Pool ☐ Child Restraint Barrier*   ☐ Spa ☐ Locking Safety Cover*

☐ Security Gate(s)   ☐ Automatic Garage Door Opener(s)* ☐ # of Remote Controls _____

☐ Garage: ☐ Attached   ☐ Not Attached   ☐ Carport

☐ Pool/Spa Heater: ☐ Gas   ☐ Solar   ☐ Electric

☐ Water Heater: ☐ Gas   ☐ Water Heater Anchored, Braced or Strapped*   ☐ Electric

☐ Water Supply: ☐ City   ☐ Well   ☐ Private Utility

                       ☐ Other _____

☐ Gas Supply: ☐ Utility ☐ Bottled

☐ Window Screens   ☐ Window Security Bars   ☐ Quick Release Mechanism on Bedroom Windows

☐ Exhaust Fan(s) in _____   ☐ 220 Volt Wiring in _____

☐ Fireplace(s) in _____   ☐ Gas Starter

☐ Roof(s): Type: _____ Age: _____ (approx.)

Other: _____

Are there, to the best of your (Seller's) knowledge, any of the above that are not in operating condition?

☐ Yes ☐ No   If yes, then describe (attach additional sheets if necessary):

_____

_____

_____

B. Are you (Seller) aware of any significant defects/malfunctions in any of the following?

☐ Yes ☐ No If yes, check appropriate box(es) below.

☐ Interior Walls   ☐ Ceilings   ☐ Floors   ☐ Exterior Walls   ☐ Insulation

☐ Roof(s)   ☐ Windows   ☐ Doors   ☐ Foundation   ☐ Slab(s)

☐ Driveways   ☐ Sidewalks   ☐ Walls/Fences   ☐ Electrical Systems   ☐ Plumbing/Sewers/Septics

☐ Other Structural Components (describe):

_____

_____

_____

If any of the above is checked, explain (attach additional sheets if necessary):

_____

_____

_____

*This garage door opener or child restraint pool barrier may not be in compliance with the safety standards relating to automatic reversing devices as set forth in Chapter 12.5 (commencing with Section 19890) of Part 3 of Division 13, or with the pool safety standards of Article 2.5 (commencing with Section 115920) of Chapter 5 of Part 10 of Division 104, of the Health and Safety Code. The water heater may not be anchored, braced or strapped in accordance with Section 19211 of the Health and Safety Code. Window security bars may not have quick release mechanisms in compliance with the 1995 Edition of the California Building Standards Code.

C. Are you (Seller) aware of any of the following:

1. Substances, materials, or products which may be an environmental hazard such as, but not limited to, asbestos, formaldehyde, radon gas, lead-based paint, fuel or chemical storage tanks, and contaminated soil or water on the subject property.   ☐ Yes   ☐ No

2. Features of the property shared in common with adjoining landowners, such as walls, fences and driveways, whose use or responsibility for maintenance may have an effect on the subject property.   ☐ Yes   ☐ No

3. Any encroachments, easements or similar matters that may affect your interest in the subject property.   ☐ Yes   ☐ No

4. Room additions, structural modifications, or other alterations or repairs made without necessary permits.   ☐ Yes   ☐ No

5. Room additions, structural modifications, or other alterations or repairs not in compliance with building codes.   ☐ Yes   ☐ No

6. Fill (compacted or otherwise) on the property or any portion thereof.   ☐ Yes   ☐ No

7. Any settling from any cause, or slippage, sliding, or other soil problems.   ☐ Yes   ☐ No

8. Flooding, drainage, or grading problems.   ☐ Yes   ☐ No

9. Major damage to the property or any other structures from fire, earthquake, floods, or landslides.   ☐ Yes   ☐ No

10. Any zoning violations, nonconforming uses, violations of "setback" requirements.   ☐ Yes   ☐ No

11. Neighborhood noise problems or other nuisances.   ☐ Yes   ☐ No

12. CC&Rs or other deed restrictions or obligations.   ☐ Yes   ☐ No

13. Homeowners' Association which has any authority over the subject property.   ☐ Yes   ☐ No

14. Any "common area" (facilities such as pools, tennis courts, walkways, or other areas co-owned in undivided interest with others).   ☐ Yes   ☐ No

15. Any notices of abatement or citations against the property.   ☐ Yes   ☐ No

16. Any lawsuits against the seller threatening to or affecting this real property, including any lawsuits alleging a defect or deficiency in this real property or "common areas" (facilities such as pools, tennis courts, walkways, or other areas co-owned in undivided interest with others).   ☐ Yes   ☐ No

If the answer to any of these is yes, explain (attach additional sheets if necessary): _____

_____

Seller certifies that the information herein is true and correct to the best of the Seller's knowledge as of the date signed by the Seller.

Seller _____   Date _____

Seller _____   Date _____

III
AGENT'S INSPECTION DISCLOSURE (LISTING AGENT)

(To be completed only if the Seller is represented by an agent in this transaction.)

THE UNDERSIGNED, BASED ON THE ABOVE INQUIRY OF THE SELLER(S) AS TO THE CONDITION OF THE PROPERTY AND BASED ON REASONABLY COMPETENT AND DILIGENT VISUAL INSPECTION OF THE ACCESSIBLE AREAS OF THE PROPERTY IN CONJUNCTION WITH THAT INQUIRY, STATES THE FOLLOWING:

☐ Agent notes no items for disclosure.

☐ Agent notes the following items: _____

Agent (Print Name of Broker Representing Seller) _____

By (Associate Licensee or Broker's Signature) _____

Date _____

IV
AGENT'S INSPECTION DISCLOSURE (SELLING AGENT)

(To be completed only if the agent who has obtained the offer is other than the agent above.)

THE UNDERSIGNED, BASED ON A REASONABLY COMPETENT AND DILIGENT VISUAL INSPECTION OF THE ACCESSIBLE AREAS OF THE PROPERTY, STATES THE FOLLOWING:

☐ Agent notes no items for disclosure.

☐ Agent notes the following items: _____

Agent (Print Name of Broker Obtaining Offer) _____

By (Associate Licensee or Broker's Signature) _____

Date _____

V

BUYER(S) AND SELLER(S) MAY WISH TO OBTAIN PROFESSIONAL ADVICE AND/OR INSPECTIONS OF THE PROPERTY AND TO PROVIDE FOR APPROPRIATE PROVISIONS IN A CONTRACT BETWEEN BUYER(S) AND SELLER(S) WITH RESPECT TO ANY ADVICE/INSPECTION/DEFECTS.
I/WE ACKNOWLEDGE RECEIPT OF A COPY OF THIS STATEMENT.

Seller _____ Date _____

Seller _____ Date _____

Buyer _____ Date _____

Buyer _____ Date _____

Agent (Print Name of Broker Representing Seller) _____

By (Associate Licensee or Broker's Signature) _____

Date _____

Agent (Print Name of Broker Obtaining the Offer) _____

By (Associate Licensee or Broker's Signature) _____

Date _____

SECTION 1102.3 OF THE CIVIL CODE PROVIDES A BUYER WITH THE RIGHT TO RESCIND A PURCHASE CONTRACT FOR AT LEAST THREE DAYS AFTER THE DELIVERY OF THIS DISCLOSURE IF DELIVERY OCCURS AFTER THE SIGNING OF AN OFFER TO PURCHASE. IF YOU WISH TO RESCIND THE CONTRACT, YOU MUST ACT WITHIN THE PRESCRIBED PERIOD. A REAL ESTATE BROKER IS QUALIFIED TO ADVISE ON REAL ESTATE. IF YOU DESIRE LEGAL ADVICE, CONSULT YOUR ATTORNEY.

2. Natural Hazard Disclosure Statement

The Transfer Disclosure Statement includes information on many hazards affecting the house, some of which require additional disclosures. The Legislature recently consolidated several disclosures regarding fire, floods and earthquakes onto one form. Effective June 1998, state law requires sellers to provide buyers with a Natural Hazard Disclosure Statement indicating if the property is in one of six hazard zones for floods, earthquakes and fire hazards. (Civil Code § 1102.6c). As with the detailed Real Estate Transfer Disclosure Form, give the Natural Hazard Disclosure Statement to anyone who looks seriously at your house. Have the prospective buyer sign two copies of the forms (keep a copy of each for yourself). Anyone who signs a contract to purchase your house should acknowledge in writing that he has received your disclosure material. (See Clause 27 in Chapter 9.)

A copy of the Natural Hazard Disclosure Statement is shown here, and a tear-out form is in the Appendix. Here's a summary of the six hazard zones included in this Statement.

Special flood hazard area designated by the Federal Emergency Management Area (FEMA). (42 U.S.C. §§ 4001 et.seq.) If your lender required you to obtain flood insurance when you bought your house, then your property is in a flood hazard area. If you financed your house privately or are otherwise unsure if your property qualifies, contact the Federal Emergency Management Agency (FEMA) and ask. Look in the government section of your white pages to find the closest office of FEMA, or check the FEMA Website at www.fema.gov/nfip. The National Flood Insurance Program (NFIP) publishes hundreds of flood zone maps for California; for information, call 800-358-9616.

Area of potential flooding due to failure of a dam as identified by the Governor's Office of Emergency Services (OES) on an "inundation map." (Government Code § 8589.5.) Check your phone book for the nearest OES office, or call their Sacramento office at 916-262-1843. You can also check the OES Website at www.oes.ca.gov.

Very high fire hazard severity zone designated by a local agency. (Government Code §§ 51178, 51179, 51182, 51183.5.) For fire safety information, call your local fire department or the Office of Emergency Services (contact information listed above).

Wildland area that may contain substantial forest fire risks and hazards. (Public Resources Code §§ 4125, 4136.) For fire safety information, call your local fire department or the Office of Emergency Services (contact information listed above).

Earthquake fault zone as identified by the California State Geologist. (Public Resources Code §§ 2621.9, 2622.) To find out if your property is within an earthquake fault zone, check with your local city or county planning department. It should have maps that show the areas. Also, contact the California Department of Conservation, Division of Mines and Geology (phone and Website below).

Seismic hazard zone, an area where landslides, liquefaction (failure of water-saturated soil), amplified or strong ground shaking or other ground failure in the event of an earthquake are most likely to occur. (Public Resources Code §§ 2694, 2696.) The California Department of Conservation, Division of Mines and Geology, publishes seismic hazard data and fault zone maps. For more information, contact their Sacramento office at 916-445-5716 and check their Website at www.consrv.ca.gov.

The designations of natural hazard areas are often puzzling, at least to a layperson. For example, San Francisco is not within an earthquake fault zone. That's because the fault line isn't in San Francisco—although San Francisco has certainly experienced the ravages of earthquakes. Also, sometimes the available

NATURAL HAZARD DISCLOSURE STATEMENT

This statement applies to the following property:

_____

The seller and his or her agent(s) disclose the following information with the knowledge that even though this is not a warranty, prospective buyers may rely on this information in deciding whether and on what terms to purchase the subject property. Seller hereby authorizes any agent(s) representing any principal(s) in this action to provide a copy of this statement to any person or entity in connection with any actual or anticipated sale of the property.

The following are representations made by the seller and his or her agent(s) based on their knowledge and maps drawn by the state. This information is a disclosure and is not intended to be part of any contract between the buyer and the seller.

THIS REAL PROPERTY LIES WITHIN THE FOLLOWING HAZARDOUS AREA(S): (Check "yes" or "no" for each area)

A SPECIAL FLOOD HAZARD AREA (Any type Zone "A" or "V") designated by the Federal Emergency Management Agency.

Yes _____   No _____   Do not know and information not available from local jurisdiction _____

AN AREA OF POTENTIAL FLOODING shown on a dam failure inundation map pursuant to Section 8589.5 of the Government Code.

Yes _____   No _____   Do not know and information not available from local jurisdiction _____

A VERY HIGH FIRE HAZARD SEVERITY ZONE pursuant to Section 51178 or 51179 of the Government Code. The owner of this property is subject to the maintenance requirements of Section 51182 of the Government Code.

Yes _____   No _____

A WILDLAND AREA THAT MAY CONTAIN SUBSTANTIAL FOREST FIRE RISKS AND HAZARDS pursuant to Section 4125 of the Public Resources Code. The owner of this property is subject to the maintenance requirements of Section 4291 of the Public Resources Code. Additionally, it is not the state's responsibility to provide fire protection services to any building or structure located within the wildlands unless the Department of Forestry and Fire Protection has entered into a cooperative agreement with a local agency for those purposes pursuant to Section 4142 of the Public Resources Code.

Yes _____   No _____

AN EARTHQUAKE FAULT ZONE pursuant to Section 2622 of the Public Resources Code.

Yes _____   No _____

A SEISMIC HAZARD ZONE pursuant to Section 2696 of the Public Resources Code.

Yes (Landslide Zone) _____   No _____   Map not yet released by state _____
Yes (Liquefaction Zone) _____   No _____   Map not yet released by state _____

THESE HAZARDS MAY LIMIT YOUR ABILITY TO DEVELOP THE REAL PROPERTY, TO OBTAIN INSURANCE, OR TO RECEIVE ASSISTANCE AFTER A DISASTER.

THE MAPS ON WHICH THESE DISCLOSURES ARE BASED ESTIMATE WHERE NATURAL HAZARDS EXIST. THEY ARE NOT DEFINITIVE INDICATORS OF WHETHER OR NOT A PROPERTY WILL BE AFFECTED BY A NATURAL DISASTER. BUYER(S) AND SELLER(S) MAY WISH TO OBTAIN PROFESSIONAL ADVICE REGARDING THOSE HAZARDS AND OTHER HAZARDS THAT MAY AFFECT THE PROPERTY.

Seller represents that the information herein is true and correct to the best of the seller's knowledge as of the date signed by the seller.

Signature of Seller _____   Date _____

Agent represents that the information herein is true and correct to the best of the agent's knowledge as of the date signed by the agent.

Signature of Agent _____   Date _____

Signature of Agent _____   Date _____

Buyer represents that he or she has read and understands this document.

Signature of Buyer _____   Date _____

maps and information are not of sufficient accuracy or scale for you to determine whether or not your property falls inside or outside of a designated hazard zone, such as a high fire hazard severity zone. In this case, the law requires a seller to mark "Yes" on the Natural Hazard Disclosure Statement—unless the seller has evidence, such as a report from a licensed engineer, that the property is not in the fire hazard zone. (Civil Code § 1102.4.)

Alternative Disclosure Form. A seller may provide these disclosures on a Local Option Real Estate Disclosure Statement, described in Section H, below.

3. Earthquake and Seismic Disclosures

Earthquakes are a fact of life in California. To help buyers make earthquake-informed decisions, state law requires sellers to provide information to buyers on the safety of the site or location of the house. As discussed in Section 2, above, you must indicate on the Natural Hazard Disclosure Statement whether or not your property is in an earthquake fault zone or a seismic hazard zone. In addition, state law requires sellers to provide information on the safety of the house itself and its ability to resist earthquakes.

You must tell buyers whether or not your property has any known seismic deficiencies, such as whether or not the house is bolted or anchored to the foundation and whether cripple walls, if any, are braced. (Government Code § 8897.) You are not required to hire anyone to help you evaluate your house, nor are you required to strengthen any weaknesses that exist. If the house was built in 1960 or later, oral disclosure is enough, although I recommend that you disclose in writing.

If the house was built before 1960, you must disclose in writing and sign the disclosure form,

Residential Earthquake Hazards Report, included in a booklet called the *Homeowner's Guide to Earthquake Safety.* You must give the buyer a copy of this booklet and disclosure "as soon as practicable before the transfer."

The *Homeowner's Guide to Earthquake Safety* is available from the Seismic Safety Commission (SCC), 1900 K Street, Suite 100, Sacramento, CA 95814. You can phone the SCC at 916-322-4917 or check their Website at www.seismic.ca.gov. This booklet provides valuable information on how to find and fix earthquake weaknesses and a detailed list of earthquake resources—everything from hiring an inspector and getting the work done to emergency planning and geologic information.

4. Water Heater Bracing

All water heaters on the property you are selling must be braced, anchored or strapped to resist falling or displacement during an earthquake. (Health and Safety Code § 19211.) You must certify in writing that the water heater complies with the law. The Real Estate Transfer Disclosure Statement in this chapter (tear-out copy in Appendix) meets this requirement.

5. Smoke Detectors

California requires all single family dwellings—and each unit of multi-unit dwellings—to have smoke detectors installed before close of escrow. (Health and Safety Code §§ 13113.7 and 13113.8.) Sellers must provide a written statement of compliance with this requirement when transferring property. The Real Estate Transfer Disclosure Statement in this chapter (tear-out copy in Appendix) meets this requirement.

DISCLOSURE OF REGISTERED SEX OFFENDERS

Contracts entered into after July 1999 must include a statement regarding the availability of a statewide database on the location of registered sex offenders. See Clause 27 of our contract in Chapter 9.

H. Complying With Local Ordinances

Some cities, including Daly City and San Francisco, require sellers to issue buyers 3R reports, showing zoning restrictions and building permits on the property. Also, some cities require energy conservation inspections prior to transfer of property. It's also a good idea to disclose to the buyer any local rent control laws. (See Clause 12 in the offer form, Chapter 9.) Sellers in communities with local disclosure requirements passed after July 1990 may be required to use a special form, the Local Option Real Estate Disclosure Statement. (Civil Code § 1102.6a.) Check with your city planning department or local title company for information on local ordinances and disclosures that affect your sale.

I. Follow-up After the Open House

When the last visitor has left your open house, you still have some work to do.

1. Retrieve your A-frame Open House signs. Store them in a place where they can be easily reached for the next time.

2. Count the number of property fact sheets you have left. If there are fewer than fifty, be sure to print another hundred during the coming week.

3. Look at the sign-up or guest list. Evaluate your marketing strategy by reviewing how many visitors came from the signs, the ads and other sources. Based on this information decide whether or not to:

- change the position of the signs for the next open house

- change the placement of the ads

- change the text of the ads. If you want to change the text, look at the weekend real estate section in your paper for ads you consider especially appealing. Incorporate what grabs you about ads for other homes—catch phrases ("ocean view," "walk to park," "bus at corner") or pieces of important information ("assumable loan").

4. Straighten up the place after the crowds have been through and check for anything that might be broken or missing. Then kick off your shoes, treat yourself to a nice dinner, and think about what you might do differently for your next open house. ■

Chapter 8

MAKING SURE THE BUYER IS FINANCIALLY QUALIFIED TO BUY YOUR HOUSE

➡️ *If you are cooperating with a real estate broker who is finding and qualifying the buyer for your home, you can either skim this chapter or skip it altogether. You can also skip this chapter if the prospective purchaser has a preapproval letter from a financial institution, approving a specified loan in advance. With preapproval, the lender has actually done a credit check on the buyer and agreed to fund the loan—pending an appraisal of the property, title report and puchase contract. This method of advance credit approval is so efficient, you should consider requiring a prospective buyer to obtain loan authorization before you accept his offer.*

Before you consider offers to purchase your house, ask yourself a basic question: "Who can afford to buy my house at my asking price?" Be honest with yourself and keep in mind that if you were a first-time homeowner, you probably could not afford your own house at your current asking price.

But why worry about the fact that many people can't afford your house? Isn't that the buyer's problem, not yours? Not necessarily. Your ability to sell your house is directly related to the ability of others to buy it. The higher your asking price, the smaller the percentage of potential home buyers who can afford to buy your house.

The unhappy truth is that most people who would like to buy your house can't afford to. And it's extremely unlikely that those people who can afford your house will pay all cash down. Not many buyers have a substantial nest egg or generous relatives to help them with a hefty down payment. The typical home buyer must borrow heavily in order to make a down payment and the monthly mortgage payments. Even then, many people can't qualify either because

their income isn't high enough or they've overextended their credit to buy a car, furniture, appliances or other items.

This chapter shows you how to determine if a prospective buyer has the income, credit and assets to financially qualify to purchase your house. Much of this information concerns the buyer more than you. It is included, however, to help you avoid accepting offers from incurable optimists who will never qualify to purchase your house. Unfortunately, the more unrealistic a potential buyer's chances are to buy a house, the more likely the person is to cloud his offer with grandiose lingo. And if you fail to see the buyer's perspective on financially qualifying to purchase your home, you could tie up your property unnecessarily and ultimately delay its sale.

MORTGAGES AND APPRAISALS

Before approving a prospective buyer's mortgage, a financial institution will have your house appraised, even if others have already done so. No matter what price you and the buyer agree on, the lender will base the loan on the appraised value, not the selling price. Lenders typically lend up to 80% of the appraised value.

Thus, if you sell your house for $200,000, but the bank appraises it at $180,000 and agrees to lend the buyer 80% (the buyer will put down 20%), the lender will lend $144,000 to the buyer, not $160,000.

If a financial institution is willing to lend more than 80% of the appraised value, the loan terms are almost always less favorable to the buyer. This may mean more points, a higher interest rate, a shorter term in which to pay off the loan (15 or 20 years instead of 30) and requiring the buyer to purchase mortgage insurance to indemnify the lender against loss in case of the buyer's default.

Example: *Martin is asking $329,000 for his home. He receives two offers—one for $320,000 and one for $295,000. He initially assumes that the $320,000 offer is stronger, but then he asks the prospective buyers some questions. The couple who offered $295,000 have a pre-approval letter from a bank for an amount that, combined with their down payment, is enough to buy Martin's house. In contrast, the prospective buyer who offered $320,000 has no pre-approval letter, offers Martin no information about her credit and wants Martin to extend some of the financing. In this scenario, the $295,000 offer is clearly the stronger one.*

For more information on financing a home purchase from the buyer's perspective, see *How to Buy a House in California,* by Ralph Warner, Ira Serkes and George Devine (Nolo Press), particularly Chapters 8 through 13.

A. House Financing Basics

Because you already own a house, you are probably familiar with the ways in which homes were financed in California when you first bought. Just the same, a short review of house financing rules won't hurt. It will help refresh your memory and explain the variations and complications that have developed in recent years.

1. Deed of Trust and Mortgage Language

In California, when you borrow money from a lender to finance the purchase of a house, the legal instrument recorded at the County Recorder's Office is called a deed of trust. When a trustor (the borrower) executes a deed of trust, he gives a trustee (often a title company) the right to sell his property (foreclose), with no court approval, if he fails to pay the beneficiary of the trust (the lender) on time. In other words, if the buyer defaults, the trustee can sell the house and pay the lender from the proceeds.

By contrast, when house purchases are made in other states—or were made many years ago in California—the recorded legal instrument is a mortgage. A mortgage normally involves only a borrower and a lender. The borrower signs a note promising to repay the loan over a specific period of time (typically 30 years) at a certain interest rate and terms. If the buyer defaults, there is no trustee (such as a title company) to foreclose. In the past, the lender had to obtain court approval to sell the house by foreclosure; today, this is seldom the case.

Despite the fact that California refers to the legal instrument showing home ownership as "deed of trust," I will use the more familiar "mortgage" throughout this chapter.

2. Types of Mortgages

Many entities, including banks, savings and loans, credit unions and mortgage companies make home loans in California. Buyers can also arrange financing through government-assisted financing programs, friends, relatives or even the seller.

Mortgages come in many varieties with different terms, interest rates and fees depending on the size and type of the loan and down payment, the borrower's income, assets and credit history. "Points" comprise the largest fee associated with getting a mortgage. One point equals 1% of a loan. Thus, if a bank charges a buyer two points for a $200,000 loan, the borrower must pay the bank $4,000 (2% of $200,000) to get the loan. With most loans, points and interest rates have a direct relationship—the more points charged, the lower the interest rate offered and vice versa.

The two main types of mortgages are fixed rate and adjustable rate. There are many variations within each type, and even hybrids that change from one to another within a period of years.

a. Fixed Rate Loans

With a fixed-rate loan, the buyer normally makes a down payment of 20% of the sales price and obtains a loan for the balance. The loan is paid off at the same amount each month over the entire mortgage term of 15 or 30 years. Some affluent buyers prefer shorter term loans in order to reduce the total amount of interest paid. These shorter term loans, which, of course, have higher monthly payments, are available for slightly lower rates than the longer term ones.

Many buyers like the security of fixed-rate loans—monthly payments don't change even if interest rates rise. But lender qualification standards may be more stringent, and initial interest rates are higher for fixed-rate loans than for adjustable rate loans. As a result, many prospective purchasers don't have the income to qualify for fixed-rate loans.

b. Adjustable Rate Loans

With an adjustable rate mortgage (ARM), interest rates fluctuate according to interest rates in the economy. The initial interest rate for an ARM is usually lower than for a fixed-rate loan. Buyers can qualify for an ARM with a lower income than for a comparably sized fixed-rate loan. For example, a buyer who is paying $220,000 for your house might pay as much as $300 less each month with an adjustable rate loan than a fixed-rate loan.

The disadvantage to the buyer is that the interest rate on an adjustable rate loan will almost certainly go up for several years, because these loans always start at a discounted interest rate. Once the discount is eliminated, and the ARM reaches its real level, it will fluctuate depending on whether interest rates in general go up or down. Most ARMs, however, regulate (cap) how much and how often the interest rate and/or payments can change in a year and over the life of the loan.

3. Government-Assisted Financing

Some buyers will suggest that they can qualify for government-guaranteed financing through the Federal Housing Administration (FHA), Veterans' Administration (VA) or a state program. By and large, your house probably won't sell under a government financing program unless the following are true:

• The house sells for $250,000 or less. In some cities, this includes the majority of houses; in other places, hardly any.

• The house is in generally good condition without serious problems or structural defects.

• The buyer is considered financially well-qualified (his gross income is at least three times the total monthly payment of the mortgage payment, property taxes and property insurance).

- The buyer, if a veteran, has the requisite amount of military service.

- If the buyer proposes taking advantage of a special program for first-time buyers, he really is a first-time homebuyer and usually must earn less than a certain maximum annual income.

B. Evaluating Potential Buyers

While you may feel uncomfortable asking people about their bank account and personal finances, start by understanding that you are in the business of selling your house and that business transactions routinely involve checking credit. This doesn't mean you need to be abrasive or insensitive in your inquiries. It does mean that you should establish a fair, but firm, procedure to check the credit of all serious prospective purchasers.

1. Informal Inquiries

Your first conversation with interested buyers will give you a rough sense of their financial position. Start with a few friendly questions about the type of work they do, how they like it, how long they have worked for their present employer, and whether they currently own a house.

Don't rush into the first gently probing conversation about finances. It makes no sense to eagerly quiz every person who pokes her nose in your door about the state of her bank balance. After all, most people who come to your house won't make an offer. When someone begins oohing and aahing over your newly built deck and starts planning to change the wallpaper in the kitchen, however, it's time to get to know both her and her financial situation a little better. If she really is serious about your house, she'll appreciate your interest.

2. Credit Information Form

Assuming the answers to your informal questions are satisfactory, your next step is to actually evaluate the prospective buyer's financial ability to purchase your house. To do this, you need to learn the criteria financial institutions use to qualify house buyers, unless, of course, the buyer can demonstrate that her credit has already been approved by a lending institution up to a level sufficient to buy your house. If the person who wants to purchase your house has such a pre-qualification letter, be sure to check the authenticity of the authorization.

To evaluate the creditworthiness of a potential buyer who does not have a preapproval letter, ask him to fill out a Credit Information Form like the one shown below and provided in the Appendix. If the offer is on behalf of more than one borrower, be sure to get information from all. You will want the prospective buyer(s) to fill it out when they present you with a formal offer. Most offers indicate the amount and type of financing the buyer(s) plan to get. Before you accept an offer, you should verify the feasibility of the financing proposal by looking into the data on the Credit Information Form.

If you conclude that the purchaser is unlikely to qualify, it's usually best not to accept the offer. There is little to be gained from dealing with a prospective buyer whose optimism has run away with his common sense. Don't waste your time signing a contract to sell the house and perhaps even taking your property off the market only to find out later that the buyer can't finance the deal.

3. Checking Credit History of Potential Home Buyers

If a potential buyer looks good on paper, you have several options in verifying their credit information, depending on how thorough you want to be. Credit reporting agencies are one good source and many will provide credit information on individuals from whom you have written permission. The Credit Information Form below provides this written permission.

One credit bureau which provides information on potential buyers of real estate is APSCREEN, 2043 Westcliff Drive, Suite 300, Newport Beach, CA 92660; 800-327-8732.

The three major national credit bureaus are:

• Equifax, P.O. Box 740241, Atlanta, GA 30374-0241; 800-685-1111; www.equifax.com.

• Experian, National Consumers Assistance Center, P.O. Box 2104, Allen, TX 75013; 888-397-3742; www.experian.com.

• Trans Union, P.O. Box 390, Springfield, PA 19064; 800-888-4213; www.tuc.com.

To locate other agencies, check the phone book Yellow Pages under "Credit Reporting Agencies."

When you contact a credit bureau, check its procedure for providing a credit bureau check and the cost and time involved. Be sure the agency agrees to honor the Credit Information Form and signatures you received from the prospective buyer. If not, you will have to delay the process by getting the agency's form and the prospective buyer's signature.

Once you submit the appropriate authorization form to the agency, you should have the credit information within a few days. The cost shouldn't exceed $25–$50 per borrower.

The Credit Information Form also gives you permission to verify employment, assets and liabilities of potential purchasers. The information you obtain from those sources should tell you whether or not the prospective buyer can afford to buy your house.

CREDIT INFORMATION FORM, PAGE 1

BACKGROUND INFORMATION		
	BORROWER	CO-BORROWER
Name (including Jr., Sr. and former names)		
Social Security number		
Driver's license number		
Home phone number		
Work phone number		
Current address		
	❏ own ❏ rent	❏ own ❏ rent
	monthly rent or mortgage payment: $	monthly rent or mortgage payment: $
Previous address if less than two years at current address		
Name of employer		
Address of employer		
Phone number of employer		
Job title		
How long with present employer		
Name, address and phone number of previous employer if less than two years at current job		
Previous job title		
How long with previous employer		

INCOME		
	BORROWER	CO-BORROWER
Current monthly gross income	$	$
Monthly amounts and sources of other income (such as interest, dividends, royalties, support and the like)	$	$
Total Monthly Income	$	$

ASSETS		
	BORROWER	CO-BORROWER
Name and address of financial institution holding deposit account, type of account (checking, savings, money market) and current balance of account	$	$
Name and address of financial institution holding deposit account, type of account (checking, savings, money market) and current balance of account	$	$
Name and address of financial institution holding marketable security, type of fund (stock, bond, annuity, life insurance, mutual fund) and current balance	$	$
Name and address of financial institution holding deposit account, type of account (checking, savings, money market) and current balance of account	$	$

CREDIT INFORMATION FORM, PAGE 2

Real Estate	value	$		value	$	
	mortgages	$		mortgages	$	
	liens	$		liens	$	
	equity	$		equity	$	
Vehicles (year, make, market value)		$			$	
Business assets (name of business, interest in business, value of interest)		$			$	
Other assets (specify asset type and value)	$	$	$			$	
TOTAL ASSETS	$	$	$			$	

LIABILITIES

	BORROWER	CO-BORROWER
Credit card—name of card, account number and current outstanding balance	$	$
Credit card—name of card, account number and current outstanding balance	$	$
Credit card—name of card, account number and current outstanding balance	$	$
Motor vehicle loan—indicate monthly payment to the right; total amount owed here: $	$	$
Real estate loan—indicate monthly payment to the right; total amount owed here: $	$	$
Child/spousal support—indicate monthly payment to the right; total amount owed here: $	$	$
Student loan—indicate monthly payment to the right; total amount owed here: $	$	$
Personal loan—indicate monthly payment to the right; total amount owed here: $	$	$
Other loan—indicate monthly payment to the right; total amount owed here: $	$	$
TOTAL LIABILITIES	$	$

Have you ever filed for bankruptcy? If yes, indicate the year, the court, the type of bankruptcy (Chapter 7, 11 or 13) and the circumstances that led you to filing.

Are there any outstanding judgments against you? If yes, please explain.

Have you had property foreclosed upon you? Have you given title or deed in lieu of foreclosure in the past ten years? If yes, please explain.

We certify that all the information given above is true and accurate. We authorize the seller to verify any and all of the information provided above, including our deposits with all financial institutions. We further authorize seller to receive any and all information about our credit from credit reporting agencies and to verify employment with the employers listed above.

_____   _____
Signature of borrower   Signature of co-borrower

_____   _____
Date   Date

4. Additional Investors and Borrowers

Today, it's not unusual for buyers to hook up with other people in order to qualify to purchase a house. The most common arrangements are equity sharing, co-investment and making a gift of funds towards a down payment. In other instances, a friend or relative agrees to co-sign a loan—that is, add his financial qualifications to the buyer's so that the buyer qualifies for the loan. The cosigner is responsible for paying if the buyer defaults.

If the prospective buyer indicates in her offer or in conversation that a relative or friend will co-sign a loan application or help finance the house through a gift, through a loan or by co-borrowing the mortgage loan, keep the following in mind:

It's important to check the creditworthiness of any friend or relative giving or lending money or acting as a co-signer or co-borrower. Ask potential buyers to provide written verification of the information provided in the Credit Information Form from the various employers, banks, brokers, creditors and the like. This may be enough; you can check further, however, if you doubt the authenticity of any of these documents.

Many financial institutions require that gift funds cannot usually exceed 95% of the down payment—that is, at least 5% of the down payment must be the borrower/buyer's own money. Banks enforce this rule by requiring that at least 70% of the down payment amount be in the buyer/borrower's own account for at least three months. Sudden increases of deposit are a red flag to lenders scrutinizing the qualifications of prospective borrowers.

If a friend or relative makes a gift, make sure the donor sends a letter to the recipient explaining that the gift is just that, and need not be paid back. Otherwise, it will be construed by lenders as a loan needing to be repaid and will make qualifying more difficult for the buyer.

C. How Bankers Qualify Buyers for Home Purchase

Now that you know the gross income and major debts of the prospective buyer, you need to figure out what the monthly payment on a loan for your house would be. As a broad generalization, most people can afford to purchase a house worth about three times their total (gross) annual income, assuming a 20% down payment and a moderate amount of other long-term debts. With no other debts, they can afford a house worth up to four or five times their income.

A much more accurate way to determine how much house someone can afford is to compare two figures:

- the monthly carrying costs (the mortgage's principal and interest, and the amounts for property taxes and insurance), plus total monthly payments on other long-term debts, and

- the prospective buyers' gross monthly income.

Lenders normally want buyers to make all monthly payments with no more than 28%–38% of their gross monthly income. Specifically, the monthly housing cost should be no more than 28% of gross monthly income. The total monthly long-term debt (including car, student loan and revolving credit account payments) should be no more than 38% of gross monthly income.

Example: *Donald and Debbie want to buy a $300,000 home, paying 10% down ($30,000) and financing the rest. If they borrow $270,000 for 30 years at a fixed rate of 9%, their monthly payments will be $2,415. Their taxes will be about $244 a month, and their home-own-ers' insurance about $75. Their total monthly payment for housing would then be $2,734. Using the 28% qualification ratio, Donald and Debbie would need to earn $9,764 a month or $117,171 a year to purchase the home. If Donald and Debbie also pay $192 a month for* *their car and $211 on Donald's student loan, their total monthly long-term outlay would be $3,137 ($2,734 + $192 + $211). At a qualification ratio of 36%, their total monthly gross income would have to be $8,713 or an annual income of $104,567 to get the mortgage. Of course, if housing is their only monthly cost of financing, and a lender applies a 36% ratio, they would then need a gross income of $7,594 a month, or $91,133 a year.*

Bankers, title companies and other financial services companies have amortization tables that show monthly payments for different mortgage amounts, depending on years and interest rate.

Lenders will vary the qualification ratio depending on the amount of the buyer's down payment, the interest rate, the buyer's credit history, employment stability and prospects, the lender's philosophy, and the money supply in the general economy. Generally, the greater the buyer's other debts, the lower the percentage of their income lenders will assume they have available to spend each month on housing. Conversely, if a buyer has no long-term debts, a great credit history and will make a larger than normal down payment, a lender may approve a ratio in excess of 36% of her monthly income. In either case, these rules aren't absolute. For example, some lenders will accept a higher monthly carrying cost if the buyer will take a less attractive loan, such as one with a higher than market interest rate or higher than usual points.

D. Seller Financing

The traditional loan, where the buyer puts down 20% of the purchase price and borrows 80% from a bank or savings and loan, won't work if the buyer doesn't have enough for a large down payment. As a result, a buyer may ask you to help finance the purchase by taking back a second mortgage on the house. This is called "seller financing," a "seller take back" or a "seller carry back."

Here's how seller financing typically works. You may extend credit for part of the down payment (often 10% of the purchase price) with payment of this money secured by a second deed of trust in your favor. For your purposes, this means that you are lending the buyer part of the purchase price. You don't actually lend him cash, like a lending institution does. Instead, during the escrow calculations, you extend the buyer a credit, against the purchase price of the home. The buyer executes a second promissory note and trust deed in your favor. The paperwork needed is prepared by the title or escrow company after you and the buyer work out the terms.

We show an example of this type of promissory note, containing the basic terms common to such notes, later in this chapter.

Some sellers take a second mortgage for tax reasons—for example, if you want to spread your receipt of profits realized from the house sale for investment purposes. Others take a second mortgage as an investment—you are investing in your old home. Many sellers, however, are reluctant to take back a second mortgage. You may want to get all your cash out of the house, particularly if you are buying another home. This "I won't take a second" position can change, however, if you find it difficult to sell your house at a decent price otherwise.

Your reluctance to take a second mortgage may stem from fear that the buyer will default. It's thus especially important to do a thorough credit check of buyers if you take a second mortgage. If the buyer doesn't make payments on either your loan or an obligation senior to it—such as the first loan or property taxes—you will be responsible for back payments on any senior obligations that are in default, before you can foreclose on your junior (second) loan. This will cost you money up front (though you will probably get it back), and about four months or so of your time and grief. In these situations, you will get your house back and then have to resell it. A title insurance company or attorney can assist you with initiating foreclosure, and will probably refer you to a specialized company that handles foreclosures.

What are the typical terms for a second deed of trust? As illustrated in the following example, you should charge higher interest than a buyer could get on a first mortgage. Compare bank mortgage rates with certificate of deposit rates, pick the higher of the two and raise it at least one full percentage point. This will usually allow you to compete favorably with mortgage brokers.

Example: *Sue and Linda are looking to buy a $300,000 house. They can borrow 80% ($240,000), but have only 10% ($30,000) for the down payment. They ask you to lend them the other 10% ($30,000). This means that you will receive $30,000 less in cash proceeds when escrow closes; instead, you will receive a second promissory note from Sue and Linda for the $30,000 they owe you.*

Because holding a second note and deed of trust is riskier than holding a first note and deed of trust, you will want a higher rate of interest than Sue and Linda are paying the first lender. If that institution is getting 9%, you should request 10% or 11% interest. In addition, although the first lender may be lending money for up to 30 years, you should lend it for only three or five years. You can allow small monthly payments and then a large "balloon payment" at the end of the term.

HOW TO PREPARE A PROMISSORY NOTE

A sample promissory note is shown below and a blank tear-out copy is provided in the Appendix. Here's how to complete each paragraph of the note:

1. Fill in the property owners' names (the persons to whom the debt is owed), the dollar amount of the second mortgage loan, the address where payment is to be made and the annual interest rate of the loan.

See if your bank will service the note (collect payments) for you; many will, if you have a large enough account balance with them.

If there are joint borrowers, this note provides that joint signers "jointly and severally" promise to pay the debt. This means that each signer is responsible both for half of the debt (that is, "jointly" promises) and the complete debt (that is, "severally" promises). It is common practice to make joint signers of a note jointly liable and severally liable so that if the debt isn't paid on time (there is a default) the person lending the money can sue and collect the whole amount due from either borrower.

The last sentence of the first paragraph lets the buyer/borrower pay off the note early without incurring any penalty.

2. Fill in the amount of the monthly payment, the length of the loan and the amount of the balloon payment to be made at the end of the loan term.

Check with a bank or title company for an amortization table which will show the monthly payment amount (principal plus interest) based on the amount, interest rate and length of your loan.

You can always agree to refinance when the balloon payment is about to come due, but if you do, be sure you get an interest rate that is both competitive and favorable.

Note that the last sentence of the second paragraph requires you to give the buyer/borrower advance warning that the balloon payment is coming due.

3. This note specifies a late charge of 6% of the monthly payment for installment payments which are ten to 30 days late.

The somewhat harsh-sounding second part of this paragraph allows you to declare the entire debt immediately due and payable in the event the borrower signing the note is more than 30 days late with an installment payment. Called an "acceleration of maturity" clause, it is commonly included in notes providing for installment payments. It allows you to immediately move to collect the debt in one lawsuit. Otherwise, you would have to wait until all of the installments should have been paid (say a year or two down the line) to bring the lawsuit, or you would have to file a separate lawsuit for each installment, which is both impractical and too expensive.

4. This note includes a provision requiring the signer of the note to pay your reasonable attorney's fees should you prevail in a court action to collect on the note. Without this clause, you and the borrower are expected to each pay your own attorney's fees should court enforcement prove necessary.

5. This note specifies the deed of trust to the property as collateral for repayment of the loan. Here you specify the address of the property (which should be the same as that specified in the sales contract), the name of the new owner, the date the deed of trust was executed and the place and county where it was recorded. The escrow agent can help you do this.

   You must record this trust deed at the office of your County Recorder in order to "perfect" your lien against the property. The escrow company can accomplish this for you. Then you will have priority over other liens that may be recorded later (with a few exceptions too complicated to explain here, and unlikely to occur in most cases).

   If you wish to change any of the terms of this promissory note, check with a real estate specialist.

One way to sell your house with a second mortgage but decrease your risk of carrying it is to sell the note and trust deed, as soon as reasonably possible, to an investor. You can do this as a private party (within the limits mentioned in Chapter 2). Usually, though, you'll need a real estate loan broker, and the procedure is beyond the scope of this book.

Suffice it to say that you will probably sell the note and trust deed for a discount of at least 20%, meaning that you will only receive about 80¢ on the dollar. Selling a $10,000 second will net you $8,000—you sell your right to collect interest along with your risk. Because of the monetary loss from selling the note and the risk in keeping it, sellers who "carry paper" often insist on a higher house selling price than they would have accepted if the buyer were not getting financing help from the seller.

There are no special legal requirements for seller financing unless you are extending credit secured by real estate six or more times a year. If so, contact the Federal Trade Commission (there are offices in San Francisco and Los Angeles) for guidelines. In addition, if a broker arranges a loan for you, including a second that you are carrying, California law requires the broker to make certain disclosures to the buyer. If no broker is in the picture, you need not worry about this.

NEGOTIABILITY OF PROMISSORY NOTE

This note is negotiable—this means it can be sold—because it contains the following provisions: the names of the borrower and lender and the borrower's address; a statement that the debt is payable "to the order of" the lender/seller; a specified principal sum to be paid and the specific rate of interest; the address where payments are to be made; the city where and date when the note is signed; and the signature of the debtor/borrower.

Should you or the borrower die, become mentally ill or otherwise not be able to pay or collect the debt, the fact that the note is negotiable increases the chance that it will be paid—because institutions in the business of purchasing uncollected notes and collecting on them may be willing to buy it.

PROMISSORY NOTE

1. For value received, ☐ I individually   ☐ we jointly and severally promise to pay to the order of

   _____

   _____

   the sum of $ _____ at _____

   at the rate of _____ %

   per year from the date this note was signed until the date it is paid in full. The signer(s) of this note has the right to pay all or a portion of the principal amount owing, without penalty, prior to the maturity date stated in this note.

2. ☐ I individually   ☐ we jointly and severally agree that this note shall be paid in equal installments, which include principal and interest, of not less than $ _____ per month, due on the first day of each month, for a period of _____ months. At the end of that period, ☐ I individually   ☐ we jointly and severally agree to make a final ("balloon") payment in the amount of $ _____. This note is subject to Civil Code Section 2966, which provides that the holder of this note shall give written notice to the signer(s) of this note of prescribed information at least 90 and not more than 150 days before any balloon payment is due.

3. If any installment payment due under this note is not received by the holder within 10 days of its due date, a late charge in the amount of 6% of the payment due shall be paid to the holder(s) of this note. If any installment payment due under this note is not received by the holder within 30 days of its due date, the entire amount of unpaid principal shall become immediately due and payable at the option of the holder without prior notice to the signer(s) of this note.

4. In the event the holder(s) of this note prevail(s) in a lawsuit to collect on it, I/we agree to pay the holder's(s') attorney fees in an amount the court finds to be just and reasonable.

5. ☐ I individually   ☐ we jointly and severally agree that until such time as the principal and interest owed under this note are paid in full, the note shall be secured by the following described mortgage, deed of trust, or security agreement:

   Deed of trust to real property commonly known as _____

   _____

   owned by _____

   executed on _____, 19_____, at _____

   _____ and recorded at _____

   _____ in the records of _____

   County, California.

   _____   _____
   Date   Date

   _____   _____
   Location (city or county)   Location (city or county)

   _____   _____
   Name of Borrower   Name of Borrower

   _____   _____
   Address of Borrower   Address of Borrower

   _____   _____
   Signature of Borrower   Signature of Borrower

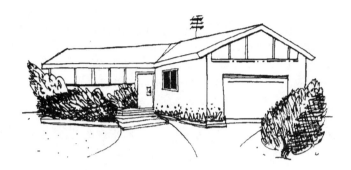

THE HOUSE SALE CONTRACT

This chapter describes the context of a typical written offer to purchase a house. Chapter 10 explains how to respond and guides you through the process of accepting and negotiating offers and counteroffers. Even if a real estate agent is preparing the paperwork for you, read both chapters carefully before responding to an offer. Many important decisions are made as a part of accepting a written offer and it's essential that you understand each one. Also, you need to know what terms are beneficial or harmful to your interests.

A. Waiting for Offers

It's common to start receiving offers a week or two after the first open house, assuming you have properly priced and advertised your house, and the market in your area isn't real flat. If you haven't received any offers within the first few weeks, consider ways to increase your marketing efforts. (See Chapters 6 and 7.)

If a full month passes and you still have no offers, consider removing your house from the market for a while and trying again later. If real estate prices are in a temporary slump and you can afford to wait, this may well be the best approach. If, however, other houses in your area are selling well or you must sell as soon as possible, an obvious alternative to taking your house off the market is to reduce your asking price. Don't get so pessimistic at this point that you reduce your price more than necessary. Study what truly comparable houses are selling for in your area before you decide how much to lower your price. That information is in Chapter 5.

You may start hearing from brokers. If your house sits on the market for some time, real estate brokers will probably assume that you're getting sick of trying to sell it yourself. Several may try to persuade you to give them the listing. If you are fed up

with handling your own sale, take a look at Chapter 4, which explains the many options of working with a real estate agent. But because the basic reason you wanted to sell your own house in the first place—to save the broker's commission—hasn't changed, you're probably better off gritting your teeth and sticking it out a while longer. If this means you have to maneuver the few persistent brokers who won't take "no" for an answer, so be it. Always keep in mind that if you price your house fairly, a buyer will materialize before long.

B. Only a Written Offer Is Legally Valid

A legal offer must be in writing (preferably typed), delivered by the prospective buyer or her agent to you (or your agent). An oral offer to purchase real property is legally worthless—meaning you can't enforce it—if the buyer wants out of the deal. In other words, people don't have to "put their money where their mouths are" unless they have also put their promises in writing.

A written offer should be detailed, covering all important issues, including price and other financial terms. Most buyers will give you a short time in which to accept their offer. During this time, the buyer may revoke her offer in writing before you respond to her or her agent.

Real estate offers almost always contain contingencies—events that must happen or else the deal won't go through. If an offer is contingent upon the buyer qualifying for financing, selling his home first, your home passing certain physical inspections, you taking back a second deed of trust or anything else, the contingencies should be clearly stated along with the time allowed to remove them.

C. Offer Form Terminology

Before you look at the offer form, here are a few words on offer terminology. The important thing to understand is that the same paperwork is called by different names, each with a different legal meaning, depending on when and by whom it's used.

- *Making an offer* is when a prospective buyer fills out an Offer to Purchase Real Property form, such as the one in this book, and gives it to the seller.

- A *counteroffer* is a form used by a seller to accept some of the buyer's terms but modify others. You can counteroffer on as many terms as you want—you may respond, for example, with a higher price or a shorter time for the buyer to arrange financing or remove inspection contingencies. (Counteroffers are covered in Chapter 10 and removing contingencies in Chapter 11.)

- A *counter counteroffer* is when the buyer accepts some of the seller's counteroffer terms, but wants to modify others. The back and forth dance can go on for a while with counter counter counteroffers, etc.

- The offer becomes a legally binding *contract* when the buyer and the seller agree on all the terms in the offer (or counteroffer) and sign it. You can both sign an offer form, such as the Offer to Purchase Real Property, or a separate written document stating that all terms of the offer (or counteroffer) are accepted. Not only must you both sign the agreement, you must both also initial every page.

Example 1: *Mitch gives Patricia a written offer to purchase her house for $300,000, which includes seven days to accept. Two days later, Patricia accepts in writing. A contract has been formed.*

Example 2: *Same offer from Mitch; however, before Patricia says yes, Mitch finds a house he likes better. He immediately calls Patricia's agent and withdraws his offer.*

Although this does revoke his offer, he puts his revocation in writing and drops it off at Patricia's agent's office so there can be no misunderstanding. Mitch's offer has now been withdrawn; no contract can be formed between them unless one or the other makes a second offer and the other accepts it in writing.

D. Types of Offer Forms

The Offer to Purchase Real Property form in this book includes all terms needed for making an offer or counteroffer, as you would be more likely to be doing, on a house in California. Many varieties of printed offer forms are in use in California, in part because many brokers design their own forms. Typically, printed forms look different from ours and from each other, but cover the same topics. Some contain numerous fine provisions, many designed to absolve all real estate professionals in the transaction (who, after all, buy the forms) from any possible liability.

Buyers who work with large brokerage firms often use their forms. Independent brokers often use forms published by Realty Publications, Inc., the Professional Publishing Corporation or the California Association of Realtors. These forms are all well written and will do the job, but you should still read this chapter to understand what the clauses mean and how to change any you don't like.

If you are interested in purchasing software that generates California real estate forms, consider purchasing Formulator, a step-by-step computer program that produces California real estate forms. Order information is at the back of this book.

Both you and the buyer must know what needs to be put into the offer form. If you are dealing with a buyer who lacks real estate knowledge and isn't working with an agent, be prepared to give the buyer the offer form discussed in detail here and set out in the Appendix.

If you are dealing with an inexperienced purchaser or someone with a language problem who obviously can't complete a written offer on his own, ask him to have his offer prepared by someone more knowledgeable. One good alternative is for the buyer to hire a real estate broker or lawyer at a reasonable hourly rate. Do not prepare or help prepare an offer for someone who can't do it himself. If trouble develops later, he will almost surely claim that you took unfair advantage of him.

In any event, no matter what the sophistication level of a person who presents an offer to you, you must understand the typical elements contained in a real estate purchase contract.

E. Understanding the Offer Form

Below is a clause-by-clause review of the Offer to Purchase Real Property form. A buyer who isn't using an agent may present a form to you just like it, especially if she is using *How to Buy a House in California*, by Ralph Warner, Ira Serkes and George Devine (Nolo Press). If the buyer presents a form drafted by a commercial publisher or real estate organization, compare the information below against the clauses of the other form and note specific points you want to be sure to include or leave out.

Heading

1. **Financial Terms**
2. **Escrow**
3. **Pre-payment Penalty and Assumption Fee**
4. **Expenses of Sale**
5. **Property Tax and Insurance Prorations; Non-Callable Bonds**
6. **Fixtures**
7. **Personal Property**
8. **Inspection Contingencies**
9. **Other Contingencies**
10. **Condition of Property**
11. **Foreign Investors**
12. **Rent Control**
13. **Title**
14. **Possession**
15. **Agency Confirmation and Commission to Brokers**
16. **Advice**
17. **Backup Offer**
18. **Duration of Offer**
19. **Other Terms and Conditions**
20. **Risk of Damage to Property**
21. **Liquidated Damages**
22. **Mediation of Disputes**
23. **Arbitration of Disputes**
24. **Attorneys' Fees**
25. **Entire Agreement**
26. **Time Is of the Essence**
27. **Disclosures**
28. **Buyer's Signature**
29. **Seller's Acceptance**

The top of the offer form includes the following basic information:

Heading

Property address, including county:

_____

_____

Date:_____.

_____ (Buyer) makes this offer to

_____ (Seller), to purchase

_____

the property described above, for the sum of _____ dollars ($_____).

Buyer includes a deposit, in the amount of _____ dollars ($_____).

evidenced by ☐ cash ☐ cashier's check ☐ personal check ☐ promissory note ☐ other,

payable to _____ to be held uncashed until the acceptance of this offer, and to

be increased to 3% of the purchase amount no later than _____ days after this offer is accepted. If this offer is accepted,

the deposit shall be delivered to a mutually agreed escrow holder and applied toward the down payment.

Address, including the county. The street number, city, county and state are sufficient—a legal description isn't required. If the property has no street address, the buyer will have to describe it the best he can ("the ten-acre Norris Ranch on County Road 305, two miles south of Andersonville").

Date of the offer.

Full names of the buyer(s) and seller(s) and their spouses. If the buyer isn't sure of your full name or marital status, he may make an educated guess. If he is wrong, you can correct it on the counteroffer. If you accept the offer as is, you can correct your name or marital status on the escrow instructions. If the prospective buyer is married but buying a house using only separate property, he may list only his name. Normally, however (as discussed in Chapter 2), some community property is used toward the down payment or monthly payments, which means both spouses' names should also appear on the offer. Be sure to ask about this.

The price offered and the deposit, both written out (such as, three hundred and seventeen thousand) and numerically ($317,000). If you accept the offer, you'll take a deposit as earnest money. This is usually about 1% of the purchase price or, sometimes, a flat $1,000

for middle-priced houses, and is often increased to 3% of the purchase price within a week after the offer is accepted. A buyer won't want to put down more in the event she gets into a dispute with a seller and has trouble getting her money back. If you feel that the deposit is too low, you can ask for more in your counteroffer.

The form of the deposit (cash, check or other—personal check is the most common) and to whom it is made out (the escrow holder). See Clause 2 for more on the escrow holder. For general information on what happens to the deposit if the purchase doesn't go through, see Clause 21.

Offers to purchase a house almost always contain contingencies, conditions that either the seller or buyer must meet (or the other party must waive) before the deal will close. For example, the buyer's acceptance is commonly contingent on arranging financing.

The buyer will specify how many days he needs to arrange financing. If he has to start from scratch (no preapproval letter), expect that he will spend five to six weeks. If all that remains is an appraisal of the property, expect the buyer to have financing set up in about two or three weeks.

1. Financial Terms

This offer is contingent upon Buyer securing financing as specified in items D, E, F and G, below, within _____ days from acceptance of this offer.

$_____   A. DEPOSIT to be applied toward the down payment.

$_____   B. DEPOSIT INCREASE to be applied toward the down payment by _____ (date).

$_____   C. DOWN PAYMENT balance, in cash, to be paid into escrow on or before the close of escrow.

$_____   D. FIRST LOAN—NEW LOAN. Buyer shall obtain a new loan, amortized over not fewer than
_____ years. Buyer's financing shall be

☐ Conventional _____ (name of lender, if known)

☐ Private _____ (name of lender, if known)

☐ Government (specify):   ☐ VA   ☐ FHA   ☐ Cal-Vet   ☐ CHFA

☐ Other: _____

Buyer's mortgage shall be ☐ at a maximum fixed rate of _____% or

☐ an adjustable rate loan with a maximum beginning rate of _____%, with the life-of-the-loan cap not to exceed _____ percentage points and the periodic cap not to be adjusted more frequently than _____ . Maximum monthly loan payment including principal, interest and, if applicable, private mortgage insurance (PMI), during the first year of the loan agreement, shall be $_____. Buyer shall pay a loan origination fee (points) of not more than _____% of the loan amount and application and appraisal fees of not more than $_____ .

$_____   E. FIRST LOAN—EXISTING LOAN. Buyer shall ☐ assume ☐ buy subject to an existing loan under the same terms and conditions that Seller has with _____ _____, the present lender. The approximate remaining balance is $_____, at the current rate of interest of _____% on a ☐ fixed ☐ adjustable rate loan, or a remaining term of approximately _____ years, secured by a First Deed of Trust.

$_____   F. SECOND LOAN—NEW LOAN. Buyer shall obtain a new loan, amortized over not fewer than _____ years. Buyer's financing shall be:

☐ Conventional _____ (name of lender, if known)

☐ Private _____ (name of lender, if known)

☐ Government (specify):   ☐ VA   ☐ FHA   ☐ Cal-Vet   ☐ CHFA

☐ Other: _____

Buyer's mortgage shall be ☐ at a maximum fixed rate of _____% or ☐ an adjustable rate loan with a maximum beginning rate of _____%, with the life-of-the-loan cap not to exceed _____ percentage points and the periodic cap not to be adjusted more frequently than _____ . Maximum monthly loan payment including principal, interest and, if applicable, private mortgage insurance (PMI), during the first year of the loan agreement, shall be $_____. Buyer shall pay a loan origination fee (points) of not more than _____% of the loan amount and application and appraisal fees of not more than $_____ .

$_____   G. SECOND LOAN—EXISTING LOAN. Buyer shall ☐ assume ☐ buy subject to an existing loan under the same terms and conditions that Seller has with _____ _____, the present lender. The approximate remaining balance is $_____, at the current rate of interest of ___% on a ☐ fixed ☐ adjustable rate loan for a remaining term of approximately _____ years, secured by a Second Deed of Trust.

$_____   H. TOTAL PURCHASE PRICE, EXCLUDING EXPENSES OF SALE AND CLOSING COSTS.

Buyer shall submit complete loan application and financial statement to lender within five days after acceptance. If Buyer, after making a good-faith effort, does not secure financing by the time specified, this contract shall become void, and all deposits shall be returned to Buyer.

In the event of FHA or VA financing, Buyer shall not be obligated to complete the purchase, nor shall Buyer forfeit the deposit, if the offer price exceeds the property's FHA or VA appraised value. Buyer shall, however, have the option of proceeding with the purchase from any above-named lender or a different lender without regard to the appraised value.

For the buyer's protection as well as yours, the terms of financing and payment should be specified in as much detail as possible. As part of doing this, the buyer should specify the maximum rate of interest and monthly payments he can make to a financial institution as well as the minimum term of years over which the loan is to be repaid (amortized). If you obtain the buyer's credit information (see Chapter 8), you should be able to get a good idea if the buyer can really afford your house.

The buyer's financing information should be outlined as follows:

Section A. The deposit amount as stated in the heading.

Section B. The deposit increase as stated in the heading, and the date by which it will be tendered, usually within a few days after the offer is accepted.

Section C. The proposed down payment balance—total down payment less the deposit and deposit increase.

Sections D-G. The amount and details of each loan. If the buyer's first (and perhaps only) loan is a new first mortgage, only Section D will be completed, specifying the minimum number of years, type of financing, maximum interest rate, maximum life-of-the-loan cap and adjustment period for an adjustable rate mortgage, maximum monthly payments and maximum fees the buyer expects to pay. If the buyer is applying for a government loan, he should be ready to demonstrate that he's eligible. The maximum number of points, and amount of application and appraisal fees the buyer is willing to pay should also be filled in.

If the buyer plans to use your existing loan as the first loan to finance his purchase, Section E will be completed. This specifies whether the buyer will assume the loan, take over the payments and become responsible for the loan or buy subject to an existing loan, make the payments without taking over formal responsibility—quite unusual. Section E also names the existing lender, the approximate remaining balance, the current interest rate, the type of loan and the approximate number of remaining years.

If the buyer proposes using a second loan to help finance the house, he will complete either Section F or G, depending on whether it's a new loan or an existing loan. Some buyers propose borrowing money from you (the seller) or from a friend or relative. Whatever the buyer plans, be sure it's spelled out clearly. Sections F and G mirror Sections D and E.

Section H. This total represents the price offered for your house.

---

2. Escrow

Buyer and Seller shall deliver signed escrow instructions to _____

_____ escrow agent located at

_____, within _____ days of

acceptance of this offer. Escrow shall close within _____ days of acceptance of this offer. A deed shall be recorded in favor of Buyer at the close of escrow.

Escrow is the process in which a disinterested third party, usually a title or escrow company, transfers the funds and documents among the buyer, seller and their lenders, following instructions provided by the buyer and seller. (See Chapter 11 for details on opening and closing escrow.)

This clause lists the name and address of the escrow holder you and the buyer choose. Although you do not actually open an escrow account until you accept an offer to purchase your house, it is wise to do some preliminary investigation in advance, so that you have at least a tentative idea as to the company you will use. After all, if you sign a contract on Sunday afternoon, the buyer will need to know to whom the deposit check should be made out.

If the buyer proposes an escrow holder, go with that person unless you are truly attached to "your"

holder and can persuade the buyer to agree. This clause also specifies the dates for delivering the written escrow instructions. These instructions authorize the escrow company to give you the money and give the buyer the deed to the property, and should be delivered a few days before the closing date.

You and the buyer need to allow enough time for the removal of all the contingencies—such as arranging financing or approving inspections—before the contract calls for the escrow to close. Unless the buyer already has her financing lined up, this should be at least 45–60 days from the date the contract is signed. If the buyer has money in hand, however, you usually need to allow only 20 to 30 days to complete physical inspections of the condition of the property.

---

3. Pre-payment Penalty and Assumption Fee

Seller shall pay any pre-payment penalty or other fees imposed by any existing lender who is paid off during escrow. Buyer shall pay any pre-payment penalty, assumption fee or other fee which becomes due after the close of escrow on any loans assumed from Seller.

This standard clause simply states that if your existing loan has a pre-payment penalty (it probably won't) and you are paying off the loan now before the end of the full term of the loan, you'll pay the penalty. It also states, however, that if your existing

loan has a pre-payment penalty and the buyer assumes the loan, she will assume the responsibility for any pre-payment penalty assessed after the close of escrow. This could occur if she sells the house, refinances the loan or pre-pays before its term runs out.

4. Expenses of Sale

Expenses of sale, settlement costs and closing costs shall be paid for as follows:

		Buyer	Seller	Share Equally	
A.		☐	☐	☐	Escrow fees
B.		☐	☐	☐	Title search
C.		☐	☐	☐	Title insurance for buyer/owner
D.		☐	☐	☐	Title insurance for buyer's lender
E.		☐	☐	☐	Deed preparation fee
F.		☐	☐	☐	Notary fee
G.		☐	☐	☐	Recording fee
H.		☐	☐	☐	Attorney's fee (if attorney hired to clarify title)
I.		☐	☐	☐	Documentary transfer tax
J.		☐	☐	☐	City transfer tax
K.		☐	☐	☐	Pest control inspection report
L.		☐	☐	☐	General contractor report
M.		☐	☐	☐	Roof inspection report
N.					Other inspections (specify):
	1.	☐	☐	☐	_____
	2.	☐	☐	☐	_____
	3.	☐	☐	☐	_____
O.		☐	☐	☐	One-year home warranty
P.					Other (specify):
	1.	☐	☐	☐	_____
	2.	☐	☐	☐	_____
	3.	☐	☐	☐	_____

When you receive an offer form, the buyer will no doubt have checked off a list of items proposing who pays for what. Review this list carefully, read the chart, below, "Who Pays for What," and make any changes in your counteroffer. Don't feel compelled to agree with whatever the buyer proposes. For example, even if the buyer checks off that you will provide (and pay for) a home warranty, don't run off and buy one unless you really think it will help with the sale. Clause 8, below, contains a list of the inspections the buyer may want to require, or which you feel are important to protect yourself from later charges by the buyer that you failed to disclose some problem with the house.

WHO PAYS FOR WHAT

Use this chart as a guide to how expenses are commonly divided; it's quite all right for you and the buyer to agree otherwise.

Item	Who usually pays	Comment
Escrow fees	Buyer customarily pays in Northern California, seller in Southern California	Not uncommon for fees to be divided
Title search	Buyer customarily pays in Northern California, seller in Southern California	Buyer benefits; not unreasonable for buyer to pay
Title insurance for buyer/owner	Buyer customarily pays in Northern California, seller in Southern California	Buyer benefits; not unreasonable for buyer to pay
Title insurance for lender	Buyer	Buyer benefits; buyer should pay
Deed preparation fee	Buyer	Buyer benefits; buyer should pay
Notary fee	Buyer usually pays for grant and trust deeds; seller usually pays for reconveyance deed on the property	Grant and trust deeds help buyer purchase and finance property; seller receives reconveyance deed when paying off existing mortgage
Recording fee	Buyer usually pays for grant and trust deeds; seller usually pays for reconveyance deed on the property	Grant and trust deeds help buyer purchase and finance property; seller receives reconveyance deed when paying off existing mortgage
Attorney's fee (if attorney hired to clarify title)	Whoever hired attorney	
Documentary transfer tax	Seller usually pays, except in probate sales where buyer is legally required to pay	
City transfer tax	Buyer and seller usually share the cost	
Pest control inspection report	Buyer usually picks inspector and pays for inspection	Buyer should pay to assure that report meets buyer's standard
General contractor report	Buyer usually picks inspector and pays for inspection	Buyer should pay to assure that report meets buyer's standard
Roof inspection report	Buyer usually picks inspector and pays for inspection	Buyer should pay to assure that report meets buyer's standard
Other inspections	Buyer usually picks inspector and pays for inspection	Buyer should pay to assure that report meets buyer's standard
One-year home warranty	Seller	Sometimes seller offers to buy a policy when he lists the property; if he doesn't, buyer can purchase one if desired
Real estate tax Fire insurance Bond liens (unless able to be paid off)	Buyer and seller usually prorate as of the date the deed is recorded (see Clause 5)	Both parties benefit; should be prorated

---

5. Property Tax and Insurance Prorations; Non-Callable Bonds

Seller shall be responsible for payment of Seller's prorated share of real estate taxes accrued until the deed transferring title to Buyer is recorded. Buyer understands that the property shall be reassessed upon change of ownership and that Buyer shall be sent a supplemental tax bill which may reflect an increase in taxes based on property value.

Any fire insurance policy carried over from Seller to Buyer and any homeowners' association fees shall be prorated, that is, Seller shall pay the portion of the premiums and fees while title is in Seller's name and Buyer shall pay the portion of the premiums and fees while title is in Buyer's name.

Buyer agrees to assume non-callable assessment bond liens (those which cannot be paid off by Seller) as follows:

_____

Clause 5 allocates payment of property taxes, fire insurance policies carried over from seller to buyer and any homeowners' association fees. Each owner pays only for the period of actual ownership. For example, if property taxes are $1,000 for a fiscal year beginning July 1, and escrow closes on the next April 1, the buyer's prorated share is $250 for the last quarter of the year (April, May and June), while the seller's share is $750 for the three previous ones (July through March).

This clause also provides that the buyer assumes any non-callable bond liens—bonds to finance local improvements such as curbs, gutters or street lights. You may not even know whether the house has any such liens, but they'll show up on the title report. Often bonds must be paid off when a house is sold, but sometimes they can't be—that is, they're non-callable. In that case, the buyer assumes responsibility to pay the lien, but the cost of doing so is credited by the seller to the buyer in escrow. Unless you know specifically what non-callable bond liens are on the house, leave it blank. If such bond liens show up in a subsequent title search, the manner of paying for them can be dealt with in escrow instructions.

---

6. Fixtures

All fixtures permanently attached to the property, including built-in appliances, electrical, plumbing, light and heating fixtures, garage door openers, attached carpets and other floor coverings, and window shades or blinds, are included in the sale except: _____

_____
_____
_____
_____

Fixtures are items permanently attached to your house and the land it's on, such as built-in appliances or bookshelves, wall-to-wall carpeting, chandeliers, drapes and landscaping. Fixtures come with the house unless you and the buyer agree that you will take them with you. If you want to take something considered a fixture, such as a built-in stove, be sure to list it in your counteroffer.

---

7. Personal Property

The following items of personal property are included in this sale:

☐ Stove   ☐ Oven   ☐ Refrigerator   ☐ Washer

☐ Dryer   ☐ Freezer   ☐ Trash Compactor   ☐ Dishwasher

_____

_____

Everything other than real property and fixtures is personal property. Personal property doesn't come with the house unless the seller agrees in writing to include it. If you promise to include items such as rugs, beds or appliances that aren't built-in, be sure they are listed in your counteroffer and final contract.

---

8. Inspection Contingencies

This offer is conditioned upon Buyer's written approval of the following inspection reports. All reports shall be carried out within _____ days of acceptance. Buyer shall deliver written approval or disapproval to Seller within 3 days of receiving each report. If Buyer does not deliver a written disapproval within the time allowed, Buyer shall be deemed to approve of the report.

Seller is to provide reasonable access to the property to Buyer, his/her agent, all inspectors and representatives of lending institutions to conduct appraisals.

A.   ☐ Pest control report

B.   ☐ General contractor report as to the general physical condition of the property including, but not limited to, heating and plumbing, electrical systems, solar energy systems, roof and appliances

C.   ☐ Plumbing contractor report

D.   ☐ Soils engineer report

E.   ☐ Energy conservation inspection report in accordance with local ordinances

F.   ☐ Geologist report

G.   ☐ Environmental inspection report

H.   ☐ City or county inspection report

I.   ☐ Roof inspection report

If Buyer and Seller, after making a good-faith effort, cannot remove in writing the above contingencies by the time specified, this contract shall become void, and all deposits shall be returned to Buyer.

Somewhere in the offer, the buyer will specify what inspections on the house she wants done—and must approve—before she will complete the purchase (close escrow). If the buyer doesn't also specify—or doesn't specify to your satisfaction—how soon the inspections must be done after the offer has been accepted, include it in your counteroffer. It's normally reasonable to allow 20 working days.

Before you get overwhelmed in reading this section, be aware that it would be unusual for a buyer to require all the inspection contingencies listed in Clause 8. Often, a buyer only asks for a general contractor and pest control report, unless she suspects problems requiring an inspection by a specialist. As a very rough rule, buyers normally want to require more inspections when a house is older and expensive or vulnerable to special problems (such as near an earthquake fault or slide zone). California laws generally require a pest control report whenever residential property is sold, unless the buyer waives it and has not been induced to do so by the seller or an agent. Even then, however, the lender may require the report. So you might as well be prepared for it. (Business and Professions Code §§ 8516, 8518, 8519 and 8614, and Civil Code § 1099.)

The clause also lets the buyer cancel the contract if the inspection reports are not to her satisfaction.

Most buyers negotiate with sellers to correct—or to monetarily compensate them for correcting—the problems before canceling the contract. (See Chapter 11 for more information on removing contingencies.)

⚠ *Never agree to pay for repairs in advance. If the buyer tries to require this in her offer, you should eliminate it in your counteroffer, or agree to a dollar limit on the amount of repairs you will compensate.*

---

9. Other Contingencies

This offer is contingent upon the following:

A. ☐ Buyer receiving and approving preliminary title report within _____ days of acceptance of this offer

B. ☐ Seller furnishing a Residential Building Record Report indicating _____ legal units within _____ days of acceptance

C. ☐ Seller furnishing declaration of restrictions, CC&Rs, bylaws, articles of incorporation, rules and regulations currently in force and a financial statement of the owners' association within _____ days of acceptance

D. ☐ Sale of Buyer's current residence, the address of which is _____,
by _____.

E. ☐ Seller furnishing rental agreements within _____ days of acceptance

F. ☐ Other: _____

Buyer shall deliver written approval or disapproval to Seller within three days of receiving each report or statement. If Buyer does not deliver a written disapproval within the time allowed, Buyer shall be deemed to approve of the report or statement. If Buyer and Seller, after making a good-faith effort, cannot remove in writing the above contingencies, this offer shall become void, and all deposits shall be returned to Buyer.

In Clause 9, the buyer specifies the other contingencies that must be met before he will close escrow. It also lets the buyer cancel the contract if the contingencies are not fulfilled to his satisfaction.

Most offers call for the removal of all contingencies within 30 to 60 days after your acceptance. There are no hard and fast rules, however; you and the buyer should decide depending on your time

constraints and how long it will realistically take to remove each contingency. If your house is in great physical shape, 30 days should be adequate to remove contingencies relating to its physical condition. You might even request that physical inspection contingencies be removed within 7–14 days. This makes sense from your point of view; sales that fall apart often do so because inspections turn up defects and the buyer and seller can't agree on who will pay for repairs. A contingency based on the buyer selling an existing house or obtaining a loan he hasn't yet applied for will normally need 30–90 days for removal.

If any contingencies aren't met in the specified time, the deal is over unless you and the buyer agree in writing to extend the contingency release time. A contingency release form and a form to extend time to satisfy a contingency are in Chapter 11.

Let's review the contingencies listed one at a time.

Item A will be selected in all sales. The buyer will want to insure that title (legal ownership) is good, that is, no one has a lien on the house or claims an easement that can't be taken care of. See Chapter 11 for a discussion of these terms and preliminary title reports.

Item B is a report on file with the local building department in some California cities indicating the number of legal (habitable under local building code standards) units on the premises. If the place has an in-law unit, or has been split to create two units, however, one may not be legal. If the buyer plans to rely on rental income, but won't be able to legally rent out the unit, she may have a problem.

Item C is for houses in developments, most of which are subject to conditions, covenants and restrictions (CC&Rs). Make sure the title company provides you and the buyer with all the rules and regulations and that you both study them carefully. If you live in a development, you must provide the buyer with the following documents, which you can get from your homeowners' association. (Civil Code § 1368.) Several of these disclosures are also required by the statutory disclosure statement discussed in Chapter 7.

- Governing documents, such as bylaws and CC&Rs.
- If residency is limited by age (for example, only people over 55 allowed), a statement that the restriction is enforceable only to the extent allowed by law. (The law allowing age restric-

tions, within limits, is the Unruh Civil Rights Act, Civil Code § 51.3.)

- A copy of the association's most recent financial report.
- A written statement from an authorized representative of the association as to the amount of any unpaid assessments that may be made against the property.

Item D is perhaps the most common non-inspection contingency. In hot (sellers') markets, sellers often reject offers contingent upon the sale of the buyer's current residence. In communities where sales have slowed, however, sellers accept this contingency more often. Obviously, before you agree to a contingency which states that the buyer must sell her existing home before closing on yours, you want to consider whether the buyer is likely to be able to sell her present home.

Start by asking the buyer some questions about her house, the location, the asking price, how long it's been on the market and similar information. If you feel that you want more assurance, you have a right to demand that the buyer list her home with a broker and put it into a Multiple Listing Service. You can also ask for the telephone number of her broker and make regular inquiries as to the progress of the sale. This may sound harsh, but it may be what you need to do to protect yourself from a would-be buyer who expresses no more than a wish to buy your home, ties it up, then tries to sell her own house at a price based on her need to buy your home and not what hers is really worth in the fair market.

Item E comes up when the place you are selling has tenants living in it whom the buyer intends to let remain after the sale—for example, you're selling a duplex or house with an already rented in-law unit. Under state rental laws, the buyer will inherit not only the tenants, but also the rental agreements. If she feels those agreements are unreasonable, she may want to be able to get out of the contracts.

10. Condition of Property

Seller represents that the heating, plumbing, air conditioning, electrical, septic, drainage, sewers, gutters and downspouts, sprinklers, as well as built-in appliances and other equipment and fixtures, are in working order. Seller agrees to maintain them in that condition, and to maintain all landscaping, grounds and pools, until possession of the property is delivered to Buyer. Seller shall, by the date of possession, replace any cracked or broken glass.

In Clause 10, you are required to assure the buyer that certain mechanical systems and appliances are in good working order and to keep them that way until you turn over possession of the property. You are also required to replace any broken glass by the time you turn over the property. Be sure that defects you list here were on your disclosure form (see Chapter 7) and vice versa.

11. Foreign Investors

If Seller is a foreign person as defined in the Foreign Investment in Real Property Tax Act, Buyer shall, absent a specific exemption, have withheld in escrow ten percent (10%) of the gross sale price of the property. Buyer and Seller shall provide the escrow holder specified in Clause 2 above with all signed documentation required by the Act.

To comply with a federal law called FIRPTA, you must complete a form (available from an escrow or title company, or the IRS) stating whether you are a foreign investor as defined by that law. (Internal Revenue Code § 1445.) If you are, the buyer must instruct the escrow holder to withhold in escrow 10% of the sale price of the house and fill out and file some papers with the IRS. The escrow agent can help with this, and your tax advisor can help you find out if you are a foreign investor. If you're a U.S. citizen, forget about this clause.

12. Rent Control

The property ☐ is ☐ is not located in a city or county subject to local rent control. A rent control ordinance may restrict the rent that can be charged for this property, limit the right of the owner to evict the occupant for other than "just cause" and control the owner's rights and responsibilities.

About 13 California cities have rent control ordinances, which may restrict the rent the owner can charge a tenant, as well as control the owner's rights and responsibilities. While this is most relevant with multi-unit buildings, it can decrease the value of houses likely to be rented in the future. Even if the buyer is not planning to rent the home now, conditions change and she may rent it out later on. You want to be sure to disclose to the buyer all local rent control laws. If you are in doubt whether your house is covered by local rent control laws, call your city or county planning office and find out.

CALIFORNIA CITIES SUBJECT TO RENT CONTROL

Berkeley	Oakland
Beverly Hills	Palm Springs
Campbell	San Francisco
East Palo Alto	San Jose
Hayward	Santa Monica
Los Angeles	Thousand Oaks
Los Gatos	West Hollywood

---

13. Title

At close of escrow, title to the property is to be clear of all liens and encumbrances of record except those listed in the preliminary title report and agreed to be assumed by Buyer. Any such liens or encumbrances assumed by Buyer shall be credited toward the purchase price. If Seller cannot remove liens or encumbrances not assumed by Buyer, Buyer shall have the right to cancel this contract and be refunded his/her deposit and costs of inspection reports.

This standard clause assures the buyer that title to the house will be in good order (clear) when you turn over possession—this means there are no legal claims against the title to the property by previous lenders or owners unknown to the present buyer. As discussed in Chapter 11, this title contingency is normally satisfied when a title company checks a title and issues a title report. If you are unable to clear up difficulties before the close of escrow, the buyer has the right to get out of the contract.

14. Possession

Buyer reserves the right to inspect the property three days before the close of escrow. Seller shall deliver physical possession of property, along with alarms, alarm codes, keys, garage door openers and all other means to operate all property locks, to Buyer:

☐ at close of escrow   ☐ no later than _____ days after the close of escrow.

If Buyer agrees to let Seller continue to occupy the property after close of escrow, Seller shall deposit into escrow for Buyer a prorated share of Buyer's monthly carrying costs (principal, interest, property taxes and insurance), for each such day, subject to the terms of a written agreement, specifying rent or security deposit, authorizing a final inspection before Seller vacates and indicating the length of tenancy, signed by both parties.

Clause 14 lets the buyer have one last look at the property right before the close of escrow to make sure that you or your tenant didn't damage the place in anticipation of moving out and that all promised repairs have been done to her satisfaction. It also specifies when the buyer can move in. Although the buyer may want to take possession on the same day escrow closes, she may give this up during your negotiations. If you are buying another house, you may insist on not moving out until 60–90 days after escrow closes, in exchange for paying the buyer rent.

Should you and the buyer agree that you can stay on after closing, you and the buyer should sign a written rental agreement specifying a daily rent or security deposit, authorizing a final inspection and indicating how long. Although the contract states a per day charge of the buyer's prorated monthly carrying costs, this can be high. You may want to counteroffer with a lower amount—for example, a flat deposit of 0.5% of the cost of the house; that's $500 on a $100,000 house.

15. Agency Confirmation and Commission to Brokers

The following agency relationship(s) are confirmed for this transaction:

Listing agent: _____ is the agent of: ☐ Seller exclusively   ☐ Buyer and Seller.

Selling agent: _____ is the agent of: ☐ Seller exclusively   ☐ Buyer and Seller

☐ Buyer exclusively.

NOTICE: The amount or rate of real estate commissions is not fixed by law. They are set by each Broker individually and may be negotiable between the Seller and Broker.

Buyer and Seller shall each pay only those broker's commissions for which Buyer and Seller have separately contracted in writing with a broker licensed by the California Commissioner of Real Estate.

$_____ or _____% of selling price to be paid to _____ by   ☐ Seller   ☐ Buyer.

$_____ or _____% of selling price to be paid to _____ by   ☐ Seller   ☐ Buyer.

Clause 15 lets you and the buyer confirm your relationships with any agents involved, to avoid misunderstandings about payments to brokers. For example, if the buyer makes her offer through a broker, she may mistakenly assume you will pay the broker's fee or split it.

Long before you fill out this offer form, if you are working with an agent you would have completed a

Confirmation: Real Estate Agency Relationships form, which contains the identical information as Clause 15. It doesn't hurt to repeat the information in the offer form.

This clause also clarifies who pays which broker, and how much. The notice is required by state law. (Business and Professions Code § 10147.5.) Your options are outlined in Chapter 4.

---

16. Advice

If Buyer or Seller wishes advice concerning the legal or tax aspects of this transaction, Buyer or Seller shall separately contract and pay for it.

This clause means that you are not liable for giving tax or legal advice to the buyer, the buyer isn't liable for giving that information to you and the real estate agents aren't liable for giving that information to you or the buyer.

---

17. Backup Offer

Should Seller accept this offer as a backup offer, the following terms and conditions apply:

If Seller accepts this offer as a primary offer, he/she must do so in writing.

Buyer has 24 hours from receipt of Seller's written acceptance to ratify it in writing. If Buyer fails to do so, Buyer's offer shall be deemed withdrawn and any contractual relationship between Buyer and Seller terminated.

It sometimes happens that contingencies in real estate contracts are never satisfied—for example, the buyer is unable to get financing. In anticipation of such a situation, you may want accept a backup offer so that you have another buyer in line. If a second offer you like comes while you and the buyer are trying to satisfy the contingencies in the first offer, you can still accept the second offer—but as a backup offer. You would check this clause in your counteroffer.

Then, if your first deal falls through, you can give the buyer who proposed the second offer an acceptance in writing. He then has 24 hours to accept or reject the deal.

Similarly, you may want to leave open the possibility that after you've already accepted an offer, a second offer will come in that is more to your liking. In that event, you will want to accept the second offer as a back-up offer. More importantly, your first contract must have a wipe-out clause, which you can add in your counteroffer. (See Chapter 10, Section H.)

A wipe-out clause does not mean you can automatically get out of the first deal. What it does mean is that any time after two weeks following the date you sign your contact, you can demand that the first buyers remove (wipe out) their contingencies within a short period of time (such as 96 hours), as opposed to giving the buyer the full number of days specified in the contract (usually 20–30 days) for the removal of contingencies. If the buyer can't, your obligations under that contract are terminated and you're free to accept the second offer as your primary offer.

---

18. Duration of Offer

This offer is submitted to Seller by Buyer on _____, at _____.M., Pacific Time, and will be considered revoked if not accepted by Seller in writing by _____.M. on _____, or, if prior to Seller's acceptance of this offer, Buyer revokes this offer in writing.

In Clause 18, the buyer gives you a deadline to accept the offer. If you don't accept by that time, the offer automatically expires unless you and the buyer extend it in writing.

In deciding how much time to give the seller, a smart buyer will pay close attention to your needs and negotiating strategy. If she's bidding high to pre-empt other bidders, she'll give you a very short time—maybe only a few hours. But if she's bidding low on a number of houses with the hope of eventually picking up a bargain, she'll leave her offer open for a considerably longer time. If she's somewhere in between these extremes, she'll give you about one to three days to respond. If she's making a backup offer, she'll need to let time pass for the other deal to fall through, thus 60–90 days is a typical length.

---

19. Other Terms and Conditions

_____
_____
_____
_____
_____
_____
_____
_____
_____
_____
_____

In the space provided in Clause 19, the buyer lists any terms or conditions not covered elsewhere in the offer. If there's not enough space, the buyer may write "Summarized on Supplement to Real Property Purchase Offer" and type up a form such as the following:

Supplement to Real Property Purchase Offer

The material set out below is hereby made a part of the offer dated _____, from

_____ (Buyer) to

_____ (Seller)

for the purchase of the real property at:

_____

Additional terms:

_____

_____

_____

_____ etc.

_____   _____
Buyer   Date

_____   _____
Buyer   Date

20. Risk of Damage to Property

If, before Buyer receives title to, or possession of, the property, it is substantially damaged by fire, flood, earthquake or other cause, Buyer shall be relieved of any obligation to buy the property and shall be refunded all deposits. When Buyer receives possession of the property, Buyer assumes sole responsibility for its physical condition. Seller shall maintain fire insurance on the property until the close of escrow.

Clause 20 states that the buyer must assume the risk of damage to, or destruction of, the property after she gets title to it. If the house is damaged or destroyed before then, it's your problem. The buyer can back out of the sale and get her deposit back.

This clause also requires you to maintain fire insurance on the property through the closing. Once the buyer takes title, however, it's her responsibility to have the insurance.

21. Liquidated Damages

If Seller accepts this offer, and Buyer later defaults on the contract, Seller shall be released from Seller's obligations under this contract. By signing their initials here, Buyer (_____) and Seller (_____) agree that if Buyer defaults, Seller shall keep all deposits, up to three percent (3%) of the purchase price stated above.

Clause 21 deals with what happens if the buyer backs out of the deal with no good reason. If she refuses to go through with the sale because a contingency can't be fulfilled—for example, the buyer fails to qualify for a loan or is dissatisfied with the pest control inspection—you must return her deposit. But if she backs out simply because she changes her mind, or doesn't try in good faith to fulfill a contingency (for instance, she doesn't apply for a loan), it's considered a default and you need not return her deposit. This approach makes sense; you should be compensated if the buyer simply decides not to go through with the purchase for a reason not covered in the contract.

This clause treats the deposit as liquidated damages, meaning you and the buyer agree in advance on the damages if she defaults. By setting the amount in advance, you and the buyer save both time and money by avoiding court or arbitration, and you are protected from the risk of a court or arbitrator awarding you a lesser amount.

California law generally prohibits sellers from keeping more than 3% of the agreed-upon sale price as liquidated damages. (Civil Code § 1675.) If you can show that a larger amount is reasonable—that is, you suffered significant monetary loss due to the buyer's default—a court might allow it. Also, the provision must be in at least 10-point boldface type (as shown) and signed or initialed by you and the seller. This makes it clear that both parties actively chose to include the provision.

---

22. Mediation of Disputes

If a dispute arises out of, or relates to, this agreement, Buyer and Seller ☐ agree ☐ do not agree to first try in good faith to settle the dispute by non-binding mediation before resorting to court action or binding arbitration. To invoke mediation, one party shall notify the other of his/her intention to proceed with mediation and shall provide the name of a chosen mediator. The other party shall have seven days to respond. If he/she disagrees with the first person's chosen mediator, the parties shall ask the escrow holder to choose the mediator or to recommend someone to choose the mediator. The mediator shall conduct the mediation session or sessions within the next three weeks. Costs of mediation shall be divided equally between Buyer and Seller.

Buyer _____   Seller _____

Buyer _____   Seller _____

Clause 22 lets you first try to settle any disputes that arise under the contract by non-binding mediation. Mediation is a process where you and the buyer pick someone to help you reach a mutually agreeable decision. The result is never imposed on either party. Mediation is cheap, fast and without the emotional drain and hostility of litigation. We highly recommend it.

Anyone can be a mediator, although it's best to have someone familiar with the real estate business. The person you choose should be fair minded and work well with people. Don't suggest your agent (if you have one) or the buyer's agent. Both of you have an interest in getting someone you agree is impartial. The escrow holder may be willing to recommend (or at least informally suggest) someone as a mediator if you and the buyer are having trouble agreeing.

23. Arbitration of Disputes*

Any dispute or claim in law or equity arising out of this agreement will be decided by neutral binding arbitration in accordance with the California Arbitration Act (C.C.P. § 1280 et seq.), and not by court action except as provided by California law for judicial review of arbitration proceedings. Judgment upon the award rendered by the arbitrator may be entered in any court having jurisdiction. The parties shall have the right to discovery in accordance with Code of Procedure § 1283.05. The parties agree that the following procedure will govern the making of the award by the arbitrator: (a) the Tentative Award will be made by the arbitrator within 30 days following submission of the matter to the arbitrator; (b) the Tentative Award will explain the factual and legal basis for the arbitrator's decision as to each of the principal controverted issues; (c) the Tentative Award will be in writing unless the parties agree otherwise; provided, however, that if the hearing is concluded within one day, the Tentative Award may be made orally at the hearing in the presence of the parties. Within 15 days after the Tentative Award has been served or announced, any party may serve objections to the Tentative Award. Upon objections being timely served, the arbitrator may call for additional evidence, oral or written argument or both. If no objections are filed, the Tentative award will become final without further action by the parties or arbitrator. Within 30 days after the filing of objections, the arbitrator will either make the Tentative Award final or modify or correct the Tentative Award, which will then become final as modified or corrected. The following matters are excluded from arbitration: (a) a judicial or non-judicial foreclosure or other action or proceeding to enforce a deed of trust, mortgage, or real property sales contract as defined in Civil Code § 2985; (b) an unlawful detainer action; (c) the filing or enforcement of a mechanic's lien; (d) any matter which is within the jurisdiction of a probate court, or small claims court; or (e) an action for bodily injury or wrongful death, or for latent or patent defects to which Code of Civil Procedure § 337.1 or § 337.15 applies. The filing of a judicial action to enable the recording of a notice of pending action, for order of attachment, receivership, injunction, or other provisional remedies, will not constitute a waiver of the right to arbitrate under this provision.

NOTICE: BY INITIALLING IN THE ["AGREE"] SPACE BELOW YOU ARE AGREEING TO HAVE ANY DISPUTE ARISING OUT OF THE MATTERS INCLUDED IN THE "ARBITRATION OF DISPUTES" PROVISION DECIDED BY NEUTRAL ARBITRATION AS PROVIDED BY CALIFORNIA LAW AND YOU ARE GIVING UP ANY RIGHTS YOU MIGHT POSSESS TO HAVE THE DISPUTE LITIGATED IN A COURT OR JURY TRIAL. BY INITIALLING IN THE ["AGREE"] SPACE BELOW YOU ARE GIVING UP YOUR JUDICIAL RIGHTS TO DISCOVERY AND APPEAL, UNLESS THOSE RIGHTS ARE SPECIFICALLY INCLUDED IN THE "ARBITRATION OF DISPUTES" PROVISION. IF YOU REFUSE TO SUBMIT TO ARBITRATION AFTER AGREEING TO THIS PROVISION, YOU MAY BE COMPELLED TO ARBITRATE UNDER THE AUTHORITY OF THE CALIFORNIA CODE OF CIVIL PROCEDURE. YOUR AGREEMENT TO THIS ARBITRATION PROVISION IS VOLUNTARY.

WE HAVE READ AND UNDERSTAND THE FOREGOING AND AGREE TO SUBMIT DISPUTES ARISING OUT OF THE MATTERS INCLUDED IN THE "ARBITRATION OF DISPUTES" PROVISION TO NEUTRAL ARBITRATION.

[_____] [_____] Buyer agrees [_____] [_____] Buyer does not agree

[_____] [_____] Seller agrees [_____] [_____] Seller does not agree

*This clause is based on a product of Professional Publishing, with permission. To find out more about Professional Publishing, its real estate products and its forms generator software (Formulator), contact them at 365 Bel Marin Keys Blvd., Suite 100, Novato, CA 94949 415-884-2164.

If you want any disputes to be decided by arbitration, you must include this exact clause in your contract. If you opt for it, you choose to resolve your dispute by arbitration should your attempt to settle any dispute informally or by mediation not succeed. You give up your right to a court trial. We recommend choosing arbitration. Like mediation, it's cheaper, faster and less hostile than litigation.

In arbitration, you submit your dispute to one or more arbitrators for a decision. Some commentators and, of course, most real estate lawyers recommend against this clause, believing you have a better chance of winning big by going to court. We don't agree. Relying on the American court system to produce an efficient, cost-effective resolution of a dispute is usually naive.

---

24. Attorneys' Fees

If litigation or arbitration arises from this contract, the prevailing party shall be reimbursed by the other party for reasonable attorneys' fees and court or arbitration costs.

In our contract, the losing party in arbitration or litigation (you could wind up in litigation if you choose arbitration and the buyer doesn't agree, or vice versa) is responsible for their own—and the other side's—attorney's fees and court costs. This clause is standard.

---

25. Entire Agreement

This document represents the entire agreement between Buyer and Seller. Any modifications to this contract shall be made in writing, signed and dated by both parties.

Clause 25, which states that this contract is the entire agreement between you and the buyer, and that all modifications to the contract must be in writing, is a statement of the law that oral real estate agreements are simply not enforceable. If you're relying on anything the buyer has told you, get it in writing.

---

26. Time is of the Essence

Time is of the essence in this transaction.

Clause 26, which is a standard clause in most contracts, emphasizes the importance of the dates you and seller agree to. It means that a missed deadline by either party is considered a substantial breach of the contract, which can result in the other party being given money damages or being allowed to cancel the contract.

 Put away your stop watch. Despite this provision, the trend is to reject cries of "she breached the 'time is of the essence' clause" for a delay of a few hours or days—for example, if the buyer fails to fulfill a financing contingency because things are backed up at her bank— unless you can show that you have suffered, or will suffer, damages as a result.

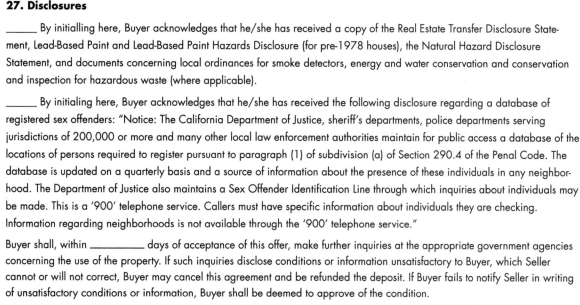

27. Disclosures

_____ By initialling here, Buyer acknowledges that he/she has received a copy of the Real Estate Transfer Disclosure State-ment, Lead-Based Paint and Lead-Based Paint Hazards Disclosure (for pre-1978 houses), the Natural Hazard Disclosure Statement, and documents concerning local ordinances for smoke detectors, energy and water conservation and conservation and inspection for hazardous waste (where applicable).

_____ By initialing here, Buyer acknowledges that he/she has received the following disclosure regarding a database of registered sex offenders: "Notice: The California Department of Justice, sheriff's departments, police departments serving jurisdictions of 200,000 or more and many other local law enforcement authorities maintain for public access a database of the locations of persons required to register pursuant to paragraph (1) of subdivision (a) of Section 290.4 of the Penal Code. The database is updated on a quarterly basis and a source of information about the presence of these individuals in any neighbor-hood. The Department of Justice also maintains a Sex Offender Identification Line through which inquiries about individuals may be made. This is a '900' telephone service. Callers must have specific information about individuals they are checking. Information regarding neighborhoods is not available through the '900' telephone service."

Buyer shall, within _____ days of acceptance of this offer, make further inquiries at the appropriate government agencies concerning the use of the property. If such inquiries disclose conditions or information unsatisfactory to Buyer, which Seller cannot or will not correct, Buyer may cancel this agreement and be refunded the deposit. If Buyer fails to notify Seller in writing of unsatisfactory conditions or information, Buyer shall be deemed to approve of the condition.

Clause 27 is included to be sure that the buyer is notified of disclosures concerning material facts about the property, potential lead-based paint haz-ards, and flood or earthquake hazards. While you must disclose these in separate forms (see Chapter 7), including this clause in the offer form may bring it to the buyer's attention if you haven't yet provided the necessary disclosure forms, and is just one more way of making sure that your disclosures are acknowl-edged. Also, if you have given the buyer a copy of the booklet on environmental hazards issued by the state (see Chapter 7), be sure to get the buyer to acknowl-edge receipt of it.

This clause also alerts the buyer to the availabil-ity of a database maintained by law enforcement au-thorities on the location of registered sex offenders. Contracts entered into after July 1, 1999, for a sale of a house or other residential property must include this notice in not less than eight-point type. (Civil Code § 2079.10a.) You are not required to provide additional information about the proximity of regis-tered sex offenders. The law clearly states, however, that it does not change a seller's existing responsibil-ity to make disclosures of "material facts" that would affect the "value and desirability" of a property. (These disclosure requirements are discussed in Chapter 7.) This means that if you know for a fact that a registered sex offender lives next door or a few houses down, you are responsible for disclosing this "material" fact to the buyer.

---

28. Buyer's Signature

This constitutes an offer to purchase the above listed property.

Broker _____   Buyer _____

by _____   Buyer _____

Address _____   Address _____

_____   _____

Telephone _____   Telephone _____

Date _____ Time _____ M.

By signing this clause, the buyer agrees to make this offer that will become a binding contract if you accept it. If the buyer is married, her spouse must also sign, unless she's purchasing the house with her separate property. If she has a broker, she'll have the broker or agent sign it too, and include his address and phone number. The date and time when the buyer presents the offer should be included also.

---

29. Seller's Acceptance

Subject to: _____

Seller agrees to sell the property to Buyer in accordance to the terms and conditions specified above.

Broker _____   Seller _____

by _____   Seller _____

Address _____   Address _____

_____   _____

Telephone _____   Telephone _____

Date _____ Time _____ M.

If you sign, you accept the buyer's offer as it stands. If you are married, you and your spouse both must sign, even if one spouse claims the house is separate property. A title company won't want to get involved in the complexities of California community property law and will want to see both signatures. ■

Chapter 10

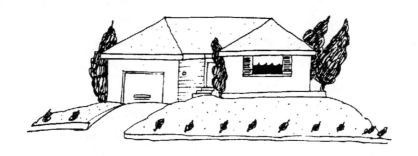

OFFERS, COUNTEROFFERS AND NEGOTIATIONS

This chapter covers responding to offers from prospective buyers and, when necessary, negotiating the price and other terms. Before reading this chapter, however, be sure to read Chapter 9 so that you can understand all terms in any offer presented to you.

A. The Legal Status of Listing Your House for Sale

You do not have to accept any offer, even one that meets or beats your price and other terms. Listing or advertising your home for sale is not a contract with the general public that you will sell it to anyone who offers the asking price. You have a legal right to reject an offer or remove your house from the market whenever you wish, within the following limits:

Broker's Rights. As discussed in Chapter 4, if you list your house with a broker under an Exclusive Authorization or Exclusive Agency contract, and the broker brings you an offer that meets or exceeds your listing price and terms, you owe a commission—whether or not you go through with the sale.

Discrimination. If you refuse to sell to buyer A but then promptly sell to buyer B at the same or a lower price or on more favorable terms, buyer A may take legal action if he is a member of a group which has historically been discriminated against. If it appears that your decision not to sell to buyer A was based on his race, ethnic background, religion, sex, marital status, age, family status or disability, you may face a lawsuit charging violation of state, federal or local laws prohibiting discrimination. For information on anti-discrimination laws, contact the California Department of Fair Employment and Housing at 800-233-3212, or check their Website at www.dfeh.ca.gov.

B. The Offer Conference

In the lingo of the real estate world, the seller receives the buyer's offer at an offer presentation or offer conference. Whether you use a fancy term or not, here are some tips on how best to conduct yourself when a prospective buyer contacts you and wants to make an offer.

Make an appointment with the prospective purchaser for the presentation of her offer. If more than one buyer contacts you close to the same time, you may wish to schedule the appointments simultaneously or shortly after one another. Although it's not legally required, I recommend entertaining offers in the order in which the prospective purchasers have contacted you.

You are very likely to hear from brokers who want to make offers on behalf of buyers, but only if you will cooperate by paying them a commission, usually 2.5% to 3.5% of the sales price. (See Chapter 4, Section E, for more on cooperating with brokers.) If you do not wish to do this, politely decline to meet with brokers. Alternatively, you may agree to cooperate and pay a commission, but only if offers to purchase are above a certain dollar amount.

Make it clear to prospective buyers that you expect offers to be in writing and accompanied by a cashier's or personal check (not cash) made out to an escrow or title company you and the buyer agree to. The buyer need only provide the check as a sign of good faith. You or your agent, if you have one, will hold the check uncashed until the offer is accepted. If you don't accept the offer, you return the check. As discussed in Chapter 9, Section E, it's typical to receive at least $1,000 as a deposit, though no amount is required by law.

If you are working with a broker hired by the hour, this person may help conduct the offer conference. At this key stage of your sale, it may be worth it to pay for several hours of professional negotiating help. Aside from having a knowledgeable friend at your side, it allows you to distance yourself a little from negotiations over price and terms. Your representative can be the tough guy and then you can step in and compromise when the time is right. (See Section D for more on negotiating.)

Prepare for a quiet, businesslike meeting. Use your study or den if you have one. Failing that, use the dining room table or a coffee table in the living room, making sure the area is quiet, private and free of clutter.

The person making the offer will present her written offer and deposit check to you. The heading of the contract provided in Chapter 9 and in the Appendix spells out your receipt of the deposit. If the prospective purchaser's offer doesn't have language like this, you'll need to provide a separate receipt for the deposit, such as the sample shown here. A tear-out copy is in the Appendix.

As the receipt states, you should hold the deposit check uncashed until you either accept or reject the offer. If you reject the offer, return the check. If you accept the offer, deposit the check with the escrow holder the check is made out to.

Sometimes the buyer will have nominated an escrow holder in his offer. (See Clause 2 in Chapter 9.) If so, go along with the buyer's choice unless you have strong reason to disagree. Otherwise, you will probably want to suggest an escrow holder. (For information on choosing the escrow holder, see Chapter 11, Section A.)

Normally, once you receive the offer, you will want to do the following:

- If the written offer is not adequately detailed—for example, if it lacks sufficient information on financial terms—suggest that the prospective purchasers redo their offer using the form in the Appendix of this book, getting independent help if necessary. Alternatively, make your own counter offer as described in Section E below.

- Pay particular attention to any time limit the buyer provides for you to respond in writing (Clause 18 of our offer form). If the offer demands a decision upon presentation or in a time period you find unreasonably short (say, less than two or three days), request a written amendment to the offer on the spot, allowing you more time. Do this by changing and

---

DEPOSIT RECEIPT

_____, Seller(s) of the property located at

_____ in

_____, California, hereby acknowledge receipt from,

_____, Offeror(s), the sum

of $_____ in the form of a: ☐ cashier's check ☐ personal check ☐ promissory note ☐ other,

payable to _____ (escrow or title insurance company),

This check will be held uncashed by the Seller until the acceptance of this offer. If this offer is accepted, the deposit shall be delivered to the mutually agreed escrow holder named above and applied toward the down payment. This deposit will be returned to the Offeror if this offer is not accepted.

_____   _____
Seller's signature   Date

_____   _____
Seller's signature   Date

initialing the time provision, and then have the
buyer initial it also. Remember, it's your house
and you are entitled to call the shots.

- Request that the buyer provide you with a credit
  information form (there's one in the Appendix)
  or lender preapproval before you make your
  final decision on the offer. If the buyer completes
  a credit information form, take a look at Chapter
  8, Section B, to see if the buyer can afford to
  purchase your house.

- Carefully study the offer, including all contingencies. This should give you a preliminary
  opinion as to whether the sale is likely to go
  through if you accept the offer.

- Make sure that the buyer has received and
  signed copies of the disclosure forms set out in
  Chapter 7 (copies are in the Appendix), along
  with all inspection reports that have been done
  in the last two years. If you haven't already given
  the Real Estate Transfer Disclosure Statement to
  the buyer, he has three days from when he
  receives it (that is, the date of the offer conference) to back out of the deal.

- Make sure the offer lists the exact time and date
  in order to avoid confusion with later counteroffers.

Typically, at this stage, you will want more information and clarification of particular aspects of the
offer. You probably won't want to debate terms, or
make an on-the-spot decision. Of course, if you are
absolutely convinced that the buyer is financially
qualified to make the purchase and is offering you a
price and terms you simply cannot refuse, you might
accept the offer right away. (See Section F, below, for
details on accepting an offer.) Alternatively, you
might reject an offer that has a ridiculously low price
or unacceptable terms. It's usually best to thank the
offerors courteously and tell them you will consider
their offers and get back to them. If they press you

for a decision, simply stand up, usher them to the
door politely, and insist on time to think.

If you immediately receive an offer after a well-
attended open house, how long should you wait for
more offers? Suppose 100 people attend your open
house on Sunday afternoon. That night, you receive
an offer for your full asking price. Do you accept it?
The answer, of course, depends on your particular
circumstances—most importantly, whether you feel
your asking price was high or low. Obviously, if
you've asked for a very high price and get it, you will
probably want to accept. Otherwise you are probably
best advised to slow things down a little and wait for
other offers. Remember, the best feedback you can
get on your asking price comes now, from potential
buyers.

If you receive multiple offers. If you receive more
than one offer, you have no obligation to disclose the
terms to other offerors. Even if the offerors do not
object, you'll have to assess your own situation.
Disclosure of offer terms to competing offerors may
work against your interest, by giving the offerors a
sense of the market which could result in lower price
offers. In some cases, however, disclosure may be
your best negotiating strategy, and lead to increased
price offers. Also, be aware of the possible negative
consequences of revealing offers *without* consent of
the offerors!

C. Revoking an Offer

A prospective buyer may revoke (literally "call back") an offer in writing any time before you communicate your response. For this reason, sellers are usually quick to accept very favorable offers. In addition, almost all offers come with a time limit during which the offer must be accepted in writing, or it automatically ends. For instance, "This offer is extended until 5:00 p.m., P.D.T., Saturday, July 10, 1993." If you try to accept after the specified date and time, the offeror may simply shrug his shoulders and say "Sorry, but you acted too late." Even if an offer contains a time limit, it can be revoked by the offeror prior to that time.

Example: Helen listed her home for sale at $235,000. She received an offer from Bill for $229,500, which allowed her four days to accept. Helen decided to wait a few days before responding because she expected offers from other people who had expressed an interest in her house. Three days after she received Bill's offer, and with no other offers in sight, Helen called him to say she was bringing over her written acceptance. Before she could do so, Bill said, "I'm so glad you called; I was just about to let you know that I'm revoking my offer, because I've found another house while you mulled over my offer." Bill's revocation is legal, although he should follow it up in writing. Fortunately for Helen, she received another attractive offer the following week. This time she promptly accepted in writing.

You and the buyer can also revoke counteroffers, as discussed in Section G.

D. The Art of Negotiating

When it comes to meeting and negotiating with potential purchasers, you may feel intimidated or unsure if you have no negotiation experience. There may even be a danger that a savvy buyer will talk you into agreeing to a contract that is not in your best interest.

Never reveal too much information, such as the lowest price you'll take or the fact that you need to sell the house as quickly as possible. Obviously, you don't want to give away as much money by negotiating poorly as you save by selling your own house. If you have any doubt as to your negotiating skill or the best strategy to follow, arrange to get help. As noted in Chapter 4, you can hire an experienced broker to help you with this crucial stage of the house selling process at a reasonable hourly rate.

If you don't want to negotiate yourself, or have a real estate professional negotiate for you, consider friends or relatives. A good negotiator doesn't need to be hard-boiled, penny-pinching or manipulative. She should pay attention to details, and have strong communication skills and common sense. Bear in mind, however, that only real estate agents and attorneys may legally be paid for negotiating a real estate transaction on your behalf.

There are several good books available on negotiation strategies, including *Getting to Yes: Negotiating Agreement Without Giving In,* by Roger Fisher and William Ury (Penguin Press).

E. Counteroffers

If you receive an offer that doesn't satisfy you, it usually makes sense to counteroffer in writing, making it clear how long the potential buyer has to accept. This normally ranges from as little as a few hours to as long as a few days, depending on the situation and your needs. Because counteroffers, like offers, are extended for a very short time, be sure that all counteroffer documents show not only the date, but the exact local time (Pacific Daylight Time or Pacific Standard Time) of presentation and expiration.

You may want to counter all the offers in an identical fashion—either simultaneously or as they come in—or tailor your responses to each offer. Either way, you will have a contract when the first counteroffer is accepted. Remember that it's illegal to discriminate on race, sex or other arbitrary grounds by giving only certain people a fair chance to meet your price and terms.

1. Common Terms in a Counteroffer

The logical way to decide what to put into a counteroffer is to review the terms of the offer. Any terms you agree with stay; those you don't are either eliminated or modified. For example, if the buyer's offer is contingent on selling an existing house or arranging financing, you will want to counteroffer with a wipeout clause if one is not already included. (See Section H, below.)

Several important issues on which you might want to base a counteroffer are discussed below.

Price. If the offer is too low, counter with a higher amount. Most potential buyers fully expect you to counteroffer on price, and thus bid a little low precisely to see what you will come back with. Many buyers may assume that you have overpriced the house slightly to leave room for bargaining and will be surprised if you aren't willing to negotiate. In fact, if your negotiating strategy is to name a price, but not bargain at all, you should go out of your way to make this clear at the offer conference.

Example: *Sally puts her house on the market for $210,000. Within two weeks, she has two offers for $195,000—not the full price, but not too bad. The buyers probably realize that Sally's house is worth around $210,000, but are trying to bargain to get it for a little less. Here are Sally's options:*

1. Sally can reject the offers and stick to her price.

2. Sally can counter with a higher price, somewhere between $195,000 and $210,000.

3. Sally can say, "I'm sorry, but because several people are interested in the house, the price is no longer $210,000—I'm raising it to $220,000." The potential buyers, of course, are likely to be shocked. This gives Sally a chance to say that she will honor the original price if someone really wants to commit to buy it immediately.

Financing. If the offer contains financing terms you believe are impractical, or if you don't feel the buyer will qualify for the amount or type of loan he proposes, change the unacceptable provisions in your counteroffer. If the buyer proposes that you carry a second deed of trust and you don't want to, counteroffer eliminating this provision.

Occupancy. If the offer doesn't give you enough time to move out, change it in your counteroffer.

Contingency of Buyer Selling Her House. Often an offeror will propose to buy your house contingent on first selling the one she already owns. Ask yourself if the buyer has a realistic chance of selling her present home during the time period allowed. If you don't think she does, refuse to accept this term. This may kill the deal, of course. But if a buyer really wants your house, she may be able to get short-term financial help from family or friends, or a bridge loan from a bank.

Inspections. Some of the buyer's inspection proposals (see Chapters 7 and 9 for more on inspections) may allow too much time. If so, propose changes.

2. Making a Counteroffer

Now it's time to make your written counteroffer, which should be presented at a conference much like the original meeting. Assuming the basic terms of the deal are specified in writing in the original offer, all you need to do is specify the items you wish to change. If the changes are minor, you can make them on the offer (initialing and dating each change) or use the short-form counteroffer included in the Appendix. Below is a completed sample.

SHORT FORM COUNTEROFFER

Helen and Robert McCloskey , Seller(s) of the real property at _291 Cornell Avenue, Culver City_ , California, accept(s) the offer to purchase the property dated _February 4, 1999_ , made by _Catherine Morris_ with the following exceptions:

     1. Price to be increased from $160,000 to $170,000

     2. Financing contingency to be removed by February 27, 19xx.

Helen McCloskey	February 4, 1999	4:00 P.M
Seller's signature	Date	Time
Robert McCloskey	February 4, 1999	4:00 P.M.
Seller's signature	Date	Time

If the offer you receive is not detailed enough to form the basis of a good contract, use the long form counteroffer in the Appendix. This is identical to the offer form discussed in Chapter 9—only the heading has been changed to read Counteroffer to Purchase Real Property. You're basically redoing the entire offer.

For many sales, the written offer-acceptance process is completed relatively quickly—the buyer makes an offer, the seller suggests a few changes, the buyer agrees. Sometimes, however, the process drags on, with counteroffers, counter counteroffers and counter counter counteroffers flying back and forth for days, or even weeks. This can work well, if you and the buyer narrow the differences with each counteroffer. But don't get so caught up in negotiating that you make a bad deal.

F. Accepting an Offer or Counteroffer

A contract is formed when either the buyer or the seller accepts all of the terms of the other's offer or counteroffer in writing within the time allowed.

You may create a valid contract if you accept an offer over the phone, but don't leave yourself vulnerable to possible disagreements in the future. A law called the statute of frauds, Civil Code § 1624, says a contract for the sale of real estate must be in writing. Technically, you can accept an offer orally, but no lender will work with you unless both the offer and acceptance are in writing. All owners, all buyers and all their spouses should sign the contract.

You and the buyer don't legally need to sign the same piece of paper. The buyer can make an offer and you can accept in writing by a separate letter or document. The usual procedure, however, is to have both signatures on one document. To go that route, you should sign the bottom of the buyer's offer or the buyer should sign the bottom of your counteroffer, stating that you accept it. If for any reason you need a separate acceptance form, use the one set out below. A tear-out copy is in the Appendix.

After you and the prospective buyer have signed the offer or counteroffer, do the following:

- Make photocopies of the contract; give one to the buyer and keep one. If you used short-form counteroffers to change a long offer, all contract terms won't be stated in one document. It's best to retype all the accepted terms onto one form.

- Make sure that the buyer gives you a deposit check made out to an escrow or title company in the amount called for in the contract.

- Keep all paperwork in a safe place.

- Give copies of documents to any real estate agent, attorney or tax advisor who is assisting you.

- Cooperate with the buyer to begin escrow proceedings.

Example: *Ito presents Monique with a typed piece of paper offering to purchase her house for $200,000 with 20% down, contingent on a satisfactory structural pest control report. This is fine with Monique, but she realizes that many other provisions should be included in the final contract. So she fills out the detailed counteroffer form in the Appendix, plugging in Ito's proposals. Ito reads her counteroffer and asks for a few minor changes. She makes these on the counteroffer form, and then initials and dates them. Ito also initials and dates the changes and then accepts in writing by signing the counteroffer form in the appropriate place; the deal is done.*

G. Revoking a Counteroffer

You or the buyer may revoke an offer or counteroffer in writing any time before the other accepts in writing. You needn't state a reason. If you want to revoke a counteroffer, do so right away. Call the buyer or her agent and tell her you're revoking your counteroffer; immediately follow up in writing. The best ways to do this are by fax (follow up by sending the original to the buyer or agent), Western Union mailgram (which contains the date and time of sending), hand delivery or overnight mail.

Obviously, one reason why you may want to withdraw your counteroffer (and return the buyer's deposit check) is if another potential buyer materializes with a better offer. If the buyer accepts in writing during the time allowed by your counteroffer before you revoke it, however, a binding legal contract has been established and you no longer can revoke your counteroffer. This is true even though you and the buyer never sit down and sign the same document.

ACCEPTANCE OF PURCHASE OFFER

_____

_____, the owner(s) of the property

at _____

_____ in the city of _____,

county of _____, California, hereby accept the offer to purchase the property

made on _____, by _____.

_____   _____
Seller's signature   Date

_____   _____
Seller's signature   Date

Example: *Jacob wanted to sell his house for $275,000. A number of prospective buyers came to his open house and seemed interested. One of them, Nancy, immediately made an offer of $269,000. Jacob counteroffered with $273,000 and gave Nancy three days to respond. While Nancy thought about whether to accept Jacob's counterof-fer, Jacob received a second offer from Susan for $276,000. Because Nancy had not yet accepted Jacob's counteroffer, Jacob gave Nancy a written revocation and accepted Susan's higher offer. Nancy lost out.*

Below is a counteroffer revocation form. A tear-out copy is in the Appendix.

COUNTEROFFER REVOCATION

_____

_____, the seller(s) of the

property at _____

_____ in the city of _____,

county of, _____ California, hereby revoke the counteroffer made on

_____ to _____

_____ buyer(s) and hereby authorize the escrow holders to return to buyer(s) any

deposit funds tendered by buyer(s).

Seller's signature	Date
Seller's signature	Date

Deposit received by:

Buyer's signature	Date
Buyer's signature	Date

H. Backup Offers and Wipe-out Clauses

If you receive an offer which meets all your needs as to price and terms and is virtually certain to result in a completed sale, then you have little reason to accept backup offers. As it often happens, however, a good offer still leaves you wondering whether or not there is a better one yet to come, which you will be turning down by accepting the present offer. Furthermore, most offers contain contingencies that, if not satisfied or removed, will cancel the deal and put you back at square one with a house to sell.

To avoid having to start all over if a deal falls through and to let you continue to search for better offers, many sellers accept backup offers. The whole idea of a backup offer is twofold: You enter a transaction contingent upon an event, such as the buyer selling her existing home or getting a loan, but you don't yet take the property off the market. Simultaneously, you accept offers that are designated backup offers. (See Chapter 9, Section E, Clause 17.) If you plan to accept backup offers, your primary contract must say so. You can use the following language in your counteroffer:

Seller's Right to Accept Backup Offers

Seller may enter into subsequent contract(s) with (an) other person(s) for sale of the property. Any such contract(s) shall be contingent on the termination of the contract between Buyer and Seller. Seller shall notify all other offerors of the existence, though not the terms, of this offer.

OPTION CONTRACTS

It is possible, but unusual, for a seller and a prospective buyer to make an enforceable agreement—a separate contract—that states that a particular offer or counteroffer will remain open (can't be revoked) for a certain period of time. This type of agreement is called an option contract. The person who gets the option to buy (or more rarely, sell) the house usually must agree to pay something in exchange for the option. I discuss—and point out the hazards of—option contracts in Chapter 13.

For additional protection, sellers may counteroffer with a wipe-out clause. In the contract with the first buyer, you state that her offer may be bumped out of its primary position if she cannot remove her contingencies within a certain time (I suggest 96 hours) of your giving her notice that you have accepted a backup offer.

This clause is often referred to by real estate agents as a 72-hour wipe-out clause, as their contracts typically allow 72 hours for the primary offeror to wipe out her contingencies or be wiped out herself. I believe 96 hours is more appropriate, given that the period in question could cover a weekend when businesses are closed.

If you want to include a wipe-out clause, use the following language in your counteroffer:

Seller's Right to Demand Removal of Contingencies

If, any time at least two weeks from the date Buyer and Seller enter into a contract for purchase of the property, Seller gives Buyer a written demand to remove all contingencies in Clause 8 of this contract concerning inspection reports and/or the Buyer's ability to arrange financing and/or get approval for assumption of loans, and/or the Buyer's ability to sell an existing residence, Buyer shall have ninety-six (96) hours from receipt of the demand if personally delivered (or five days from the date of mailing, if the demand is mailed by certified mail) in which to remove all these contingencies. If Buyer cannot do so, then the contract shall be terminated immediately. Buyer and Seller shall sign a mutual release, and all deposits shall be returned to Buyer.

Be aware that you're essentially saying to the buyer: "I'm giving you 20 (or thereabout) days to remove contingencies, but you better act quickly. Because if I get a better offer, just two weeks from now, I can demand immediate removal of the remaining contingencies or the deal is off." Some buyers may balk—and you risk losing the deal if you insist on a wipe-out clause.

Example: *Harry offered his home for sale for $225,000, thinking he'd be delighted to accept $215,000. After his first open house, Harry was surprised to receive an offer from Eddie and Ethel for $1,000 more than his full asking price. The offer included contingencies that Eddie and Ethel sell their existing home as part of arranging financing and that Harry's home pass a termite inspection.*

Harry called a broker friend who gave him this advice: "If you believe you priced the property accurately, accept the offer, subject to all its conditions and provisions, but make sure the buyer's offer or your counteroffer contains a 96-hour wipe-out clause. This way, if your deal with Eddie and Ethel is stalled and you receive another offer, you can ask Eddie and Ethel to remove their contingencies within

96 hours. On the other hand, if you believe that you may have underpriced the property, you might want to wait a week or even raise the price to Eddie and Ethel in a counteroffer."

Below is a form to use to exercise your right to accept a backup offer and demand that the buyer remove contingencies as you included in your counteroffer. A copy is in the Appendix.

SELLER'S DEMAND FOR REMOVAL OF CONTINGENCIES

Under the terms of the contract dated _____ , between

_____ (Buyer) and

_____ (Seller) for the

purchase of the real property at _____

_____ (address), Seller hereby

demands that Buyer remove the following contingencies specified in Clause(s) _____ of the contract:

_____

_____

_____

_____

_____

_____

_____

_____

_____

_____

_____

_____ within

☐ ninety-six (96) hours from receipt of this demand, if personally delivered.

☐ five (5) days from mailing this demand, if mailed by certified mail.

If Buyer does not remove this contingency within the time specified, the contract shall become void. Seller shall promptly return Buyer's deposit upon Buyer's execution of a release, releasing Buyer and Seller from all obligations under the contract.

_____   _____
Seller's signature   Date

_____   _____
Seller's signature   Date

Personally delivered on: _____

Mailed by certified mail on: _____

Example: *Jane accepted Toby's offer to purchase her house for $210,000, although, she would have been delighted to get $195,000. She had asked $215,000, hoping to take advantage of an upward hop in the market, and was delighted to find that the hop turned out to be more like a jump. The problem was that Jane wasn't 100% sure of Toby's ability to secure a loan, even though the financial information he provided looked pretty decent. One problem was that Toby was hoping to obtain a bank loan for 90% of the purchase price, with only a 10% down payment.*

Jane insisted on a 96-hour wipe-out clause in her contract with Toby. This allowed her to realistically deal with backup offers while keeping Toby's deal on the front burner. Of course, Jane disclosed the fact of the contract with Toby to backup offerors. Two weeks later, a second offer came in for $215,000. This buyer was willing to make a 20% down payment and had the necessary cash in hand. In a counteroffer, Jane gave Toby 96 hours to wipe out the contingency that he be able to arrange the financing his offer described. As it turned out, Toby's bank told him that, despite his good credit, it would not make a loan on the terms he could afford with only 10% down. Unable to wipe out this contingency, and aware that he wouldn't be able to complete the transaction, Toby was out of the deal quickly. He signed a form releasing Jane from obligation under the contract, got his deposit back, and Jane was able to sell to the other buyer without delay. ■

Chapter 11

AFTER THE CONTRACT IS SIGNED: PROCEEDING THROUGH ESCROW

Congratulations! You've sold your house! But it's not yet time to move out. After signing a contract, you're usually still a month or more away from a final house sale. This chapter covers all the technical tasks involved in closing escrow or transferring ownership—including opening an escrow account, obtaining title insurance and removing contingencies.

The time it takes between the contract signing and the close of escrow depends on what remains to be done following the signing. If you're waiting for a buyer to sell his existing house, the process could take a long time. If you don't have such unpredictable contingencies and foresee no serious problems with financing or inspections, you can expect to close escrow in one to three months.

You must understand the escrow process before you begin. Opening and successfully closing escrow involves detailed, picky and often overlapping steps. Before taking any concrete action, read this entire chapter carefully to be sure you understand both the big picture and the small details of the escrow process.

A. Opening Escrow

In finalizing the sale of your house, you and the buyer need a neutral third party, the escrow holder, to:

- hold onto, and then exchange, deeds and money
- pay off existing loans
- record deeds
- prorate the property tax payments, and
- help with other transfer details.

To begin this process, you and the buyer open an escrow account with a person or organization legally empowered to act as an escrow agent. In many eastern and mid-western states, escrow is commonly handled by lawyers, and is often termed settlement. Lawyers need not be involved with escrow in

California, and usually aren't, unless an unusual problem arises (for example, your title isn't clear), in which case either buyer or seller may wish to consult an attorney. By custom, escrow is done differently in Northern and Southern California.

Northern California. An escrow account is normally opened with a title insurance or title company by the buyer immediately after the purchase contract is signed. In some circumstances, the buyer and seller may together select the escrow agent. Title companies not only provide the necessary title insurance, but also handle financing arrangements such as collecting the buyer's down payment and funds from the buyer's lender, paying off the seller's existing lender and preparing and recording a deed from the seller to the buyer and a deed of trust for the buyer's lender.

ESCROW TERMINOLOGY

The following are common real estate terms used during escrow:

Close of escrow or closing: The final transfer of ownership of the house to the buyer. It occurs after both the buyer and seller have met all terms of the contract and the deed is recorded. Closing also refers to the time when the transfer will occur, such as, "the closing on my house will happen on January 27 at 10:00 a.m."

Closing costs: The expenses involved in the closing process, including escrow fees and title insurance.

Closing date: The date the escrow closes. Until all contingencies in the buyer's offer are removed, no firm closing date can be set. Thus, during the early and middle stages of an escrow, the closing date is projected, not firm.

Closing statement: A document prepared by the escrow holder containing a complete accounting of all funds, credits and debts involved in the escrow process. Basically this amounts to a statement of the amount of cash the buyer and the buyer's lender have put into escrow, how much the seller has received and how much money was used for other expenses.

Demand or request for beneficiary statement: A letter from the seller's lender to the escrow holder telling how much the escrow holder must send the lender to pay the seller's existing mortgage in full. The lender sends it after being notified by the escrow holder that the seller is selling the house and expects to close escrow by a certain date. If the time between opening and closing escrow is reasonably short, the seller will want to receive the demand fast in order to include the calculations in the closing. If the time between opening and closing will take some time, however, the seller won't rush the demand. A demand is typically good for only 30 days; if it comes too soon, it will expire before escrow closes and the seller will have to request a second one.

Final title report or final: Just before the close of escrow, the title company rechecks the condition of the title established in the preliminary title report. If it's the same (it usually is), the preliminary title report becomes the final report, and title insurance policies are issued.

Funding the loan: After the lender issues a loan commitment letter, the lender must actually fund the loan—that is, deliver the money to the escrow holder. California law requires that checks and drafts be collected prior to disbursement. This means that to close escrow, funds must be deposited one or more days prior to the close of escrow.

Legal description or legal: The description of the parcel of land being sold which appears on the deed to the property. It has nothing to do with the buildings, but rather the land itself. The legal may specify lot and block numbers or metes and bounds (a complicated exercise in map-reading), none of which should concern you. (If you want to know more about legally describing California real property, see *The Deeds Book*, by Mary Randolph (Nolo Press).)

Loan commitment: A written statement from a lender promising to lend the buyer a certain sum of money on certain terms.

Opening escrow: Escrow is opened when you and the buyer select an escrow agent to hold onto and transfer documents and money during the house purchase process.

Preliminary, prelim or pre: The preliminary title report issued by a title company soon after escrow opens. It shows current ownership information on the property (including any liens or encumbrances on the property). If any problems are found, you can take steps to resolve them before escrow closes. The title insurance policy issued at the close of escrow is usually based on this report.

Taking title: Describes the transfer of ownership from seller to buyer. For example, "The buyer takes title [gets his name on the deed] next Tuesday."

Southern California. An escrow account is usually opened by the buyer and seller with an escrow company, which prepares the necessary papers and exchanges the seller's ownership interest for the buyer's money after deducting the amount needed to pay off the seller's existing mortgage, past taxes and other liens. Title insurance is obtained from a title insurance company, which isn't usually otherwise involved in the escrow process.

Other Escrow Holders. Although it's unusual, escrow can be legally handled by someone other than a title or escrow company. The buyer or seller's attorney, a real estate broker participating in the transaction who has a trust account for supervising escrows or the escrow department of a bank are legally empowered to do the job.

1. When to Open Escrow

When you accept the buyer's offer to purchase the house or the buyer accepts your counteroffer, a deposit is usually taken to the title or escrow company and an escrow account is opened by the buyer or seller, depending on local custom. If a real estate agent procured the offer, she is responsible for taking care of this. The deposit is usually in the form of a check accompanying the offer. (For more information on deposits, see Chapter 9, Section E.)

2. How to Find an Escrow Holder

The escrow clause (Clause 2) of the offer contract discussed in Chapter 9 has a place to enter the name and address of the escrow holder. In some situations, you may disagree with the buyer. As the basic task to be accomplished and prices charged are similar, this should not be an issue to hold up the acceptance of an offer; unless you feel very strongly about using "your" escrow agent or not using the buyer's, give in.

You don't want the buyer to later take legal action against you if she feels you forced an escrow holder on her and that this worked against her interests.

How do you know which title company or escrow company to enter on the offer form? As with finding any service provider, it's best to get a recommendation from someone you trust, particularly someone who has sold his own home. If you are working with a real estate professional on any aspect of your house sale, she'll almost surely have some recommendations.

If you are considering several recommended firms, you may be inclined to call around and compare prices, but prices tend to be pretty similar. Because of the small potential savings involved, it normally makes more sense to concentrate on finding a company that offers superior service, especially if you're handling the purchase without professional help. Be sure that the escrow company you choose will be supportive to the self-help home seller, not someone who thinks it's beneath its dignity to work with a non-professional. If you understand the basic escrow terminology (see chart, above), you'll have an easier time dealing with escrow and title companies.

3. How to Work With the Escrow Holder

What happens after escrow opens depends to a considerable extent on your escrow agent and your contract with the buyer. If the contract contains contingencies, the escrow holder will do very little until you and the buyer remove them.

The buyer's salesperson, if any, should help to see that the escrow process goes smoothly. If neither you nor the buyer is working with a salesperson, however, you'll need to handle the details yourselves. You should clearly understand what the company needs from you and when it needs it. Fortunately, it's not difficult. Make an initial appointment with the escrow agent. Bring the contract with you and use it as your guide to ask questions. Check in regularly—about once a week—to be sure you're doing what's expected and that the process is on track.

TYPICAL TITLE INSURANCE AND ESCROW FEES	
Sale Price of House	Insurance & Fees
$100,000	$1,000
$200,000	$1,500
$300,000	$2,000

Your contract with the buyer will contain a clause specifying the date for delivering written escrow instructions to the escrow holder. These instructions authorize the escrow company to give you the money and give the buyer the deed to the property, and should be delivered a few days before the closing date.

4. Order Title Insurance

Ordering title insurance from a title insurance company, usually the same company handling the escrow in Northern California, is the buyer's responsibility. The title company issues a preliminary title report, and then just before closing, a final title report and two title insurance policies. Title insurance is discussed in Section C, below.

5. The Cost of Escrow

Generally, escrow costs, which are considered to be part of closing costs, are under 1.5% of the purchase price. Included in the escrow costs are the preliminary and final title reports, recording of the deed, notarization, the title company's fees, the escrow

company's fees (if applicable) and title insurance policies. In Southern California, the costs are divided between the escrow company and a title insurance company. In Northern California, all costs are paid to the title company.

No law specifies who pays escrow costs; you and the buyer negotiate as part of the forming of the contract. For our discussion on who *customarily* pays what fees, see the chart Who Pays for What and Clause 4 in our offer form in Chapter 9.

B. Removing Contingencies

Depending on the exact provisions of the contract you and the buyer sign, there will probably be several contingencies that must be removed before your sale becomes final. (See Chapter 9, Section E, Clauses 8 and 9.) As buyers and sellers satisfy, or waive, a contingency, they must remove or release it in writing.

You remove a contingency by executing a contingency release form such as the one below. (A tear-out copy is in the Appendix.) Give the original to the buyer and keep a copy for yourself.

Don't wait until all contingencies are met to do this. Remove each one as it is satisfied or abandoned. Make several copies of the release form so that you can remove each contingency as soon as possible. If the structural pest control report and general contractor's report are made within a couple of weeks after the real estate sale contract is signed, but financing hasn't yet been approved, the buyer should still remove these first two contingencies. This is because the time limits for removing inspection contingencies are usually shorter than those involving financing or the sale of an existing house.

CONTINGENCY RELEASE

_____, (Buyer) of the property

at _____ _____

_____ (address), hereby removes

the following contingency(ies) from the purchase contract dated _____:

_____

_____

_____

_____

_____

_____

If this release is based on accepting any inspection report, a copy of the report, signed by Buyer, is attached, and Buyer releases Seller from liability for any physical defects disclosed by the attached report.

_____   _____
Buyer's signature   Date

_____   _____
Buyer's signature   Date

_____   _____
Seller's signature   Date

_____   _____
Seller's signature   Date

---

1. Inspection Contingencies

Most house purchase contracts give the buyer the right to have the house inspected by specified inspectors, and approve the results of their reports, before going through with the sale. To do this, buyers hire and normally pay inspectors. You must let the inspectors have access to your house, as spelled out in Clause 8 of the contract in Chapter 9. There is no compelling reason for you to accompany inspectors on their rounds, but if you wish to, there should be no objection. Inspectors should have copies of your Real Estate Transfer Disclosure Statement (see Chapter 7) and all other inspection reports done in the last few years.

Sometimes problems are discovered during an inspection. For example, your house may have termite damage, or need new wiring, new plumbing, a new roof or foundation repairs. If the problems will be expensive to fix, the buyer may refuse to go ahead with the deal unless you are willing to pay all or part of the repair costs.

At this point, you and the buyer should negotiate over who pays for what repairs. While many sellers agree to pay for most or all repairs, all sorts of financial arrangements are possible. If you've gotten a great price for your house, you might readily agree to pay for all or most of the repairs. If, however, you feel that you underpriced the house, you will not want to pay for a lot of fix-up work. You would be better off letting the buyer walk away from the deal and putting the house back on the market at a higher price.

In many situations, negotiating to remove contingencies can be emotionally difficult. Understandably, neither you nor the buyer will want to spend large sums of money at a point where you each probably feel you've already compromised enough. In a sense this is really the crunch point where the deal will either fall apart or a binding contract will go through. You may benefit from the advice of someone experienced in negotiating real estate deals, especially if serious problems are discovered during the inspections and the removal of contingencies appears complicated.

Usually, the buyer will ask for an escrow credit, which is the amount you are willing to reduce the price to take into account necessary repairs. In other words the buyer gets a credit against the price of the house for the amount of the repairs. In some instances the buyer's lender will require that the buyer uses the money you credit to make the repairs before escrow closes.

If the buyer assumes the responsibility of paying for some or all repairs, however, one or two scenarios will probably take place. One, she will take title to the house in its substandard condition and have to make repairs later. Or, two, her lender will insist that the repairs be made before the sale closes, in which case she will have to come up with the necessary cash. The more work that needs to be done, the more likely it is that a financial institution will require that it be done prior to closing. If repairs are major, this can be an impossible burden for a buyer whose finances are already stretched to come up with the down payment. If you are carrying the first deed of trust or the buyer is borrowing the money from a friend or relative, you can agree to close escrow and keep the money (credit) there until you and the buyer sign off on a notice of completion issued by the contractor who does the work. In this situation, make sure there is a cutoff date by which the work must be done. If the buyer (now the new owner)

doesn't get around to doing the work by that date, the escrow credit will be given back to you.

As inspections are done on your house and reports are issued, have the buyer date and sign the inspection report and write "approved as read" somewhere on the document, assuming she is satisfied that the house passes the inspection. Attach the signed report to the contingency release form and keep a copy.

If you agree to credit the buyer for the cost of any repairs, add the following to the contingency release, after the word "report":

provided that by _____ .M. on _____, Seller agrees in writing to extend to Buyer an escrow credit in the amount of $_____ against the purchase price to cover the cost of needed repair and rehabilitation work to be paid by Buyer.

Example: *Mary listed her house for $225,000, and agreed to sell it to Albert for $221,000. Albert's offer was contingent upon having a satisfactory pest control inspection. The inspection turned up $10,000 worth of problems. Albert wrote Mary a memo, stating that he wouldn't remove the inspection contingency unless she agreed to credit him in escrow with the amount of work recommended by the inspector. Mary refused, feeling that she had given Albert a good deal on the price of the house and he should pay for the problems.*

After negotiating, Albert and Mary signed a contingency release form to split the difference. In other words, Mary gave Albert a $5,000 escrow credit. This means that by keeping the sales price at $221,000, Albert, in effect, paid Mary $216,000. Because Albert's lender did not require him do the repairs prior to the close of escrow, he was free to do them at a convenient future date, but before the cutoff date. If he didn't do the work by that date, the $5,000 would be returned to Mary.

2. Financing Contingencies

To remove a financing contingency, the buyer must provide you with written evidence that he has obtained financing needed to purchase your house. Usually, this is in the form of a written loan commitment letter from a lender or a bank confirmation if the buyer has arranged private financing. It can also be a check for the amount of the purchase price not yet paid. To remove a financing contingency, the buyer should sign a contingency release form.

3. Extending Time to Meet a Contingency

Buyers frequently need extra time to satisfy a contract contingency. Without the extra time, the contract ends (that is, the deal falls through) unless you and the buyer agree to extend it. If you want out at this point, don't extend the time. More commonly, however, you'll want the deal to go through, but will need reassurance that the buyer is still serious about buying your house. You may demand that the buyer increase his deposit in exchange for you granting an extension. The amounts vary, but to extend a $300,000 offer for two weeks, $500–$1,000 is reasonable.

Example: *Julie agrees to buy Shawn's house for $300,000, contingent upon her securing an adjustable rate mortgage at 8% or lower for 80% of the purchase price and selling her own house within 90 days. Julie arranges the financing easily, but is having trouble selling her house. Shawn feels Julie is asking too much for her house. He's also considering putting his house back on the market for $310,000 if Julie doesn't meet the 90-day closing deadline. Julie really wants Shawn's house and knows she's in danger of losing it. She offers to increase her deposit by $3,000 and to lower her listing price by $15,000 if Shawn will extend her time to purchase (to let her sell her existing house) for another 60 days. Shawn agrees.*

Any agreement to extend the time to meet a contingency (or to change any other term of the contract) must be in writing and signed. You can use Clause 19, "Other Terms and Conditions" of our offer form in Chapter 9 or you can use a separate form like

---

EXTENDING TIME TO MEET CONTINGENCIES

The material set out below is hereby made a part of the offer dated _____

from _____ (Buyer) to

_____ (Seller) for

the purchase of the real property located at: _____

_____

The final date for Buyer's removal of all contingencies set out in Clause _____ of the contract, is hereby extended until

_____ (month, day and year), at _____ M. (time).

_____   _____
Buyer's signature   Date

_____   _____
Buyer's signature   Date

_____   _____
Seller's signature   Date

_____   _____
Seller's signature   Date

the one below. Blank copies of both forms are in the Appendix.

If the buyer needs just a few extra days to remove her contingencies because the pest control report is slow in coming or the loan approval letter is delayed over a holiday weekend, you should certainly agree to extend the time allowed. If, however, the buyer is facing more serious obstacles in removing her contingencies that jeopardize the entire deal, you may want to entertain any backup offer you have accepted and issue a "Seller's Demand for Removal of Contingencies" to the primary buyer. A copy of the form and a full discussion on backup offers is in Chapter 10, Section H.

4. If a Contingency Cannot Be Met

If, after trying in good faith, you or the buyer can't meet a contingency, the deal is over. The most common reasons sales fall through are:

- An inspection turns up extensive physical problems and the buyer no longer wants the house, or the two of you can't agree on who will pay for repairs.

- The buyer is unable to sell his existing house within the time provided or give you the time you need to find another house.

- The buyer can't secure adequate financing within the time provided.

If the buyer made a deposit, you and the buyer should sign a release canceling the contract and authorizing the return of his deposit. You do not have the right to keep the deposit if the deal falls through for failure to meet a contingency spelled out in the contract. If, however, an inspection turns up no problems and the prospective buyer refuses to go ahead with the purchase (or refuses to proceed for another non-legitimate reason), you can keep the deposit. Most sellers rarely keep an entire deposit, however, because they often can't complete a subsequent sale until the escrow with the first prospective buyer terminates; this normally can't happen until the buyer's deposit is released. Thus, even if a buyer withdraws for a non-legitimate reason, it's common for the buyer and seller to compromise, with the seller keeping part of the deposit and returning some of it to the buyer.

Below is a release form; a tear-out copy is included in the Appendix.

RELEASE OF REAL ESTATE PURCHASE CONTRACT

_____ (Seller)

and _____ (Buyer)

hereby mutually release each other from any and all claims with respect to the real estate purchase contract dated
_____, for the property located at _____
_____.

It is the intent of this release to declare all rights and obligations arising out of the real estate purchase contract null and void.

☐   Buyer has received his/her deposit.

☐   _____ has directed the escrow holder to return Buyer's deposit.

_____   Date _____

_____   Date _____

_____   Date _____

_____   Date _____

C. Title Report and Title Insurance

Title insurance is meant to insure both the buyer and his lender against certain clouds on the legal title to the property. The title insurance company—depending upon the policy included—insures against the possibility of undisclosed legal challenges or liens against the property, such as a forged deed or an unrecorded easement. If a claim arises and is covered by the title insurance policy, the title insurance company will pay it off. The result is that the buyer will still own the property and the particular claim will be extinguished, or the buyer or lender is paid off if the claim is honored.

Financial institutions require a California Land Title Association (CLTA) policy and an American Land Title Association (ALTA) policy. The CLTA policy covers items in the public record, such as mortgage liens, trust deed liens or judgment liens. The ALTA policy is more extensive, insuring against claims found both in the public record and by physically inspecting the house, such as unrecorded easements, boundary disputes and physical encroachments.

The policies also differ regarding how much they cover and whom they benefit. The CLTA policy insures to the amount of the purchase price and benefits the buyer. The ALTA policy insures to the amount of the loan and benefits the lender. The buyer can usually buy the extended coverage for about 30% above the standard policy cost, and has to have a survey of the property done.

As soon as you and the buyer sign the house purchase contract, the buyer should order a preliminary title report (also called a prelim or pre) on the property. This report is a statement summarizing the current condition of the title to the property, especially liens, encumbrances and easements. The buyer will want the prelim early in escrow so that he, you and lender have time to address any problems that turn up.

... require you to pay ... ese problems ... ate the lien and ... to pay the lien- ... wly discovered ... ndary line or ... nants, conditions ... ir (if the previ- ... se situations ... of a lawyer. ... t you cannot ...

- ... you an extension of time, or

- buy the house with less than perfect title.

If the prelim showed no problems, or all problems have been remedied or the buyer is agreeing to take less than perfect title, when escrow is ready to close the title insurance company checks the public records for any changes since the prelim was issued. If all is the same (as is the usual case), the prelim becomes the final title report. Any changes are reported in a supplemental title report. The buyer and lender must decide whether to close or call the deal off under the contract provision requiring you to provide clear title.

D. Buyer's Final Physical Inspection of the Property

A few days before escrow closes, the buyer may wish to re-inspect the property to make sure everything is in order. This is her right. She'll want to make sure that:

- no damage has occurred to the house since she agreed to buy it

- the fixtures and personal property you agreed to sell are still in the house

- all work called for in the contract is done to her satisfaction.

If the buyer discovers a problem during this final inspection, she can:

- insist that the closing be delayed until you fix the problem

- insist that you credit her in escrow with a sum of money sufficient to remedy the problem—this means she pays that much less for the house

- conclude that the problem isn't significant and close anyway.

E. Closing Escrow

Escrow cannot close until the escrow holder records a deed naming the buyer the new owner and issues checks to the seller and all others entitled to be paid from the proceeds, such as the seller's lender and any lienholders. If work must be done to repair damage or substandard conditions discovered in an inspection report, money may be held by the escrow holder after the sale closes to pay the contractor.

The paperwork necessary for closing escrow should be completed a minimum of four working days before the expected closing date. You and the buyer—not necessarily together—must go to the escrow holder's office to review and sign the papers. The four-day gap allows for delays in the transmittal of the loan documents between the lender(s) and the escrow holder.

The forms you'll be required to sign include:

- grant deed to buyer

- final escrow instructions, which need to be delivered to the escrow holder a few days before the closing date

- settlement sheet, which lists all disbursements, such as your mortgage company, any

lienholders, any broker fees, the money you get,
as well as the closing fees

- copy of the preliminary title report

- deed of trust (and other forms) from the lender

- copies of structural pest control and other
  inspection reports

- FIRPTA (Foreign Investment in Real Property
  Tax Act) statement (see Clause 11 of the offer
  forms in Chapter 9), and

- any rental agreement between you and the buyer
  if you will live in the house for a while after the
  close. ■

Chapter 12

WHAT IF SOMETHING GOES WRONG DURING ESCROW?

The likelihood of a major disaster—such as the buyer dying or an earthquake destroying the house—befalling your sale is slim. But it's possible during escrow something will go wrong. This chapter presents only a brief overview of what may happen if your deal threatens to unravel. In any case, you'll need the expeditious help of an experienced real estate lawyer.

Difficulties in removing contingencies are not covered by this chapter. If you or the buyer have trouble removing a contingency, such as the buyer obtaining financing, the buyer selling another house or you closing on a new house, see Chapter 11.

A. The Seller Backs Out

Backing out of the deal, or breaching the contract, technically means failing to perform without a legal excuse. What a court might consider a legal excuse, and therefore allow the termination of the contract, depends on the application of contract law principles to the circumstances of the transaction. The many twists and turns of that subject are well beyond the scope of this book.

But suppose you back out of the deal after the buyer has met or waived all contingencies simply because you change your mind about selling your house or you get a better offer. Isn't that a clear breach of contract? Yes, and the buyer's remedy is normally to mediate, arbitrate (if you opted for either in the house purchase contract) or sue, requesting that you sell the house and pay the buyer damages based on his out-of-pocket costs.

Example: *Alex and Mack signed a contract for Alex to sell his home to Mack for $250,000. Alex wasn't completely happy with the price and Mack knew he'd gotten a good deal. Mack quickly removed the contingencies and was ready to close the deal. But Alex received an offer for*

$270,000, which he wanted to accept. He tried to cancel the deal with Mack, offering to return his deposit. Mack refused and pointed out that if Alex didn't complete the deal, he'd be in breach of the contract.

Alex's lawyer advised him that if he accepted the other offer, Mack would probably pursue arbitration (they had checked it off on their contract) and win, and the arbitrators would order Alex to sell the house to Mack and pay Mack's court costs, attorney's fees, costs of storing furniture and costs of living elsewhere. Even though he was unhappy, Alex honored his contract with Mack.

B. The Buyer Backs Out

If the buyer refuses to go through with the deal without a good reason, you can pursue mediation, arbitration or a lawsuit, requesting he pay your damages. Damages aren't always easy to determine, however, because you have a duty to try to limit (mitigate, in legalese) your losses by selling the house to someone else. To avoid arguing over the amount of the loss, most house purchase contracts provide a specific figure (liquidated damages) for the seller's damages if the buyer breaches the contract. (See Clause 21 in our contract in Chapter 9.)

A liquidated damages clause means that you are theoretically entitled to the stated amount. In practice, however, disputes are often settled by the buyer agreeing to allow you to keep part, but not all, of the deposit.

Example: *Alison was ecstatic when she accepted Lori's offer of $185,000 for her home, along with a deposit check for $1,000. She was confident that the sale would go through easily because the house was in great condition and Lori had prequalified for her loan. A week after Lori and Alison signed the contract, but before the inspections occurred, Lori told Alison that she was canceling the contract because she had found another house she liked just as much for $170,000.*

Alison was irate and told Lori this constituted a default. Not so, insisted Lori, since the required inspections had yet to be made and approved, and there would probably be something wrong with the house anyway. Alison told Lori she could not disapprove of the inspection reports until they were made, and only then if they turned up real problems. Because the reports (including a roofing report, contractor's walkthrough and plumber's inspection, as called for in the contract) would likely cost Lori almost $1,000, Alison suggested that Lori agree that she (Alison) could keep the $1,000 deposit as consideration for ending the contract. Although this annoyed Lori, she finally agreed when she realized that if the inspection reports didn't turn up any problems, she might be out both the cost of the reports and the deposit.

C. The Buyer or Seller Dies

Technically, a contract for real property is enforceable even if the buyer or the seller dies because a deceased person's estate is responsible for fulfilling that person's lawful obligations. Just the same, you can bet your bottom dollar the title insurance and/or es-

crow company will put on the brakes and call in their attorneys if the buyer dies. You should do exactly the same. Chances are the executors of the buyer's estate, and possibly the buyer's inheritors, may want to get out of the deal and will be willing to pay you something for a release.

D. The House Is Destroyed by Natural Disaster

As explained in Clause 20 of the purchase contract in Chapter 9, destruction of the house is normally handled as follows: If the buyer has either physical possession or legal title to the property, he is responsible for the physical condition of the property and insurance. Otherwise, you are responsible. To protect yourself, make sure your homeowner's policy is in force until the close of escrow, at which moment the buyer's policy goes into effect.

If the house is flooded three days before escrow closes, you can pay for the repairs and deliver the property in the condition it was in before the flood. If the buyer wants out of the deal, however, he can simply refuse to grant an extension to make the repairs.

E. The Escrow Holder's Role in a Dispute

If a dispute arises between you and the buyer during escrow, don't look to the escrow holder to resolve it—or to transfer the money and deed. The escrow holder is a neutral party. You'll have to solve the problem yourselves—for example, through mediation or arbitration as indicated in the purchase contract (Clauses 22 and 23 in Chapter 9). Until then, the escrow holder sits still. If the dispute drags on long enough, the escrow holder may get tired of being stuck in the middle and may initiate a lawsuit, called an interpleader, to have the court resolve the dispute and direct the distribution of the deposited money. ■

WHEN YOUR HOUSE IS DIFFICULT TO SELL: LEASE-OPTION AGREEMENTS

If the real estate market isn't to your liking—that is, it favors buyers—or your house is in a bad location or in poor shape, don't assume you won't sell or will sell for far too little. Selling will probably take more effort on your part than for most sellers, but there is a creative strategy you can use to help you sell—the lease-option contract.

A. Lease-Option

A lease-option is a contract where an owner leases her house for a set period of time—usually from one to five years—to a tenant for a specific monthly rent. The contract gives the tenant the right (option) to buy the house for a price established in advance. The rent paid by the tenant under the lease may increase during the contract term. In addition, the tenant pays some money for the option: a lump sum payment at the start of the contract, or periodically. The tenant may pay only a few dollars or thousands of dollars for the option, as long as it fulfills the legal require-ment of paying consideration for a contract—in this case, for tying up the property with the option. Because the person holding the option has the right to complete the purchase—whether or not she does—the tenant is not entitled to a refund of her option fee if she does not exercise the option.

Depending on the contract, the tenant normally can exercise the option to buy at any of the following times:

- any time during the lease period
- at a date specified in the contract, or
- when another prospective buyer makes an offer on the house, the offer made by the other prospective buyer must give the tenant a right of first refusal to match the offered price.

When the tenant exercises his option—that is, he buys your house—you can follow the procedures in Chapters 9 and 10 for preparing a house sales contract.

A lease-option often is a good deal in two situations:

1. You and the would-be buyer can't bring off an actual sale at the present time, but are in general agreement about price and terms. This may arise, for example, if you need to move but the buyer can't come up with the necessary financing.

2. You need to move now, but don't want the profit to be taxed in the current fiscal year. For example, the retirement community you've been waiting to move to finally has an opening. You don't want to pass it up, but you also want to defer receiving money on your house, as it would raise your tax bracket.

Lease-options aren't all positive. There are risks and other negatives, such as:

The tenant may not be willing or able to exercise the option to buy the property. As a result, although you receive a fee, your property is tied up. When the tenant fully rejects exercising her option, you're back to square one.

During the period of the lease-option contract, you may run across landlord-tenant difficulties. We deal with some in the contract provided and recommend that you obtain Nolo's *Landlord's Law Book*. But be aware that problems may arise with your tenant.

If you enter into a lease-option agreement, you become a landlord—a position heavily regulated in California. To help you relate to your tenant, Nolo Press publishes The Landlord's Law Book, Volume 1: Rights and Responsibilities, *by David Brown and Ralph Warner. The book covers the practical and legal rules associated with renting residential real property— including information on leases, rental agreements, rent control, security deposits, discrimination, invasion of privacy, the landlord's duty to maintain the premises and much more. Written specifically for California landlords, it provides practical, easy-to-use checklists and forms for rental property.*

During the lease period, the tenant is not likely to take care of the property the way you have as owner. Consequently, if he does not exercise the option to buy the property, you may have to sell the property in a somewhat deteriorated condition or spend time and money making repairs.

Lease-options also have tax ramifications. That information is beyond the scope of this book, however, and if you're seriously considering pursuing this option, discuss it first with your tax consultant. You might also take a look at Chapter 22 of *How to Sell Your House in a Buyer's Market,* by Martin Shenkman and John Boroson (John Wiley & Sons).

Example: *Ed and Robin lease Jane's house for $1,700 per month for two years. In addition, they pay Jane $2,000 for the option to purchase the house for $180,000 at any time during the two years. If Ed and Robin decide to buy, the $2,000 will be credited against the purchase price; if not, Jane keeps it.*

This example is deliberately simple to give you the general idea. Many lease-option deals are more complicated. For example, the house purchase price might be a fixed dollar amount, plus an amount tied to any increase over time in the Consumer Price Index. Or instead of an upfront option fee, the rent might be set higher than market rates, with the extra money applied to the purchase price when the option to purchase is exercised. This is the more common method of paying for the right of the option, and provides an incentive for the tenant/optionee to exercise the option and complete the purchase as quickly as possible.

If a lease-option contract sounds feasible, take a look at the sample and directions for completing it below. A tear-out copy is in the Appendix. If you are concerned that it doesn't cover all your needs, consult an attorney before offering a lease-option agreement to a tenant.

B. Provisions to Include in a Lease-Option Contract

Your lease-option contract should clearly specify:

- the price at which the property can be purchased under the option
- the amount being paid for the option
- the rent being paid under the lease
- the terms and conditions of the lease, and
- the time limits for the option and the lease.

Below I discuss each clause in the lease-option agreement form provided in this book. Clauses 1 through 16 cover the lease; Clauses 17 through 24 cover the option.

Clause 1.   Identification of Owner and Tenant

This Agreement to create a Lease with Option to Purchase is made and entered into on _____,

between _____ (Owner or Lessor/Optionor) and

_____ (Tenant or Lessee/Optionee).

In Clause 1, indicate both the date on which the contract is made and the names of the parties to the agreement. Be sure to list the names of all adults who will live on the premises, even if they are husband and wife.

In legalese, the person who owns the property and hopes to sell it, but is now renting it out, is called the lessor; because she is also extending an option, she is called an optionor. The prospective buyer of the property who is now leasing it is called the lessee; because he also receives an option to buy the property, he is called an optionee. As much as possible, our contract simplifies the language by using owner and tenant except when the other words are necessary for clarity.

Clause 2.   Identification of the Premises

Subject to the terms and conditions below, Owner rents to Tenant, and Tenant rents from Owner, for residential purposes only,

the premises at _____

_____, California.

In Clause 2, simply fill in the blank with the address of the house you are renting out and planning to sell. You don't need a formal legal description like an assessor's parcel or lot and block number. If the house has no street address, use the best descrip-tion you can, such as "the ten acre Norris Ranch on County Road 305, two miles south of Andersonville."

The words "for residential purposes only" are included to prevent the tenant from using the property for conducting a business that might affect your insurance or violate zoning laws.

Clause 3.   Defining the Term of the Tenancy

The term of the rental shall begin on _____, and shall continue for a period of _____

months, expiring on _____.

Should Tenant vacate before expiration of the term, Tenant shall be liable for the balance of the rent for the remainder of the

term, less any rent Owner collects or could have collected from a replacement tenant by reasonably attempting to re-rent. Tenant

who vacates before expiration of the term is also responsible for Owner's costs of advertising for a replacement tenant.

In Clause 3, you indicate the specific length of your contract and specify the date on which the lease will end. Because you want to encourage a purchase, a year is a good length to give the tenant incentive to buy. This provision includes a warning that explains the tenant's liability for breaking the lease. California law allows for easy renewal of the lease beyond its original term, if both parties agree, but also protects against automatic renewal when at least one party opposes it.

Clause 4.   Amount and Schedule for the Payment of Rent

On signing this Agreement, Tenant shall pay to Owner the sum of $_____ as rent, payable in advance, for the period of

_____ through _____. Thereafter, Tenant shall pay to Owner a monthly rent of

$_____, payable in advance on the first day of each month, except when the first falls on a weekend or legal

holiday, in which case rent is due on the next business day. Rent shall be paid to _____

at_____, California.

In Clause 4, specify the amount of the monthly rent and where and to whom the rent is paid. Rent is the amount NOT paid directly for the option. (The option amount is covered in Clause 19.) Money paid directly for the option is usually credited against the purchase price when the option is exercised.

The due date for rent payment needs to be made clear, and the date the first month's rent is due is the date the lease contract is signed.

Clause 5.   Late Fees

If Tenant fails to pay the rent in full within five days after it is due, Tenant shall pay Owner a late charge of $_____

plus $_____ for each additional day that the rent continues to be unpaid. The total late charge for any one month

shall not exceed $_____. By this provision, Owner does not waive the right to insist on payment of the rent in full on

the day it is due.

Clause 6.   Returned Check Charges

In the event any check offered by Tenant to Owner in payment of rent or any other amount due under this Agreement is returned

for lack of sufficient funds, Tenant shall pay to Owner a returned check charge in the amount of $_____.

It's legal to charge the tenant an extra fee if the rent is late or if his rent check bounces—if the fee is reasonable. A typical late charge provision is $10 after the fifth day the rent is due, plus $5.00 for each additional day, up to a maximum of $50.

As for fees when the tenant's rent check bounces, you should charge no more than the amount your bank charges you for a returned check plus a few dollars for your trouble.

Clause 7.   Amount and Payment of Deposits

On signing this Agreement, Tenant shall pay to Owner the sum of $_____, which is equal to two months'
rent, as and for security as that term is defined by Section 1950.5 of the California Civil Code, namely any payment, fee,
deposit or charge to be used to compensate Owner for:

(a)   Tenant's default in the payment of rent

(b)   repair of damages to the premises, exclusive of ordinary wear and tear, or

(c)   cleaning of the premises on termination of tenancy.

Tenant may not, without Owner's prior written consent, apply this security deposit to rent or to any other sum due under this
Agreement.

Within three weeks after Tenant has vacated the premises, Owner shall furnish Tenant with an itemized written statement of the
basis for, and the amount of, any of the security deposit retained by the Owner, including accounting for any interest required
by local security deposit laws. Owner may withhold only that portion of Tenant's security deposit:

(a)   to remedy any default by Tenant in the payment of rent

(b)   to repair damages to the premises exclusive of ordinary wear and tear, or

(c)   to clean the premises, if necessary.

The amount and use of security deposits is limited by state law and some local rent control regulations. This provision summarizes the main security deposit rules and acknowledges your receipt of the tenant's deposit.

Clause 8.   Utilities

Tenants shall be responsible for payment of all utility charges, except for the following, which shall be paid by Owner:

_____

_____

_____

_____ .

This provision avoids misunderstandings concerning utilities. Normally, a tenant pays for all services except garbage collection, and sometimes water, especially if the landlord maintains a yard. If you are leasing a single-family home, it is not unreasonable to expect the tenant to pay for all utilities and services. In any event, you must notify a prospective tenant, before he signs a lease, if the gas or electric meter serves any areas outside the actual dwelling. (Civil Code § 1940.9.)

Clause 9.   Prohibition of Assignment and Subletting

Tenant shall not sublet any part of the premises or assign this lease without the prior written consent of Owner.

Because the intent under this contract is to eventually sell your house, and because you've agreed to lease only to the tenant in question, this clause bars the tenant from subletting the property or assigning his lease rights to another person without your express permission.

Clause 10.   Condition of the Premises

Tenant acknowledges that (s)he has examined the premises, including appliances, fixtures, carpets, drapes and paint, and has found them to be in good, safe and clean condition and repair, except as otherwise noted on the written inventory of furniture and furnishings on the premises which Tenant has completed and given Owner, a copy of which Tenant acknowledges receipt of, and which is deemed to be incorporated into this Agreement by this reference.

Tenant agrees to:

(a) keep the premises in good order and repair and, upon termination of tenancy, to return the premises to Owner in a condition identical to that which existed when Tenant took occupancy, except for ordinary wear and tear

(b) immediately notify Owner of any defects or dangerous conditions in and about the premises of which (s)he becomes aware, and

c) reimburse Owner, on demand by Owner or his or her agent, for the cost of any repairs to the premises damaged by Tenant or his or her guests or invitees.

The parties agree that the following appliances and fixtures will be included with the property:

☐   for sale if the option is exercised: _____

_____

☐   for rent only during the period of the lease: _____.

Clause 10 makes it clear that if the tenant damages the premises—for example, breaks a window or scratches hardwood floors—it is his responsibility to pay for fixing the problem.

You and the tenant should agree on an inventory of the condition, furnishings and personal property on the premises at the time the lease-option begins. If you and the tenant acknowledge a defect in the property's condition, specify it in the Transfer Disclosure Statement that accompanies the sales contract. (See Chapter 7.) And be sure it's noted in the checklist you give the tenant. (See Nolo's *Landlord's Law Book*.)

The tenant should also agree to return the premises, at the end of the lease, in the same condition in which she found it, except for ordinary wear and tear and circumstances beyond her control, such as vandalism or fire.

In order to avoid disputes, be sure to state which appliances and fixtures are part of the property and which, if any, are to be included in the eventual sale, which will be specified in the purchase contract that is drawn up later.

Clause 11. Possession of Premises

The failure of Tenant to take possession of the premises shall not relieve him or her of the obligation to pay rent. In the event Owner is unable to deliver possession of the premises to Tenant for any reason not within Owner's control, including but not limited to failure of prior occupants to vacate as agreed or required by law, or partial or complete destruction of the premises, Owner shall not be liable to Tenant, except for the return of all sums previously paid by Tenant to Owner, in the event Tenant chooses to terminate this Agreement because of Owner's inability to deliver possession.

Clause 11 protects you if you're unable, for reasons beyond your control, to turn over possession after having signed a lease or rental agreement—for example, if workers doing repairs did not finish as scheduled.

Clause 12. Pets

No animal or other pet shall be kept on the premises without Owner's prior written consent, except: properly trained dogs needed by blind, deaf or physically disabled persons, and

☐ _____ , under the following conditions:

_____

_____ .

It is illegal to forbid a disabled person to keep a trained guide dog for the blind, a trained signal dog for the deaf or a trained service dog for the otherwise physically disabled on the premises. (Civil Code § 54.1.) Except for these situations, you can prevent a tenant from keeping pets without your written permission.

Clause 13. Owner's Access for Inspection and Emergency

Owner or Owner's agents may enter the premises in the event of an emergency, or to make repairs or improvements, supply agreed services, or exhibit the premises to prospective purchasers or tenants. Except in case of emergency, Owner shall give Tenant reasonable notice of intent to enter and shall enter only during regular business hours of Monday through Friday from 9:00 a.m. to 6:00 p.m. and Saturday from 9:00 a.m. to noon. In order to facilitate Owner's right of access, Tenant shall not, without Owner's prior written consent, alter or re-key any lock to the premises or install any burglar alarm system. At all times Owner or Owner's agent shall be provided with a key or keys capable of unlocking all such locks and gaining entry. Tenant further agrees to provide instructions on how to disarm any burglar alarm system should Owner so request.

The law limits the owner's right to enter rental property in the tenant's absence or without her permission. (Nolo's *Landlord's Law Book* includes a whole chapter on tenants' privacy rights. See the box at the beginning of the chapter.) Clause 13 makes it clear to the tenant that you, as the owner, have a legal right of access to the property—for example, to make repairs—provided you give the tenant reasonable notice.

Clause 14.   Prohibitions Against Violating Laws and Causing Disturbances

Tenant shall be entitled to quiet enjoyment of the premises. Tenant shall not use the premises in such a way as to violate any law or ordinance, including laws prohibiting the use, possession or sale of illegal drugs, commit waste or nuisance, or annoy, disturb, inconvenience or interfere with the quiet enjoyment of any other tenant or nearby resident.

A clause similar to Clause 14 is found in most form leases and puts the tenant on notice to be a good neighbor.

Clause 15.   Repairs and Alterations

Except as provided by law or as authorized by the prior written consent of Owner, Tenant shall not make any repairs or alterations to the premises.

Clause 15 makes it clear that alterations and repairs without your consent aren't allowed. The except-as-provided-by-law language is a reference to the "repair and deduct" remedy the tenant may use to repair health- or safety-threatening defects when a landlord doesn't. (See *The Landlord's Law Book*, described at the beginning of the chapter, for details.)

Be sure to let the tenant know whom she should call when repairs are needed.

Clause 16.   Damage to Premises, Financial Responsibility and Renter's Insurance

In the event the premises are damaged by fire or other casualty covered by insurance, Owner shall have the option either to:

(a)   repair such damage and restore the premises, this Agreement continuing in full force and effect, or

(b)   give notice to Tenant at any time within thirty (30) days after such damage terminating this Agreement as of a date to be specified in such notice. In the event of the giving of such notice, this Agreement shall expire and all rights of Tenant pursuant to this Agreement shall terminate.

Owner shall not be required to make any repair or replacement of any property brought onto the premises by Tenant. Tenant agrees to accept financial responsibility for any damage to the premises from fire or casualty caused by Tenant's negligence. Tenant shall carry a standard renter's insurance policy from a recognized insurance firm, or, as an alternative, warrant that (s)he will be financially responsible for losses not covered by Owner's fire and extended coverage insurance policy. Repair of damage or plumbing stoppages caused by Tenant's negligence or misuse will be paid for by Tenant.

This clause speaks to what happens if the premises are seriously damaged by fire or other calamity. Basically, it limits your risk to thirty days' rental value, even if the damage was your responsibility, and eliminates your risk entirely if the damage was caused by the tenant. This provision forces the tenant to assume responsibility for damage to her own belongings and for certain types of damage to your property caused by her acts.

This clause gives tenants the option of obtaining renter's insurance or being held personally responsible for damages they or their guests cause.

Clause 17.   Option Terms

Tenant shall have the option to purchase the property for the sum of _____ and no/100 dollars ($_____), providing the Tenant exercises this option by giving written notice of that exercise to Owner at the above address, not later than _____ and completes the purchase not later than ninety (90) days from the above notice. The purchase shall be completed according to the terms of a purchase contract and escrow instructions mutually executed by the parties within thirty (30) days of Tenant's notice to Owner that Tenant intends to exercise the option.

This clause specifies the price at which you agree the tenant may purchase the property. In some contracts, this price is a fixed amount plus an adjustment for appreciation. This clause also gives the specific date for completing the purchase or closing escrow (discussed in Chapter 11). Make the option period (during which time the potential buyer may exercise the option) as short as reasonably possible. You don't want the property tied up indefinitely.

Clause 18.   Right to Record Option

This option may be recorded in favor of Tenant (Optionee) and for that purpose Owner (Optionor) agrees to sign this Agreement in the presence of a notary. .

Because the tenant has the right to record the option agreement at the county recorder's office, thereby giving notice to the world that he has the right to buy the house for an agreed-upon amount before anyone else, you should sign the lease-option contract before a notary public. A notary's signature and seal are usually required by the recorder's office in order for a document to be recorded.

Clause 19.   Right to Assign or Sell Option

This option may be assigned or sold by Tenant to another party. For this right, Tenant agrees to:

a.   ☐ pay Owner, with this agreement, the sum of _____ and no/100 dollars

($_____), which is not refundable to Tenant under any circumstance, even if Tenant does not exercise this

option.

b.   ☐ pay Owner, in addition to monthly rent stated above, the sum of $_____ and no/100

dollars ($_____), each month, beginning on_____, and ending on _____.

This sum is not to be considered as rent but is to be in consideration of the right of option, and is not refundable to the

Tenant under any circumstance, even if Tenant does not exercise the option. The parties agree that any sums paid by

Tenant to Owner under Clause 21 below, shall be credited against the purchase price in the event Tenant exercises the

option to buy.

Some of the money paid by the tenant to you is not rent, but payment for the right of the option. Here, the contract specifies this amount and the manner in which it is paid: at the time the contract is signed, in installments like rent, or a combination of those two.

Clause 20.   Costs of Exercising Option

The parties agree that general financing and transaction costs at the time the option is exercised cannot be estimated in advance, and are therefore not contingencies of this contract. However, the parties agree that at the time this option is exercised:

• Expenses of owning the property (real estate taxes, insurance and special assessments) shall be prorated or divided between the parties as to the date of close of escrow.

• Tenant shall order a title search on the property and pay for title insurance satisfactory to Tenant and any lenders involved in the purchase transaction, and will pay for any necessary escrow, notary and recording fees. Tenant shall have ten days from the exercise of the option in which to report in writing any objections to the condition of title, and Owner shall make every effort in good faith to remove such exceptions to clear title within ten days thereafter, or else this contract may be cancelled at the option of either party.

• Tenant may, at any time prior to the exercise of this option, have the property inspected at his or her own expense by a licensed general contractor, pest control operator or any other professional deemed necessary to advise Tenant concerning the physical condition of the property. If Tenant notifies Owner in writing, on or before the above date for exercise of the option, of objections on the part of Tenant concerning the condition of the property, and the parties cannot reach an agreement concerning these objections, the Tenant need not exercise this option.

Because the option contract is being signed some time in advance of an actual purchase, this part of the contract puts off until that time the actual expenses of the transaction. Specific costs are covered in the following paragraphs.

Some expenses in a real estate transfer, by their nature, lend themselves to proration, which is a division according to time. This contract provides for the proration of real estate taxes, insurance policies and special assessments.

The tenant will probably want a title search and title insurance policy on the property, at least for his own protection; in addition, any lender(s) extending financing for the purchase will require it. It doesn't need to be done until it is time to exercise the option. (See Chapter 11 for details on title insurance and escrow.)

The tenant has the right to arrange and pay for inspections on the property at any time. If inspections turn up negative information and convince her not to go ahead with exercising the option, you will have already been compensated for your loss of having kept your house off the market by the option payment or increased monthly payments you've received. To avoid this problem, you could suggest to the tenant that she commission inspections of the property before signing the option contract.

Clause 21.   Summary of Funds Received From Tenant by Owner

Nonrefundable option fee $_____

Refundable security deposit $_____

Nonrefundable rent $_____

TOTAL $_____

Because you will be receiving several types of money from the tenant—some refundable and some not—it is good to list which is which.

Clause 22.   Time

Time shall be of the essence of this agreement.

Time is of the essence, meaning that all the obligations of the parties need to be met by certain dates in order for the contract to be fulfilled, unless the parties both agree to extend the deadlines involved.

Example: *Norma, your tenant, has until February 4 to exercise the option to buy. On January 27, she notifies you that she's waiting for approval on a loan, but doesn't expect a final answer until February 6. You write a simple agreement extending the date for the exercise of the option from February 4 until February 8. Of course, if you no longer want to sell to Norma—for example, the value of your property has skyrocketed and you'd like to find a new buyer who will pay what it's worth—you wouldn't want to grant an extension. A third possibility is to grant an extension, but at a higher price.*

Clause 23. Entire Agreement

This document constitutes the entire Agreement between the parties, and no promises or representations, other than those contained here and implied in law, have been made by Owner or Tenant.

The meaning of this provision is obvious. Get everything you want included in your agreement in writing before you sign. Any agreements made later will have to be in writing.

Clause 24. Additional Provisions

_____

_____

_____

_____

_____

If you want to include additional clauses in your lease agreement, list them here. You may, for example, want to include a clause on how to deal with disputes that may arise between you and the tenant/optionee. The situation is complicated, because you are dealing with two simultaneous contracts—a lease and an option. Many landlord-tenant disputes are best resolved by mediation. For that purpose, look at Chapter 8 of Nolo's _Landlord's Law Book_ (described in the box at the beginning of this chapter) which includes a section on mediating disputes with tenants. Some of the mediation mechanisms mentioned there will also help with option contract disputes. If, however, you want to include specific language on mediation and arbitration, you can include Clauses 22 and 23 from the house purchase contract (see Chapter 9) in this section of additional provisions of the lease option contract.

If you have no additional provisions, simply put a large "X" through this section.

If you need to make more extensive changes to the lease-option agreement, see Section C, below.

C. Modifying and Signing the Option Agreement

Our lease-option contract is designed to protect your interests, but it may not fit your exact situation. If you need to change the lease-option contract, use the following guidelines.

1. Before Signing the Lease-Option Agreement

The easiest way to change our lease-option contract is to cross out unwanted portions and write in desired changes at Clause 24. If the changes are lengthy, use a separate sheet of paper. Type the same heading as used on the original document, identify the parties, and make it clear that you are adding provisions to the lease or rental agreement.

If you want to make major alterations, retype the form and add your own provisions. Also consider having the new agreement reviewed by an experienced real estate lawyer.

2. Signing the Lease-Option Agreement

The end of the lease-option agreement contains space for the signatures and street address of the owner and tenant. Be sure the tenant reviews the lease-option agreement before signing and is clear about the terms. If you've altered a standard form, be sure that you and all tenants initial the changes when you sign the document. Give the tenant a copy of the signed lease or rental agreement.

3. After Signing the Lease-Option Agreement

If you want to change any terms of the lease-option agreement, you must put them in writing and make sure both parties sign them. There are two good ways to make mutually agreed-upon changes to a written agreement after it is signed. The first is to agree to substitute a whole new agreement for the old one. The second is to add the new provision as an amendment to the original agreement. An amendment need not have any special form, so long as it clearly refers to the agreement it's changing and is signed by the same people who signed the original agreement. ■

APPENDIX

Recording requested by	
and when recorded mail this deed and tax statements to:	For recorder's use

QUITCLAIM DEED

☐ This transfer is exempt from the documentary transfer tax.

    ☐ The documentary transfer tax is $_____ and is computed on

        ☐ the full value of the interest or property conveyed.

        ☐ the full value less the value of liens or encumbrances remaining thereon at the time of sale.

The property is located in   ☐ an unincorporated area.

                         ☐ the city of _____.

For a valuable consideration, receipt of which is hereby acknowledged,

hereby quitclaim(s) to _____

the following real property in the City of _____, County of

_____, California:

Date: _____

_____

_____

_____

_____

State of California

County of   } ss.

On _____, _____, known to me or proved by satisfactory evidence to be the person(s) whose name(s) is/are subscribed above, personally appeared before me, a Notary Public for California, and acknowledged that _____ executed this deed.

[SEAL]

_____
Signature of Notary

TAX DEDUCTIBLE MOVING EXPENSES

Direct moving expenses	
Airline/train/boat/bus tickets	$
Car use	$
Gas and oil for car	$
Car or truck rental	$
Gas and oil for truck	$
Professional mover's fee	$
Lodging during trip	$
Storing possessions before moving into new home	$
Costs of selling home (when paid by seller)	
Real estate commissions or hourly fees	$
Advertising	$
Documentary transfer tax	$
Appraisal fees	$
Escrow fees	$
Title fees	$
Points (as in FHA or VA transactions)	$
This book, when used to help sell home	$
Costs of buying home (when paid by buyer; not deductible presently, but add to basis)	
Real estate commissions or fees	$
Documentary transfer tax	$
Appraisal fees	$
Attorneys and/or accountant's fees	$
Escrow fees	$
Title fees	$
Costs of financing home purchase: points (deductible by buyer in year paid by buyer)	
Loan points not fully deducted on prior tax returns	$

HOURLY BROKER FEE AGREEMENT

_____ ,

the seller(s) of the real property located at _____

_____ , in the City of

_____ , County of _____ , California, hereby engage

_____ , a licensed real estate broker in the State of California, to advise

them as to the mechanics involved in selling their own house, with the intention that the broker shall act as needed as an

advisor as to typical sales procedures, the preparation of routine forms, comparable sales prices, information on

available financing, and suggestions as to competent professionals, such as attorneys, accountants, pest control inspec-

tors, general contractors, etc., as needed.

Broker shall not receive a commission but shall be compensated at $_____ per hour, not to exceed a total

amount of $_____ , based on the broker's estimate that the advice required shall not call for more than

_____ hours of the broker's labor. Broker shall be paid as follows:

_____

_____

If the seller and broker agree that more of the broker's time is needed, an additional written contract will be prepared.

It is understood that sellers are handling their own sale and are solely responsible for all decisions made and paperwork

prepared. In addition, it is expressly agreed that broker will not provide any legal direction or tax or estate planning

advice, and shall make no representation concerning the physical condition of the property or the legal condition of title

to any party. Broker expressly recommends that sellers seek the appropriate professional advice offered by attorneys, tax

accountants, pest control inspectors, and/or general contractors as needed.

Agreed this date of _____ , by:

_____

_____

Seller(s)

_____

Broker

_____

By

SIGN-IN SHEET

Thank you for coming. Please take a fact sheet on our house and sign in before going through our home. Please print clearly.

Name	Address	Phone	How did you learn about this house?

Sample Disclosure Format for Target Housing Sales

DISCLOSURE OF INFORMATION ON LEAD-BASED PAINT AND LEAD-BASED PAINT HAZARDS

Lead Warning Statement

Every purchaser of any interest in residential real property on which a residential dwelling was built prior to 1978 is notified that such property may present exposure to lead from lead-based paint that may place young children at risk of developing lead poisoning. Lead poisoning in young children may produce permanent neurological damage, including learning disabilities, reduced intelligence quotient, behavioral problems, and impaired memory. Lead poisoning also poses a particular risk to pregnant women. The seller of any interest in residential real property is required to provide the buyer with any information on lead-based paint hazards from risk assessments or inspections in the seller's possession and notify the buyer of any known lead-based paint hazards. A risk assessment or inspection for possible lead-based paint hazards is recommended prior to purchase.

Seller's Disclosure (initial)

_____ (a) Presence of lead-based paint and/or lead-based paint hazards (check one below):

❑ Known lead-based paint and/or lead-based paint hazards are present in the housing (explain).

_____

_____

❑ Seller has no knowledge of lead-based paint and/or lead-based paint hazards in the housing.

_____ (b) Records and reports available to the seller (check one below):

❑ Seller has provided the purchaser with all available records and reports pertaining to lead-based paint and/or lead-based paint hazards in the housing (list documents below).

_____

_____

❑ Seller has no reports or records pertaining to lead-based paint and/or lead-based paint hazards in the housing.

Purchaser's Acknowledgment (initial)

_____ (c) Purchaser has received copies of all information listed above.

_____ (d) Purchaser has received the pamphlet *Protect Your Family from Lead in Your Home.*

_____ (e) Purchaser has (check one below):

❑ Received a 10-day opportunity (or mutually agreed upon period) to conduct a risk assessment or inspection for the presence of lead-based paint and/or lead-based paint hazards; or

❑ Waived the opportunity to conduct a risk assessment or inspection for the presence of lead-based paint and/or lead-based paint hazards.

Agent's Acknowledgment (initial)

_____ (f) Agent has informed the seller of the seller's obligations under 42 U.S.C. 4852(d) and is aware of his/her responsibility to ensure compliance.

Certification of Accuracy

The following parties have reviewed the information above and certify, to the best of their knowledge, that the information provided by the signatory is true and accurate.

Seller	Date	Seller	Date
Agent	Date	Agent	Date
Purchaser	Date	Purchaser	Date

Are You Planning To Buy, Rent, or Renovate a Home Built Before 1978?

Many houses and apartments built before 1978 have paint that contains lead (called lead-based paint). Lead from paint, chips, and dust can pose serious health hazards if not taken care of properly.

By 1996, federal law will require that individuals receive certain information before renting, buying, or renovating pre-1978 housing:

LANDLORDS will have to disclose known information on lead-based paint hazards before leases take effect. Leases will include a federal form about lead-based paint.

SELLERS will have to disclose known information on lead-based paint hazards before selling a house. Sales contracts will include a federal form about lead-based paint in the building. Buyers will have up to 10 days to check for lead hazards.

RENOVATORS will have to give you this pamphlet before starting work.

IF YOU WANT MORE INFORMATION on these requirements, call the National Lead Information Clearinghouse at **1-800-424-LEAD**.

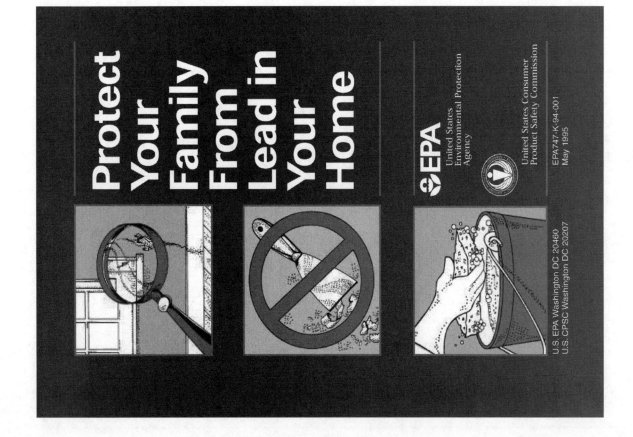

Protect Your Family From Lead in Your Home

EPA

United States Environmental Protection Agency

United States Consumer Product Safety Commission

EPA747-K-94-001
May 1995

U.S. EPA Washington DC 20460
U.S. CPSC Washington DC 20207

IMPORTANT!

Lead From Paint, Dust, and Soil Can Be Dangerous If Not Managed Properly

FACT: **Lead exposure can harm young children and babies even before they are born.**

FACT: Even children that seem healthy can have high levels of lead in their bodies.

FACT: People can get lead in their bodies by breathing or swallowing lead dust, or by eating soil or paint chips with lead in them.

FACT: People have many options for reducing lead hazards. In most cases, lead-based paint that is in good condition is not a hazard.

FACT: Removing lead-based paint improperly can increase the danger to your family.

If you think your home might have lead hazards, read this pamphlet to learn some simple steps to protect your family.

Lead Gets in the Body in Many Ways

People can get lead in their body if they:

◆ Put their hands or other objects covered with lead dust in their mouths.

◆ Eat paint chips or soil that contains lead.

◆ Breathe in lead dust (especially during renovations that disturb painted surfaces).

1 out of every 11 children in the United States has dangerous levels of lead in the bloodstream.

Even children who appear healthy can have dangerous levels of lead.

Lead is even more dangerous to children than adults because:

◆ Babies and young children often put their hands and other objects in their mouths. These objects can have lead dust on them.

◆ Children's growing bodies absorb more lead.

◆ Children's brains and nervous systems are more sensitive to the damaging effects of lead.

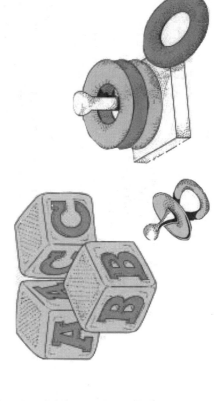

Lead's Effects

If not detected early, children with high levels of lead in their bodies can suffer from:

◆ Damage to the brain and nervous system

◆ Behavior and learning problems (such as hyperactivity)

◆ Slowed growth

◆ Hearing problems

◆ Headaches

Lead is also harmful to adults. Adults can suffer from:

◆ Difficulties during pregnancy

◆ Other reproductive problems (in both men and women)

◆ High blood pressure

◆ Digestive problems

◆ Nerve disorders

◆ Memory and concentration problems

◆ Muscle and joint pain

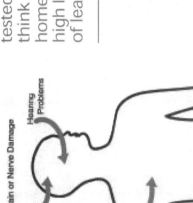

Brain or Nerve Damage

Hearing Problems

Slowed Growth

Digestive Problems

Reproductive Problems (Adults)

Lead affects the body in many ways.

Checking Your Family for Lead

A simple blood test can detect high levels of lead. Blood tests are important for:

◆ Children who are 6 months to 1 year old (6 months if you live in an older home with cracking or peeling paint).

◆ Family members that you think might have high levels of lead.

If your child is older than 1 year, talk to your doctor about whether your child needs testing.

Your doctor or health center can do blood tests. They are inexpensive and sometimes free. Your doctor will explain what the test results mean. *Treatment can range from changes in your diet to medication or a hospital stay.*

Get your children tested if you think your home has high levels of lead.

Where Lead-Based Paint Is Found

Many homes built before 1978 have lead-based paint. The federal government banned lead-based paint from housing in 1978. Some states stopped its use even earlier. Lead can be found:

◆ In homes in the city, country, or suburbs.

◆ In apartments, single-family homes, and both private and public housing.

◆ Inside *and* outside of the house.

◆ In soil around a home. (Soil can pick up lead from exterior paint, or other sources such as past use of leaded gas in cars.)

In general, the older your home, the more likely it has lead-based paint.

Where Lead Is Likely To Be a Hazard

Lead-based paint that is in good condition is usually not a hazard.

Peeling, chipping, chalking, or cracking lead-based paint is a hazard and needs immediate attention.

Lead-based paint may also be a hazard when found on surfaces that children can chew or that get a lot of wear-and-tear. These areas include:

◆ Windows and window sills.

◆ Doors and door frames.

◆ Stairs, railings, and banisters.

◆ Porches and fences.

Lead dust can form when lead-based paint is dry scraped, dry sanded, or heated. Dust also forms when painted surfaces bump or rub together. Lead chips and dust can get on surfaces and objects that people touch. Settled lead dust can reenter the air when people vacuum, sweep, or walk through it.

Lead in soil can be a hazard when children play in bare soil or when people bring soil into the house on their shoes. Call your state agency (see page 12) to find out about soil testing for lead.

Lead from paint chips, which you can see, and lead dust, which you can't always see, can both be serious hazards

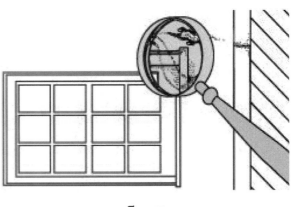

Checking Your Home for Lead Hazards

You can get your home checked for lead hazards in one of two ways, or both:

◆ A paint inspection tells you the lead content of every painted surface in your home. It won't tell you whether the paint is a hazard or how you should deal with it.

◆ A risk assessment tells you if there are any sources of serious lead exposure (such as peeling paint and lead dust). It also tells you what actions to take to address these hazards.

Have qualified professionals do the work. *The federal government is writing standards for inspectors and risk assessors. Some states might already have standards in place.* Call your state agency for help with locating qualified professionals in your area (see page 12).

Trained professionals use a range of methods when checking your home, including:

◆ Visual inspection of paint condition and location.

◆ Lab tests of paint samples.

◆ Surface dust tests.

◆ A portable x-ray fluorescence machine.

Home test kits for lead are available, but recent studies suggest that they are not always accurate. Consumers should not rely on these tests before doing renovations or to assure safety.

Just knowing that a home has lead-based paint may not tell you if there is a hazard.

What You Can Do Now To Protect Your Family

If you suspect that your house has lead hazards, you can take some immediate steps to reduce your family's risk:

◆ **If you rent, notify your landlord of peeling or chipping paint.**

◆ **Clean up paint chips immediately.**

◆ **Clean floors, window frames, window sills, and other surfaces weekly.** Use a mop or sponge with warm water and a general all-purpose cleaner or a cleaner made specifically for lead. REMEMBER: NEVER MIX AMMONIA AND BLEACH PRODUCTS TOGETHER SINCE THEY CAN FORM A DANGEROUS GAS.

◆ **Thoroughly rinse sponges and mop heads after cleaning dirty or dusty areas.**

◆ **Wash children's hands often, especially before they eat and before nap time and bed time.**

◆ **Keep play areas clean.** Wash bottles, pacifiers, toys, and stuffed animals regularly.

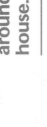

◆ **Keep children from chewing window sills or other painted surfaces.**

◆ **Clean or remove shoes before entering your home to avoid tracking in lead from soil.**

◆ **Make sure children eat nutritious, low-fat meals high in iron and calcium,** such as spinach and low-fat dairy products. Children with good diets absorb less lead.

How To Significantly Reduce Lead Hazards

In addition to day-to-day cleaning and good nutrition:

◆ You can **temporarily** reduce lead hazards by taking actions such as repairing damaged painted surfaces and planting grass to cover soil with high lead levels. These actions (called "interim controls") are not permanent solutions and will need ongoing attention.

◆ To **permanently** remove lead hazards, you must hire a lead "abatement" contractor. Abatement (or permanent hazard elimination) methods include removing, sealing, or enclosing lead-based paint with special materials. Just painting over the hazard with regular paint is not enough.

Removing lead improperly can increase the hazard to your family by spreading even more lead dust around the house.

Always use a professional who is trained to remove lead hazards safely.

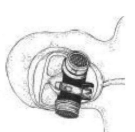

Always hire a person with special training for correcting lead problems—someone who knows how to do this work safely and has the proper equipment to clean up thoroughly. If possible, hire a certified lead abatement contractor. Certified contractors will employ qualified workers and follow strict safety rules as set by their state or by the federal government.

Call your state agency (see page 12) for help with locating qualified contractors in your area and to see if financial assistance is available.

Remodeling or Renovating a Home With Lead-Based Paint

Take precautions before you begin remodeling or renovations that disturb painted surfaces (such as scraping off paint or tearing out walls):

◆ **Have the area tested for lead-based paint.**

◆ **Do not use a dry scraper, belt-sander, propane torch, or heat gun** to remove lead-based paint. These actions create large amounts of lead dust and fumes. Lead dust can remain in your home long after the work is done.

◆ **Temporarily move your family** (especially children and pregnant women) out of the apartment or house until the work is done and the area is properly cleaned. If you can't move your family, at least completely seal off the work area.

◆ **Follow other safety measures to reduce lead hazards.** You can find out about other safety measures by calling 1-800-424-LEAD. Ask for the brochure "Reducing Lead Hazards When Remodeling Your Home." This brochure explains what to do before, during, and after renovations.

If you have already completed renovations or remodeling that could have released lead-based paint or dust, get your young children tested and follow the steps outlined on page 7 of this brochure.

If not conducted properly, certain types of renovations can release lead from paint and dust into the air.

Other Sources of Lead

◆ **Drinking water.** Your home might have plumbing with lead or lead solder. Call your local health department or water supplier to find out about testing your water. You cannot see, smell, or taste lead, and boiling your water will not get rid of lead. If you think your plumbing might have lead in it:

- Use only cold water for drinking and cooking.

- Run water for 15 to 30 seconds before drinking it, especially if you have not used your water for a few hours.

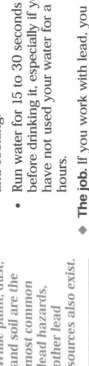

While paint, dust, and soil are the most common lead hazards, other lead sources also exist.

◆ **The job.** If you work with lead, you could bring it home on your hands or clothes. Shower and change clothes before coming home. Launder your clothes separately from the rest of your family's.

◆ Old painted **toys** and **furniture.**

◆ Food and liquids stored in **lead crystal** or **lead-glazed pottery or porcelain.**

◆ **Lead smelters** or other industries that release lead into the air.

◆ **Hobbies** that use lead, such as making pottery or stained glass, or refinishing furniture.

◆ **Folk remedies** that contain lead, such as "greta" and "azarcon" used to treat an upset stomach.

For More Information

The National Lead Information Center

Call **1-800-LEAD-FYI** to learn how to protect children from lead poisoning.

For other information on lead hazards, call the center's clearinghouse at **1-800-424-LEAD**. For the hearing impaired, call, TDD **1-800-526-5456** (FAX: **202-659-1192,** Internet: **EHC@CAIS.COM**).

EPA's Safe Drinking Water Hotline

Call **1-800-426-4791** for information about lead in drinking water.

Consumer Product Safety Commission Hotline

To request information on lead in consumer products, or to report an unsafe consumer product or a product-related injury call **1-800-638-2772.** (Internet: info@cpsc.gov). For the hearing impaired, call **TDD 1-800-638-8270.**

Local Sources of Information

State Health and Environmental Agencies

Some cities and states have their own rules for lead-based paint activities. Check with your state agency (listed below) to see if state or local laws apply to you. Most state agencies can also provide information on finding a lead abatement firm in your area, and on possible sources of financial aid for reducing lead hazards.

State/Region	Phone Number	State/Region	Phone Number
Alabama	(205) 242-5661	Missouri	(314) 526-4911
Alaska	(907) 465-5152	Montana	(406) 444-3671
Arkansas	(501) 661-2534	Nebraska	(402) 471-2451
Arizona	(602) 542-7307	Nevada	(702) 687-6615
California	(510) 450-2424	New Hampshire	(603) 271-4507
Colorado	(303) 692-3012	New Jersey	(609) 633-2043
Connecticut	(203) 566-5808	New Mexico	(505) 841-8024
Washington, DC	(202) 727-9850	New York	(800) 458-1158
Delaware	(302) 739-4735	North Carolina	(919) 715-3293
Florida	(904) 488-3385	North Dakota	(701) 328-5188
Georgia	(404) 657-6514	Ohio	(614) 466-1450
Hawaii	(808) 832-5860	Oklahoma	(405) 271-5220
Idaho	(208) 332-5544	Oregon	(503) 248-5240
Illinois	(800) 545-2200	Pennsylvania	(717) 782-2884
Indiana	(317) 382-6662	Rhode Island	(401) 277-3424
Iowa	(800) 972-2026	South Carolina	(803) 935-7945
Kansas	(913) 296-0189	South Dakota	(605) 773-3153
Kentucky	(502) 564-2154	Tennessee	(615) 741-5683
Louisiana	(504) 765-0219	Texas	(512) 834-6600
Massachusetts	(800) 532-9571	Utah	(801) 536-4000
Maryland	(410) 631-3859	Vermont	(802) 863-7231
Maine	(207) 287-4311	Virginia	(800) 523-4019
Michigan	(517) 335-8885	Washington	(206) 753-2556
Minnesota	(612) 627-5498	West Virginia	(304) 558-2981
Mississippi	(601) 960-7463	Wisconsin	(608) 266-5885
		Wyoming	(307) 777-7391

Simple Steps To Protect Your Family From Lead Hazards

If you think your home has high levels of lead:

- Get your young children tested for lead, even if they seem healthy.

- Wash children's hands, bottles, pacifiers, and toys often.

- Make sure children eat healthy, low-fat foods.

- Get your home checked for lead hazards.

- Regularly clean floors, window sills, and other surfaces.

- Wipe soil off shoes before entering house.

- Talk to your landlord about fixing surfaces with peeling or chipping paint.

- Take precautions to avoid exposure to lead dust when remodeling or renovating (call 1-800-424-LEAD for guidelines).

- Don't use a belt-sander, propane torch, dry scraper, or dry sandpaper on painted surfaces that may contain lead.

- Don't try to remove lead-based paint yourself.

EPA Regional Offices

Your Regional EPA Office can provide further information regarding regulations and lead protection programs.

EPA Regional Offices

Region 1 (Connecticut, Massachusetts, Maine, New Hampshire, Rhode Island, Vermont)
John F. Kennedy Federal Building
One Congress Street
Boston, MA 02203
(617) 565-3420

Region 2 (New Jersey, New York, Puerto Rico, Virgin Islands)
Building 5
2890 Woodbridge Avenue
Edison, NJ 08837-3679
(908) 321-6671

Region 3 (Delaware, Washington DC, Maryland, Pennsylvania, Virginia, West Virginia)
841 Chestnut Building
Philadelphia, PA 19107
(215) 597-9800

Region 4 (Alabama, Florida, Georgia, Kentucky, Mississippi, North Carolina, South Carolina, Tennessee)
345 Courtland Street, NE
Atlanta, GA 30365
(404) 347-4727

Region 5 (Illinois, Indiana, Michigan, Minnesota, Ohio, Wisconsin)
77 West Jackson Boulevard
Chicago, IL 60604-3590
(312) 886-6003

Region 6 (Arkansas, Louisiana, New Mexico, Oklahoma, Texas)
First Interstate Bank Tower
1445 Ross Avenue, 12th Floor, Suite 1200
Dallas, TX 75202-2733
(214) 665-7244

Region 7 (Iowa, Kansas, Missouri, Nebraska)
726 Minnesota Avenue
Kansas City, KS 66101
(913) 551-7020

Region 8 (Colorado, Montana, North Dakota, South Dakota, Utah, Wyoming)
999 18th Street, Suite 500
Denver, CO 80202-2405
(303) 293-1603

Region 9 (Arizona, California, Hawaii, Nevada)
75 Hawthorne Street
San Francisco, CA 94105
(415) 744-1124

Region 10 (Idaho, Oregon, Washington, Alaska)
1200 Sixth Avenue
Seattle, WA 98101
(206) 553-1200

CPSC Regional Offices

Eastern Regional Center
6 World Trade Center
Vesey Street, Room 350
New York, NY 10048
(212) 466-1612

Central Regional Center
230 South Dearborn Street
Room 2944
Chicago, IL 60604-1601
(312) 353-8260

Western Regional Center
600 Harrison Street, Room 245
San Francisco, CA 94107
(415) 744-2966

REAL ESTATE TRANSFER DISCLOSURE STATEMENT

(CALIFORNIA CIVIL CODE § 1102, ET SEQ.)

THIS DISCLOSURE STATEMENT CONCERNS THE REAL PROPERTY SITUATED IN THE CITY OF _____ , COUNTY OF _____ , STATE OF CALIFORNIA, DESCRIBED AS _____

_____ .

THIS STATEMENT IS A DISCLOSURE OF THE CONDITION OF THE ABOVE DESCRIBED PROPERTY IN COMPLIANCE WITH SECTION 1102 OF THE CIVIL CODE AS OF _____ , 19——. IT IS NOT A WARRANTY OF ANY KIND BY THE SELLER(S) OR ANY AGENT(S) REPRESENTING ANY PRINCIPAL(S) IN THIS TRANSACTION, AND IT IS NOT A SUBSTITUTE FOR ANY INSPECTIONS OR WARRANTIES THE PRINCIPAL(S) MAY WISH TO OBTAIN.

I

COORDINATION WITH OTHER DISCLOSURE FORMS

This Real Estate Transfer Disclosure Statement is made pursuant to Section 1102 of the Civil Code. Other statutes require disclosures, depending upon the details of the particular real estate transaction (for example: special study zone and purchase-money liens on residential property).

Substituted Disclosures: The following disclosures have or will be made in connection with this real estate transfer, and are intended to satisfy the disclosure obligations on this form, where the subject matter is the same:

☐ Inspection reports completed pursuant to the contract of sale or receipt for deposit.

☐ Additional inspection reports or disclosures:

_____ .

(List all substituted disclosure forms to be used in connection with this transaction.)

II

SELLER'S INFORMATION

The Seller discloses the following information with the knowledge that even though this is not a warranty, prospective Buyers may rely on this information in deciding whether and on what terms to purchase the subject property. Seller hereby authorizes any agent(s) representing any principal(s) in this transaction to provide a copy of this statement to any person or entity in connection with any actual or anticipated sale of the property.

THE FOLLOWING ARE REPRESENTATIONS MADE BY THE SELLER(S) AND ARE NOT THE REPRESENTATIONS OF THE AGENT(S), IF ANY. THIS INFORMATION IS A DISCLOSURE AND IT IS NOT INTENDED TO BE PART OF ANY CONTRACT BETWEEN THE BUYER AND SELLER.

Seller ☐ is ☐ is not occupying the property.

A. The subject property has the items checked below (read across):

☐ Range	☐ Oven	☐ Microwave
☐ Dishwasher	☐ Trash Compactor	☐ Garbage Disposal
☐ Washer/Dryer Hookups	☐ Rain Gutters	☐ Smoke Detector(s)
☐ Fire Alarm	☐ T.V. Antenna	☐ Satellite Dish
☐ Intercom	☐ Central Heating	☐ Central Air Conditioning
☐ Evaporator Cooler(s)	☐ Wall/Window Air Conditioning	☐ Sprinklers
☐ Public Sewer System	☐ Septic Tank	☐ Sump Pump

☐ Water Softener   ☐ Patio/Decking   ☐ Built-in Barbecue

☐ Sauna   ☐ Gazebo   ☐ Burglar Alarms

☐ Hot Tub ☐ Locking Safety Cover*   ☐ Pool ☐ Child Restraint Barrier*   ☐ Spa ☐ Locking Safety Cover*

☐ Security Gate(s)   ☐ Automatic Garage Door Opener(s)*   ☐ # of Remote Controls _____

☐ Garage: ☐ Attached   ☐ Not Attached   ☐ Carport

☐ Pool/Spa Heater: ☐ Gas   ☐ Solar   ☐ Electric

☐ Water Heater: ☐ Gas   ☐ Water Heater Anchored, Braced or Strapped*   ☐ Electric

☐ Water Supply: ☐ City   ☐ Well   ☐ Private Utility

                         ☐ Other _____

☐ Gas Supply: ☐ Utility   ☐ Bottled

☐ Window Screens   ☐ Window Security Bars   ☐ Quick Release Mechanism on Bedroom Windows

☐ Exhaust Fan(s) in _____   ☐ 220 Volt Wiring in _____

☐ Fireplace(s) in _____   ☐ Gas Starter

☐ Roof(s): Type: _____ Age: _____ (approx.)

Other: _____

Are there, to the best of your (Seller's) knowledge, any of the above that are not in operating condition?

☐ Yes ☐ No   If yes, then describe (attach additional sheets if necessary):

_____

_____

_____

B. Are you (Seller) aware of any significant defects/malfunctions in any of the following?

☐ Yes ☐ No   If yes, check appropriate box(es) below.

☐ Interior Walls   ☐ Ceilings   ☐ Floors   ☐ Exterior Walls   ☐ Insulation

☐ Roof(s)   ☐ Windows   ☐ Doors   ☐ Foundation   ☐ Slab(s)

☐ Driveways   ☐ Sidewalks   ☐ Walls/Fences   ☐ Electrical Systems   ☐ Plumbing/Sewers/Septics

☐ Other Structural Components (describe):

_____

_____

If any of the above is checked, explain (attach additional sheets if necessary):

_____

_____

_____

*This garage door opener or child restraint pool barrier may not be in compliance with the safety standards relating to automatic reversing devices as set forth in Chapter 12.5 (commencing with Section 19890) of Part 3 of Division 13, or with the pool safety standards of Article 2.5 (commencing with Section 115920) of Chapter 5 of Part 10 of Division 104, of the Health and Safety Code. The water heater may not be anchored, braced or strapped in accordance with Section 19211 of the Health and Safety Code. Window security bars may not have quick release mechanisms in compliance with the 1995 Edition of the California Building Standards Code.

C. Are you (Seller) aware of any of the following:

1. Substances, materials, or products which may be an environmental hazard such as, but not limited to, asbestos, formaldehyde, radon gas, lead-based paint, fuel or chemical storage tanks, and contaminated soil or water on the subject property. ☐ Yes ☐ No

2. Features of the property shared in common with adjoining landowners, such as walls, fences and driveways, whose use or responsibility for maintenance may have an effect on the subject property. ☐ Yes ☐ No

3. Any encroachments, easements or similar matters that may affect your interest in the subject property. ☐ Yes ☐ No

4. Room additions, structural modifications, or other alterations or repairs made without necessary permits. ☐ Yes ☐ No

5. Room additions, structural modifications, or other alterations or repairs not in compliance with building codes. ☐ Yes ☐ No

6. Fill (compacted or otherwise) on the property or any portion thereof. ☐ Yes ☐ No

7. Any settling from any cause, or slippage, sliding, or other soil problems. ☐ Yes ☐ No

8. Flooding, drainage, or grading problems. ☐ Yes ☐ No

9. Major damage to the property or any other structures from fire, earthquake, floods, or landslides. ☐ Yes ☐ No

10. Any zoning violations, nonconforming uses, violations of "setback" requirements. ☐ Yes ☐ No

11. Neighborhood noise problems or other nuisances. ☐ Yes ☐ No

12. CC&Rs or other deed restrictions or obligations. ☐ Yes ☐ No

13. Homeowners' Association which has any authority over the subject property. ☐ Yes ☐ No

14. Any "common area" (facilities such as pools, tennis courts, walkways, or other areas co-owned in undivided interest with others). ☐ Yes ☐ No

15. Any notices of abatement or citations against the property. ☐ Yes ☐ No

16. Any lawsuits against the seller threatening to or affecting this real property, including any lawsuits alleging a defect or deficiency in this real property or "common areas" (facilities such as pools, tennis courts, walkways, or other areas co-owned in undivided interest with others). ☐ Yes ☐ No

If the answer to any of these is yes, explain (attach additional sheets if necessary): _____

_____

Seller certifies that the information herein is true and correct to the best of the Seller's knowledge as of the date signed by the Seller.

Seller _____ Date _____

Seller _____ Date _____

III

AGENT'S INSPECTION DISCLOSURE (LISTING AGENT)

(To be completed only if the Seller is represented by an agent in this transaction.)

THE UNDERSIGNED, BASED ON THE ABOVE INQUIRY OF THE SELLER(S) AS TO THE CONDITION OF THE PROPERTY AND BASED ON REASONABLY COMPETENT AND DILIGENT VISUAL INSPECTION OF THE ACCESSIBLE AREAS OF THE PROPERTY IN CONJUNCTION WITH THAT INQUIRY, STATES THE FOLLOWING:

☐ Agent notes no items for disclosure.

☐ Agent notes the following items: _____

Agent (Print Name of Broker Representing Seller):_____

By (Associate Licensee or Broker's Signature) _____

Date _____

IV

AGENT'S INSPECTION DISCLOSURE (SELLING AGENT)

(To be completed only if the agent who has obtained the offer is other than the agent above.)

THE UNDERSIGNED, BASED ON A REASONABLY COMPETENT AND DILIGENT VISUAL INSPECTION OF THE ACCESSIBLE AREAS OF THE PROPERTY, STATES THE FOLLOWING:

☐ Agent notes no items for disclosure.

☐ Agent notes the following items: _____

Agent (Print Name of Broker Obtaining Offer) _____

By (Associate Licensee or Broker's Signature) _____

Date _____

V

BUYER(S) AND SELLER(S) MAY WISH TO OBTAIN PROFESSIONAL ADVICE AND/OR INSPECTIONS OF THE PROPERTY AND TO PROVIDE FOR APPROPRIATE PROVISIONS IN A CONTRACT BETWEEN BUYER(S) AND SELLER(S) WITH RESPECT TO ANY ADVICE/INSPECTION/DEFECTS.

I/WE ACKNOWLEDGE RECEIPT OF A COPY OF THIS STATEMENT.

Seller _____ Date _____

Seller _____ Date _____

Buyer _____ Date _____

Buyer _____ Date _____

Agent (Print Name of Broker Representing Seller) _____

By (Associate Licensee or Broker's Signature) _____

Date _____

Agent (Print Name of Broker Obtaining the Offer) _____

By (Associate Licensee or Broker's Signature) _____

Date _____

SECTION 1102.3 OF THE CIVIL CODE PROVIDES A BUYER WITH THE RIGHT TO RESCIND A PURCHASE CONTRACT FOR AT LEAST THREE DAYS AFTER THE DELIVERY OF THIS DISCLOSURE IF DELIVERY OCCURS AFTER THE SIGNING OF AN OFFER TO PURCHASE. IF YOU WISH TO RESCIND THE CONTRACT, YOU MUST ACT WITHIN THE PRESCRIBED PERIOD. A REAL ESTATE BROKER IS QUALIFIED TO ADVISE ON REAL ESTATE. IF YOU DESIRE LEGAL ADVICE, CONSULT YOUR ATTORNEY.

NATURAL HAZARD DISCLOSURE STATEMENT

This statement applies to the following property:

_____

The seller and his or her agent(s) disclose the following information with the knowledge that even though this is not a warranty, prospective buyers may rely on this information in deciding whether and on what terms to purchase the subject property. Seller hereby authorizes any agent(s) representing any principal(s) in this action to provide a copy of this statement to any person or entity in connection with any actual or anticipated sale of the property.

The following are representations made by the seller and his or her agent(s) based on their knowledge and maps drawn by the state. This information is a disclosure and is not intended to be part of any contract between the buyer and the seller.

THIS REAL PROPERTY LIES WITHIN THE FOLLOWING HAZARDOUS AREA(S): (Check "yes" or "no" for each area)

A SPECIAL FLOOD HAZARD AREA (Any type Zone "A" or "V") designated by the Federal Emergency Management Agency.

Yes _____   No _____   Do not know and information not available from local jurisdiction _____

AN AREA OF POTENTIAL FLOODING shown on a dam failure inundation map pursuant to Section 8589.5 of the Government Code.

Yes _____   No _____   Do not know and information not available from local jurisdiction _____

A VERY HIGH FIRE HAZARD SEVERITY ZONE pursuant to Section 51178 or 51179 of the Government Code. The owner of this property is subject to the maintenance requirements of Section 51182 of the Government Code.

Yes _____   No _____

A WILDLAND AREA THAT MAY CONTAIN SUBSTANTIAL FOREST FIRE RISKS AND HAZARDS pursuant to Section 4125 of the Public Resources Code. The owner of this property is subject to the maintenance requirements of Section 4291 of the Public Resources Code. Additionally, it is not the state's responsibility to provide fire protection services to any building or structure located within the wildlands unless the Department of Forestry and Fire Protection has entered into a cooperative agreement with a local agency for those purposes pursuant to Section 4142 of the Public Resources Code.

Yes _____   No _____

AN EARTHQUAKE FAULT ZONE pursuant to Section 2622 of the Public Resources Code.

Yes _____   No _____

A SEISMIC HAZARD ZONE pursuant to Section 2696 of the Public Resources Code.

Yes (Landslide Zone) _____   No _____   Map not yet released by state _____
Yes (Liquefaction Zone) _____   No _____   Map not yet released by state _____

THESE HAZARDS MAY LIMIT YOUR ABILITY TO DEVELOP THE REAL PROPERTY, TO OBTAIN INSURANCE, OR TO RECEIVE ASSISTANCE AFTER A DISASTER.

THE MAPS ON WHICH THESE DISCLOSURES ARE BASED ESTIMATE WHERE NATURAL HAZARDS EXIST. THEY ARE NOT DEFINITIVE INDICATORS OF WHETHER OR NOT A PROPERTY WILL BE AFFECTED BY A NATURAL DISASTER. BUYER(S) AND SELLER(S) MAY WISH TO OBTAIN PROFESSIONAL ADVICE REGARDING THOSE HAZARDS AND OTHER HAZARDS THAT MAY AFFECT THE PROPERTY.

Seller represents that the information herein is true and correct to the best of the seller's knowledge as of the date signed by the seller.

Signature of Seller _____   Date _____

Agent represents that the information herein is true and correct to the best of the agent's knowledge as of the date signed by the agent.

Signature of Agent _____   Date _____

Signature of Agent _____   Date _____

Buyer represents that he or she has read and understands this document.

Signature of Buyer _____   Date _____

CREDIT INFORMATION FORM

BACKGROUND INFORMATION

	BORROWER	CO-BORROWER
Name (including Jr., Sr. and former names)		
Social Security number		
Driver's license number		
Home phone number		
Work phone number		
Current address		
	❑ own ❑ rent	❑ own ❑ rent
	monthly rent or mortgage payment: $	monthly rent or mortgage payment: $
Previous address if less than two years at current address		
Name of employer		
Address of employer		
Phone number of employer		
Job title		
How long with present employer		
Name, address and phone number of previous employer if less than two years at current job		
Previous job title		
How long with previous employer		

INCOME

	BORROWER	CO-BORROWER
Current monthly gross income	$	$
Monthly amounts and sources of other income (such as interest, dividends, royalties, support and the like)	$	$
Total Monthly Income	$	$

ASSETS

	BORROWER	CO-BORROWER
Name and address of financial institution holding deposit account, type of account (checking, savings, money market) and current balance of account	$	$
Name and address of financial institution holding deposit account, type of account (checking, savings, money market) and current balance of account	$	$
Name and address of financial institution holding marketable security, type of fund (stock, bond, annuity, life insurance, mutual fund) and current balance	$	$
Name and address of financial institution holding deposit account, type of account (checking, savings, money market) and current balance of account	$	$

Real Estate	value	$		value	$	
	mortgages	$		mortgages	$	
	liens	$		liens	$	
	equity	$		equity	$	
Vehicles (year, make, market value)		$				
Business assets (name of business, interest in business, value of interest)						
Other assets (specify asset type and value)		$				
TOTAL ASSETS						

LIABILITIES

	BORROWER	CO-BORROWER
Credit card—name of card, account number and current outstanding balance	$	$
Credit card—name of card, account number and current outstanding balance	$	$
Credit card—name of card, account number and current outstanding balance	$	$
Motor vehicle loan—indicate monthly payment to the right; total amount owed here: $	$	$
Real estate loan—indicate monthly payment to the right; total amount owed here: $	$	$
Child/spousal support—indicate monthly payment to the right; total amount owed here: $	$	$
Student loan—indicate monthly payment to the right; total amount owed here: $	$	$
Personal loan—indicate monthly payment to the right; total amount owed here: $	$	$
Other loan—indicate monthly payment to the right; total amount owed here: $	$	$
TOTAL LIABILITIES	$	$

Have you ever filed for bankruptcy? If yes, indicate the year, the court, the type of bankruptcy (Chapter 7, 11 or 13) and the circumstances that led you to filing.

Are there any outstanding judgments against you? If yes, please explain.

Have you had property foreclosed upon you? Have you given title or deed in lieu of foreclosure in the past ten years? If yes, please explain.

We certify that all the information given above is true and accurate. We authorize the seller to verify any and all of the information provided above, including our deposits with all financial institutions. We further authorize seller to receive any and all information about our credit from credit reporting agencies and to verify employment with the employers listed above.

_____

Signature of borrower

_____

Date

_____

Signature of co-borrower

_____

Date

PROMISSORY NOTE

1. For value received, ☐ I individually   ☐ we jointly and severally promise to pay to the order of

    _____

    _____

    the sum of $ _____ at _____

    at the rate of _____ %

    per year from the date this note was signed until the date it is paid in full. The signer(s) of this note has the right to pay all or a portion of the principal amount owing, without penalty, prior to the maturity date stated in this note.

2. ☐ I individually   ☐ we jointly and severally agree that this note shall be paid in equal installments, which include principal and interest, of not less than $ _____ per month, due on the first day of each month, for a period of _____ months. At the end of that period, ☐ I individually   ☐ we jointly and severally agree to make a final ("balloon") payment in the amount of $ _____. This note is subject to Civil Code Section 2966, which provides that the holder of this note shall give written notice to the signer(s) of this note of prescribed information at least 90 and not more than 150 days before any balloon payment is due.

3. If any installment payment due under this note is not received by the holder within 10 days of its due date, a late charge in the amount of 6% of the payment due shall be paid to the holder(s) of this note. If any installment payment due under this note is not received by the holder within 30 days of its due date, the entire amount of unpaid principal shall become immediately due and payable at the option of the holder without prior notice to the signer(s) of this note.

4. In the event the holder(s) of this note prevail(s) in a lawsuit to collect on it, I/we agree to pay the holder's(s') attorney fees in an amount the court finds to be just and reasonable.

5. ☐ I individually   ☐ we jointly and severally agree that until such time as the principal and interest owed under this note are paid in full, the note shall be secured by the following described mortgage, deed of trust, or security agreement:

    Deed of trust to real property commonly known as _____

    _____

    owned by _____

    executed on _____ at _____

    _____ and recorded at _____

    _____ in the records of _____

    County, California.

    _____   _____
    Date   Date

    _____   _____
    Location (city or county)   Location (city or county)

    _____   _____
    Name of Borrower   Name of Borrower

    _____   _____
    Address of Borrower   Address of Borrower

    _____   _____
    Signature of Borrower   Signature of Borrower

OFFER TO PURCHASE REAL PROPERTY

Heading

Property address, including county: _____

_____

Date:_____.

_____ (Buyer) makes this offer to

_____ (Seller), to purchase

_____

the property described above, for the sum of _____dollars ($_____).

Buyer includes a deposit, in the amount of _____ dollars ($_____).

evidenced by ☐ cash ☐ cashier's check ☐ personal check ☐ promissory note ☐ other,

payable to _____ to be held uncashed until the acceptance of this offer, and

to be increased to 3% of the purchase amount no later than _____ days after this offer is accepted. If this offer is

accepted, the deposit shall be delivered to a mutually agreed escrow holder and applied toward the down payment.

1. Financial Terms

This offer is contingent upon Buyer securing financing as specified in items D, E, F and G, below, within _____ days
from acceptance of this offer.

$_____ A. DEPOSIT to be applied toward the down payment.

$_____ B. DEPOSIT INCREASE to be applied toward the down payment by _____ (date).

$_____ C. DOWN PAYMENT balance, in cash, to be paid into escrow on or before the close of escrow.

$_____ D. FIRST LOAN—NEW LOAN. Buyer shall obtain a new loan, amortized over not fewer than
_____ years. Buyer's financing shall be

    ☐ Conventional _____ (name of lender, if known)

    ☐ Private _____ (name of lender, if known)

    ☐ Government (specify): ☐ VA ☐ FHA ☐ Cal-Vet ☐ CHFA

    ☐ Other: _____

Buyer's mortgage shall be ☐ at a maximum fixed rate of _____% or

☐ an adjustable rate loan with a maximum beginning rate of _____%, with the life-of-

the-loan cap not to exceed _____ percentage points and the periodic cap not to be

adjusted more frequently than _____ . Maximum monthly loan payment

including principal, interest and, if applicable, private mortgage insurance (PMI), during

the first year of the loan agreement, shall be $_____. Buyer shall pay a loan origination

fee (points) of not more than _____% of the loan amount and application and appraisal

fees of not more than $_____.

$_____ E. FIRST LOAN—EXISTING LOAN. Buyer shall ☐ assume ☐ buy subject to an existing
loan under the same terms and conditions that Seller has with _____

_____, the present lender. The approximate remaining balance is

$_____, at the current rate of interest of _____% on a ☐ fixed ☐ adjustable rate

loan, or a remaining term of approximately _____ years, secured by a First Deed of Trust.

$_____ F. SECOND LOAN—NEW LOAN. Buyer shall obtain a new loan, amortized over not fewer
than _____ years. Buyer's financing shall be:

    ☐ Conventional _____ (name of lender, if known)

    ☐ Private _____ (name of lender, if known)

    ☐ Government (specify): ☐ VA ☐ FHA ☐ Cal-Vet ☐ CHFA

    ☐ Other: _____

Buyer's mortgage shall be ☐ at a maximum fixed rate of _____% or ☐ an adjustable rate loan with a maximum beginning rate of _____%, with the life-of-the-loan cap not to exceed_____ percentage points and the periodic cap not to be adjusted more frequently than _____. Maximum monthly loan payment including principal, interest and, if applicable, private mortgage insurance (PMI), during the first year of the loan agreement, shall be $_____. Buyer shall pay a loan origination fee (points) of not more than _____% of the loan amount and application and appraisal fees of not more than $_____.

$_____ G. SECOND LOAN—EXISTING LOAN. Buyer shall ☐ assume ☐ buy subject to an existing loan under the same terms and conditions that Seller has with _____

_____, the present lender. The approximate remaining balance is $_____, at the current rate of interest of _____% on a ☐ fixed ☐ adjustable rate loan, for a remaining term of approximately _____ years, secured by a Second Deed of Trust.

$_____ H. TOTAL PURCHASE PRICE, EXCLUDING EXPENSES OF SALE AND CLOSING COSTS.

Buyer shall submit complete loan application and financial statement to lender within five days after acceptance. If Buyer, after making a good-faith effort, does not secure financing by the time specified, this contract shall become void, and all deposits shall be returned to Buyer.

In the event of FHA or VA financing, Buyer shall not be obligated to complete the purchase, nor shall Buyer forfeit the deposit, if the offer price exceeds the property's FHA or VA appraised value. Buyer shall, however, have the option of proceeding with the purchase from any above-named lender or a different lender without regard to the appraised value.

2. Escrow

Buyer and Seller shall deliver signed escrow instructions to _____
_____ escrow agent located at
_____, within _____ days of acceptance of this offer. Escrow shall close within _____ days of acceptance of this offer. A deed shall be recorded in favor of Buyer at the close of escrow.

3. Pre-payment Penalty and Assumption Fee

Seller shall pay any pre-payment penalty or other fees imposed by any existing lender who is paid off during escrow. Buyer shall pay any pre-payment penalty, assumption fee or other fee which becomes due after the close of escrow on any loans assumed from Seller.

4. Expenses of Sale

Expenses of sale, settlement costs and closing costs shall be paid for as follows:

	Buyer	Seller	Share Equally	
A.	☐	☐	☐	Escrow fees
B.	☐	☐	☐	Title search
C.	☐	☐	☐	Title insurance for buyer/owner
D.	☐	☐	☐	Title insurance for buyer's lender
E.	☐	☐	☐	Deed preparation fee

F.	☐	☐	☐	Notary fee
G.	☐	☐	☐	Recording fee
H.	☐	☐	☐	Attorney's fee (if attorney hired to clarify title)
I.	☐	☐	☐	Documentary transfer tax
J.	☐	☐	☐	City transfer tax
K.	☐	☐	☐	Pest control inspection report
L.	☐	☐	☐	General contractor report
M.	☐	☐	☐	Roof inspection report
N.				Other inspections (specify):
1.	☐	☐	☐	_____
2.	☐	☐	☐	_____
3.	☐	☐	☐	_____
O.	☐	☐	☐	One-year home warranty
P.				Other (specify):
1.	☐	☐	☐	_____
2.	☐	☐	☐	_____
3.	☐	☐	☐	_____

5. Property Tax and Insurance Prorations; Non-Callable Bonds

Seller shall be responsible for payment of Seller's prorated share of real estate taxes accrued until the deed transferring title to Buyer is recorded. Buyer understands that the property shall be reassessed upon change of ownership and that Buyer shall be sent a supplemental tax bill which may reflect an increase in taxes based on property value.

Any fire insurance policy carried over from Seller to Buyer and any homeowners' association fees shall be prorated, that is, Seller shall pay the portion of the premiums and fees while title is in Seller's name and Buyer shall pay the portion of the premiums and fees while title is in Buyer's name.

Buyer agrees to assume non-callable assessment bond liens (those which cannot be paid off by Seller) as follows:

_____

6. Fixtures

All fixtures permanently attached to the property, including built-in appliances, electrical, plumbing, light and heating fixtures, garage door openers, attached carpets and other floor coverings, and window shades or blinds, are included in the sale except: _____

_____

_____

_____

_____

7. Personal Property

The following items of personal property are included in this sale:

☐ Stove	☐ Oven	☐ Refrigerator	☐ Washer
☐ Dryer	☐ Freezer	☐ Trash Compactor	☐ Dishwasher

_____

_____

8. Inspection Contingencies

This offer is conditioned upon Buyer's written approval of the following inspection reports. All reports shall be carried out within _____ days of acceptance. Buyer shall deliver written approval or disapproval to Seller within 3 days of receiving each report. If Buyer does not deliver a written disapproval within the time allowed, Buyer shall be deemed to approve of the report.

Seller is to provide reasonable access to the property to Buyer, his/her agent, all inspectors and representatives of lending institutions to conduct appraisals.

A. ☐ Pest control report

B. ☐ General contractor report as to the general physical condition of the property including, but not limited to, heating and plumbing, electrical systems, solar energy systems, roof and appliances

C. ☐ Plumbing contractor report

D. ☐ Soils engineer report

E. ☐ Energy conservation inspection report in accordance with local ordinances

F. ☐ Geologist report

G. ☐ Environmental inspection report

H. ☐ City or county inspection report

I. ☐ Roof inspection report

If Buyer and Seller, after making a good-faith effort, cannot remove in writing the above contingencies by the time specified, this contract shall become void, and all deposits shall be returned to Buyer.

9. Other Contingencies

This offer is contingent upon the following:

A. ☐ Buyer receiving and approving preliminary title report within _____ days of acceptance of this offer

B. ☐ Seller furnishing a Residential Building Record Report indicating _____ legal units within _____ days of acceptance

C. ☐ Seller furnishing declaration of restrictions, CC&Rs, bylaws, articles of incorporation, rules and regulations currently in force and a financial statement of the owners' association within _____ days of acceptance

D. ☐ Sale of Buyer's current residence, the address of which is _____, _____ by _____.

E. ☐ Seller furnishing rental agreements within _____ days of acceptance

F. ☐ Other: _____

Buyer shall deliver written approval or disapproval to Seller within three days of receiving each report or statement. If Buyer does not deliver a written disapproval within the time allowed, Buyer shall be deemed to approve of the report or statement. If Buyer and Seller, after making a good-faith effort, cannot remove in writing the above contingencies, this offer shall become void, and all deposits shall be returned to Buyer.

10. Condition of Property

Seller represents that the heating, plumbing, air conditioning, electrical, septic, drainage, sewers, gutters and downspouts, sprinklers, as well as built-in appliances and other equipment and fixtures, are in working order. Seller agrees to maintain them in that condition, and to maintain all landscaping, grounds and pools, until possession of the property is delivered to Buyer. Seller shall, by the date of possession, replace any cracked or broken glass.

11. Foreign Investors

If Seller is a foreign person as defined in the Foreign Investment in Real Property Tax Act, Buyer shall, absent a specific exemption, have withheld in escrow ten percent (10%) of the gross sale price of the property. Buyer and Seller shall provide the escrow holder specified in Clause 2 above with all signed documentation required by the Act.

12. Rent Control

The property ☐ is ☐ is not located in a city or county subject to local rent control. A rent control ordinance may restrict the rent that can be charged for this property, limit the right of the owner to evict the occupant for other than "just cause" and control the owner's rights and responsibilities.

13. Title

At close of escrow, title to the property is to be clear of all liens and encumbrances of record except those listed in the preliminary title report and agreed to be assumed by Buyer. Any such liens or encumbrances assumed by Buyer shall be credited toward the purchase price. If Seller cannot remove liens or encumbrances not assumed by Buyer, Buyer shall have the right to cancel this contract and be refunded his/her deposit and costs of inspection reports.

14. Possession

Buyer reserves the right to inspect the property three days before the close of escrow. Seller shall deliver physical possession of property, along with alarms, alarm codes, keys, garage door openers and all other means to operate all property locks, to Buyer:

☐ at close of escrow   ☐ no later than _____ days after the close of escrow.

If Buyer agrees to let Seller continue to occupy the property after close of escrow, Seller shall deposit into escrow for Buyer a prorated share of Buyer's monthly carrying costs (principal, interest, property taxes and insurance), for each such day, subject to the terms of a written agreement, specifying rent or security deposit, authorizing a final inspection before Seller vacates and indicating the length of tenancy, signed by both parties.

15. Agency Confirmation and Commission to Brokers

The following agency relationship(s) are confirmed for this transaction:

Listing agent: _____ is the agent of: ☐ Seller exclusively   ☐ Buyer and Seller.

Selling agent: _____ is the agent of: ☐ Seller exclusively   ☐ Buyer and Seller

☐ Buyer exclusively.

NOTICE: The amount or rate of real estate commissions is not fixed by law. They are set by each Broker individually and may be negotiable between the Seller and Broker.

Buyer and Seller shall each pay only those broker's commissions for which Buyer and Seller have separately contracted in writing with a broker licensed by the California Commissioner of Real Estate.

$_____ or _____% of selling price to be paid to _____ by ☐ Seller ☐ Buyer.

$_____ or _____% of selling price to be paid to _____ by ☐ Seller ☐ Buyer.

16. Advice

If Buyer or Seller wishes advice concerning the legal or tax aspects of this transaction, Buyer or Seller shall separately contract and pay for it.

17. Backup Offer

Should Seller accept this offer as a backup offer, the following terms and conditions apply:

If Seller accepts this offer as a primary offer, he/she must do so in writing.

Buyer has 24 hours from receipt of Seller's written acceptance to ratify it in writing. If Buyer fails to do so, Buyer's offer shall be deemed withdrawn and any contractual relationship between Buyer and Seller terminated.

18. Duration of Offer

This offer is submitted to Seller by Buyer on _____, at _____.M., Pacific Time, and will be considered revoked if not accepted by Seller in writing by _____.M. on _____, or, if prior to Seller's acceptance of this offer, Buyer revokes this offer in writing.

19. Other Terms and Conditions

_____

_____

_____

_____

_____

_____

_____

_____

_____

20. Risk of Damage to Property

If, before Buyer receives title to, or possession of, the property, it is substantially damaged by fire, flood, earthquake or other cause, Buyer shall be relieved of any obligation to buy the property and shall be refunded all deposits. When Buyer receives possession of the property, Buyer assumes sole responsibility for its physical condition. Seller shall maintain fire insurance on the property until the close of escrow.

21. Liquidated Damages

If Seller accepts this offer, and Buyer later defaults on the contract, Seller shall be released from Seller's obligations under this contract. By signing their initials here, Buyer (_____) and Seller (_____) agree that if Buyer defaults, Seller shall keep all deposits, up to three percent (3%) of the purchase price stated above.

22. Mediation of Disputes

If a dispute arises out of, or relates to, this agreement, Buyer and Seller ☐ agree ☐ do not agree to first try in good faith to settle the dispute by non-binding mediation before resorting to court action or binding arbitration. To invoke mediation, one party shall notify the other of his/her intention to proceed with mediation and shall provide the name of a chosen mediator. The other party shall have seven days to respond. If he/she disagrees with the first person's chosen mediator, the parties shall ask the escrow holder to choose the mediator or to recommend someone to choose the mediator. The mediator shall conduct the mediation session or sessions within the next three weeks. Costs of mediation shall be divided equally between Buyer and Seller.

Buyer _____   Seller _____

Buyer _____   Seller _____

23. Arbitration of Disputes*

Any dispute or claim in law or equity arising out of this agreement will be decided by neutral binding arbitration in accordance with the California Arbitration Act (C.C.P. § 1280 et seq.), and not by court action except as provided by California law for judicial review of arbitration proceedings. Judgment upon the award rendered by the arbitrator may be entered in any court having jurisdiction. The parties shall have the right to discovery in accordance with Code of Procedure § 1283.05. The parties agree that the following procedure will govern the making of the award by the arbitrator: (a) the Tentative Award will be made by the arbitrator within 30 days following submission of the matter to the arbitrator; (b) the Tentative Award will explain the factual and legal basis for the arbitrator's decision as to each of the principal controverted issues; (c) the Tentative Award will be in writing unless the parties agree otherwise; provided, however, that if the hearing is concluded within one day, the Tentative Award may be made orally at the hearing in the presence of the parties. Within 15 days after the Tentative Award has been served or announced, any party may serve objections to the Tentative Award. Upon objections being timely served, the arbitrator may call for additional evidence, oral or written argument or both. If no objections are filed, the Tentative award will become final without further action by the parties or arbitrator. Within 30 days after the filing of objections, the arbitrator will either make the Tentative Award final or modify or correct the Tentative Award, which will then become final as modified or corrected. The following matters are excluded from arbitration: (a) a judicial or non-judicial foreclosure or other action or proceeding to enforce a deed of trust, mortgage, or real property sales contract as defined in Civil Code § 2985; (b) an unlawful detainer action; (c) the filing or enforcement of a mechanic's lien; (d) any matter which is within the jurisdiction of a probate court, or small claims court; or (e) an action for bodily injury or wrongful death, or for latent or patent defects to which Code of Civil Procedure § 337.1 or § 337.15 applies. The filing of a judicial action to enable the recording of a notice of pending action, for order of attachment, receivership, injunction, or other provisional remedies, will not constitute a waiver of the right to arbitrate under this provision.

NOTICE: BY INITIALLING IN THE ["AGREE"] SPACE BELOW YOU ARE AGREEING TO HAVE ANY DISPUTE ARISING OUT OF THE MATTERS INCLUDED IN THE "ARBITRATION OF DISPUTES" PROVISION DECIDED BY NEUTRAL ARBITRATION AS PROVIDED BY CALIFORNIA LAW AND YOU ARE GIVING UP ANY RIGHTS YOU MIGHT POSSESS TO HAVE THE DISPUTE LITIGATED IN A COURT OR JURY TRIAL. BY INITIALLING IN THE ["AGREE"] SPACE BELOW YOU ARE GIVING UP YOUR JUDICIAL RIGHTS TO DISCOVERY AND APPEAL, UNLESS THOSE RIGHTS ARE SPECIFICALLY INCLUDED IN THE "ARBITRATION OF DISPUTES" PROVISION. IF YOU REFUSE TO SUBMIT TO ARBITRATION AFTER AGREEING TO THIS PROVISION, YOU MAY BE COMPELLED TO ARBITRATE UNDER THE AUTHORITY OF THE CALIFORNIA CODE OF CIVIL PROCEDURE. YOUR AGREEMENT TO THIS ARBITRATION PROVISION IS VOLUNTARY.

WE HAVE READ AND UNDERSTAND THE FOREGOING AND AGREE TO SUBMIT DISPUTES ARISING OUT OF THE MATTERS INCLUDED IN THE "ARBITRATION OF DISPUTES" PROVISION TO NEUTRAL ARBITRATION.

[_____] [_____] Buyer agrees   [_____] [_____] Buyer does not agree

[_____] [_____] Seller agrees   [_____] [_____] Seller does not agree

* This clause is based on a product of Professional Publishing, with permission. To find out more about Professional Publishing, its real estate products and its forms generator software *(Formulator)*, contact them at 365 Bel Marin Keys Blvd., Suite 100, Novato, CA 94949, at 415-884-2164.

24. Attorneys' Fees

If litigation or arbitration arises from this contract, the prevailing party shall be reimbursed by the other party for reasonable attorneys' fees and court or arbitration costs.

25. Entire Agreement

This document represents the entire agreement between Buyer and Seller. Any modifications or amendments to this contract shall be made in writing, signed and dated by both parties.

26. Time is of the Essence

Time is of the essence in this transaction.

27. Disclosures

_____ By initialling here, Buyer acknowledges that he/she has received a copy of the Real Estate Transfer Disclosure Statement, Lead-Based Paint and Lead-Based Paint Hazards Disclosure (for pre-1978 houses), the Natural Hazard Disclosure Statement, and documents concerning local ordinances for smoke detectors, energy and water conservation and conservation and inspection for hazardous waste (where applicable).

_____ By initialing here, Buyer acknowledges that he/she has received the following disclosure regarding a database of registered sex offenders: "Notice: The California Department of Justice, sheriff's departments, police departments serving jurisdictions of 200,000 or more and many other local law enforcement authorities maintain for public access a database of the locations of persons required to register pursuant to paragraph (1) of subdivision (a) of Section 290.4 of the Penal Code. The database is updated on a quarterly basis and a source of information about the presence of these individuals in any neighborhood. The Department of Justice also maintains a Sex Offender Identification Line through which inquiries about individuals may be made. This is a '900' telephone service. Callers must have specific information about individuals they are checking. Information regarding neighborhoods is not available through the '900' telephone service."

Buyer shall, within _____ days of acceptance of this offer, make further inquiries at the appropriate government agencies concerning the use of the property. If such inquiries disclose conditions or information unsatisfactory to Buyer, which Seller cannot or will not correct, Buyer may cancel this agreement and be refunded the deposit. If Buyer fails to notify Seller in writing of unsatisfactory conditions or information, Buyer shall be deemed to approve of the condition.

28. Buyer's Signature

This constitutes an offer to purchase the above listed property.

Broker _____   Buyer _____

by _____   Buyer _____

Address _____   Address _____

_____   _____

Telephone _____   Telephone _____

Date _____ Time _____ M.

29. Seller's Acceptance

Subject to: _____

Seller agrees to sell the property to Buyer in accordance to the terms and conditions specified above.

Broker _____   Seller _____

by _____   Seller _____

Address _____   Address _____

_____   _____

Telephone _____   Telephone _____

Date _____ Time _____ M.

DEPOSIT RECEIPT

_____, Seller(s) of the property located at

_____ in

_____, California, hereby acknowledge receipt from,

_____, Offeror(s), the sum

of $_____ in the form of a: ☐ cashier's check   ☐ personal check   ☐ promissory note   ☐ other,

payable to _____ (escrow or title insurance company).

This check will be held uncashed by the Seller until the acceptance of this offer. If this offer is accepted, the deposit shall

be delivered to the mutually agreed escrow holder named above and applied toward the down payment. This deposit

will be returned to the Offeror if this offer is not accepted.

_____   _____
Seller's signature   Date

_____   _____
Seller's signature   Date

SHORT FORM COUNTEROFFER

_____

_____, Seller(s) of the real property

at _____

_____, California, accept(s) the offer

to purchase the property dated _____ made by _____

_____ with the following exceptions:

_____   _____   _____
Seller's signature   Date   Time

_____   _____   _____
Seller's signature   Date   Time

COUNTEROFFER TO PURCHASE REAL PROPERTY

Heading

Property address, including county: _____

_____

Date: _____.

_____ (Buyer) makes this offer to

_____ (Seller), to purchase

the property described above, for the sum of _____ dollars ($_____).

Buyer includes a deposit, in the amount of _____ dollars ($_____).

evidenced by ☐ cash ☐ cashier's check ☐ personal check ☐ promissory note ☐ other,

payable to _____ to be held uncashed until the acceptance of this offer, and

to be increased to 3% of the purchase amount no later than _____ days after this offer is accepted. If this offer is

accepted, the deposit shall be delivered to a mutually agreed escrow holder and applied toward the down payment.

1. Financial Terms

This offer is contingent upon Buyer securing financing as specified in items D, E, F and G, below, within _____ days

from acceptance of this offer.

$_____ A. DEPOSIT to be applied toward the down payment.

$_____ B. DEPOSIT INCREASE to be applied toward the down payment by _____ (date).

$_____ C. DOWN PAYMENT balance, in cash, to be paid into escrow on or before the close of escrow.

$_____ D. FIRST LOAN—NEW LOAN. Buyer shall obtain a new loan, amortized over not fewer than

_____ years. Buyer's financing shall be

☐ Conventional _____ (name of lender, if known)

☐ Private _____ (name of lender, if known)

☐ Government (specify): ☐ VA   ☐ FHA   ☐ Cal-Vet   ☐ CHFA

☐ Other: _____

Buyer's mortgage shall be ☐ at a maximum fixed rate of _____% or ☐ an adjustable

rate loan with a maximum beginning rate of _____%, with the life-of-the-loan cap not to

exceed _____ percentage points and the periodic cap not to be adjusted more frequently

than _____ . Maximum monthly loan payment including principal, interest

and, if applicable, private mortgage insurance (PMI), during the first year of the loan

agreement, shall be $_____. Buyer shall pay a loan origination fee (points) of not more

than _____% of the loan amount and application and appraisal fees of not more than

$_____.

$_____ E. FIRST LOAN—EXISTING LOAN. Buyer shall ☐ assume ☐ buy subject to an existing

loan under the same terms and conditions that Seller has with _____

_____, the present lender. The approximate remaining balance is

$_____, at the current rate of interest of _____% on a ☐ fixed ☐ adjustable rate

loan, or a remaining term of approximately _____ years, secured by a First Deed of Trust.

$_____ F. SECOND LOAN—NEW LOAN. Buyer shall obtain a new loan, amortized over not fewer

than _____ years. Buyer's financing shall be:

☐ Conventional _____ (name of lender, if known)

☐ Private _____ (name of lender, if known)

☐ Government (specify): ☐ VA   ☐ FHA   ☐ Cal-Vet   ☐ CHFA

☐ Other: _____

Buyer's mortgage shall be ☐ at a maximum fixed rate of _____% or ☐ an adjustable rate loan with a maximum beginning rate of _____%, with the life-of-the-loan cap not to exceed_____ percentage points and the periodic cap not to be adjusted more frequently than _____. Maximum monthly loan payment including principal, interest and, if applicable, private mortgage insurance (PMI), during the first year of the loan agreement, shall be $_____. Buyer shall pay a loan origination fee (points) of not more than _____% of the loan amount and application and appraisal fees of not more than $_____.

$_____ G. SECOND LOAN—EXISTING LOAN. Buyer shall ☐ assume ☐ buy subject to an existing loan under the same terms and conditions that Seller has with _____ _____, the present lender. The approximate remaining balance is $_____, at the current rate of interest of _____% on a ☐ fixed ☐ adjustable rate loan, for a remaining term of approximately _____ years, secured by a Second Deed of Trust.

$_____ H. TOTAL PURCHASE PRICE, EXCLUDING EXPENSES OF SALE AND CLOSING COSTS.

Buyer shall submit complete loan application and financial statement to lender within five days after acceptance. If Buyer, after making a good-faith effort, does not secure financing by the time specified, this contract shall become void, and all deposits shall be returned to Buyer.

In the event of FHA or VA financing, Buyer shall not be obligated to complete the purchase, nor shall Buyer forfeit the deposit, if the offer price exceeds the property's FHA or VA appraised value. Buyer shall, however, have the option of proceeding with the purchase from any above-named lender or a different lender without regard to the appraised value.

2. Escrow

Buyer and Seller shall deliver signed escrow instructions to _____
_____ escrow agent located at
_____, within _____ days of
acceptance of this offer. Escrow shall close within _____ days of acceptance of this offer. A deed shall be recorded in favor of Buyer at the close of escrow.

3. Pre-payment Penalty and Assumption Fee

Seller shall pay any pre-payment penalty or other fees imposed by any existing lender who is paid off during escrow. Buyer shall pay any pre-payment penalty, assumption fee or other fee which becomes due after the close of escrow on any loans assumed from Seller.

4. Expenses of Sale

Expenses of sale, settlement costs and closing costs shall be paid for as follows:

	Buyer	Seller	Share Equally	
A.	☐	☐	☐	Escrow fees
B.	☐	☐	☐	Title search
C.	☐	☐	☐	Title insurance for buyer/owner
D.	☐	☐	☐	Title insurance for buyer's lender
E.	☐	☐	☐	Deed preparation fee

F.	☐	☐	☐	Notary fee
G.	☐	☐	☐	Recording fee
H.	☐	☐	☐	Attorney's fee (if attorney hired to clarify title)
I.	☐	☐	☐	Documentary transfer tax
J.	☐	☐	☐	City transfer tax
K	☐	☐	☐	Pest control inspection report
L.	☐	☐	☐	General contractor report
M.	☐	☐	☐	Roof inspection report
N.				Other inspections (specify):

N.
1. ☐ ☐ ☐

_____   2. ☐ ☐ ☐

_____   3. ☐ ☐ ☐

_____

O.	☐	☐	☐	One-year home warranty
P.				Other (specify):

P.
1. ☐ ☐ ☐

_____   2. ☐ ☐ ☐

_____   3. ☐ ☐ ☐

_____

5. Property Tax and Insurance Prorations; Non-Callable Bonds

Seller shall be responsible for payment of Seller's prorated share of real estate taxes accrued until the deed transferring title to Buyer is recorded. Buyer understands that the property shall be reassessed upon change of ownership and that Buyer shall be sent a supplemental tax bill which may reflect an increase in taxes based on property value.

Any fire insurance policy carried over from Seller to Buyer and any homeowners' association fees shall be prorated, that is, Seller shall pay the portion of the premiums and fees while title is in Seller's name and Buyer shall pay the portion of the premiums and fees while title is in Buyer's name.

Buyer agrees to assume non-callable assessment bond liens (those which cannot be paid off by Seller) as follows:

_____

6. Fixtures

All fixtures permanently attached to the property, including built-in appliances, electrical, plumbing, light and heating fixtures, garage door openers, attached carpets and other floor coverings, and window shades or blinds, are included in the sale except: _____

_____

_____

_____

_____

7. Personal Property

The following items of personal property are included in this sale:

☐ Stove	☐ Oven	☐ Refrigerator	☐ Washer
☐ Dryer	☐ Freezer	☐ Trash Compactor	☐ Dishwasher

_____

_____

8. Inspection Contingencies

This offer is conditioned upon Buyer's written approval of the following inspection reports. All reports shall be carried out within _____ days of acceptance. Buyer shall deliver written approval or disapproval to Seller within 3 days of receiving each report. If Buyer does not deliver a written disapproval within the time allowed, Buyer shall be deemed to approve of the report.

Seller is to provide reasonable access to the property to Buyer, his/her agent, all inspectors and representatives of lending institutions to conduct appraisals.

A. ☐ Pest control report

B. ☐ General contractor report as to the general physical condition of the property including, but not limited to, heating and plumbing, electrical systems, solar energy systems, roof and appliances

C. ☐ Plumbing contractor report

D. ☐ Soils engineer report

E. ☐ Energy conservation inspection report in accordance with local ordinances

F. ☐ Geologist report

G. ☐ Environmental inspection report

H. ☐ City or county inspection report

I. ☐ Roof inspection report

If Buyer and Seller, after making a good-faith effort, cannot remove in writing the above contingencies by the time specified, this contract shall become void, and all deposits shall be returned to Buyer.

9. Other Contingencies

This offer is contingent upon the following:

A. ☐ Buyer receiving and approving preliminary title report within _____ days of acceptance of this offer

B. ☐ Seller furnishing a Residential Building Record Report indicating _____ legal units within _____ days of acceptance

C. ☐ Seller furnishing declaration of restrictions, CC&Rs, bylaws, articles of incorporation, rules and regulations currently in force and a financial statement of the owners' association within _____ days of acceptance

D. ☐ Sale of Buyer's current residence, the address of which is _____ , _____ by _____

E. ☐ Seller furnishing rental agreements within _____ days of acceptance

F. ☐ Other: _____

Buyer shall deliver written approval or disapproval to Seller within three days of receiving each report or statement. If Buyer does not deliver a written disapproval within the time allowed, Buyer shall be deemed to approve of the report or statement. If Buyer and Seller, after making a good-faith effort, cannot remove in writing the above contingencies, this offer shall become void, and all deposits shall be returned to Buyer.

10. Condition of Property

Seller represents that the heating, plumbing, air conditioning, electrical, septic, drainage, sewers, gutters and downspouts, sprinklers, as well as built-in appliances and other equipment and fixtures, are in working order. Seller agrees to maintain them in that condition, and to maintain all landscaping, grounds and pools, until possession of the property is delivered to Buyer. Seller shall, by the date of possession, replace any cracked or broken glass.

11. Foreign Investors

If Seller is a foreign person as defined in the Foreign Investment in Real Property Tax Act, Buyer shall, absent a specific exemption, have withheld in escrow ten percent (10%) of the gross sale price of the property. Buyer and Seller shall provide the escrow holder specified in Clause 2 above with all signed documentation required by the Act.

12. Rent Control

The property ☐ is ☐ is   not located in a city or county subject to local rent control. A rent control ordinance may restrict the rent that can be charged for this property, limit the right of the owner to evict the occupant for other than "just cause" and control the owner's rights and responsibilities.

13. Title

At close of escrow, title to the property is to be clear of all liens and encumbrances of record except those listed in the preliminary title report and agreed to be assumed by Buyer. Any such liens or encumbrances assumed by Buyer shall be credited toward the purchase price. If Seller cannot remove liens or encumbrances not assumed by Buyer, Buyer shall have the right to cancel this contract and be refunded his/her deposit and costs of inspection reports.

14. Possession

Buyer reserves the right to inspect the property three days before the close of escrow. Seller shall deliver physical possession of property, along with alarms, alarm codes, keys, garage door openers and all other means to operate all property locks, to Buyer:

☐ at close of escrow   ☐ no later than _____ days after the close of escrow.

If Buyer agrees to let Seller continue to occupy the property after close of escrow, Seller shall deposit into escrow for Buyer a prorated share of Buyer's monthly carrying costs (principal, interest, property taxes and insurance), for each such day, subject to the terms of a written agreement, specifying rent or security deposit, authorizing a final inspection before Seller vacates and indicating the length of tenancy, signed by both parties.

15. Agency Confirmation and Commission to Brokers

The following agency relationship(s) are confirmed for this transaction:

Listing agent: _____ is the agent of: ☐ Seller exclusively   ☐ Buyer and Seller.

Selling agent: _____ is the agent of: ☐ Seller exclusively   ☐ Buyer and Seller

☐ Buyer exclusively.

NOTICE: The amount or rate of real estate commissions is not fixed by law. They are set by each Broker individually and may be negotiable between the Seller and Broker.

Buyer and Seller shall each pay only those broker's commissions for which Buyer and Seller have separately contracted in writing with a broker licensed by the California Commissioner of Real Estate.

$_____ or ____% of selling price to be paid to _____ by ☐ Seller ☐ Buyer.

$_____ or ____% of selling price to be paid to _____ by ☐ Seller ☐ Buyer.

16. Advice

If Buyer or Seller wishes advice concerning the legal or tax aspects of this transaction, Buyer or Seller shall separately contract and pay for it.

17. Backup Offer

Should Seller accept this offer as a backup offer, the following terms and conditions apply:

If Seller accepts this offer as a primary offer, he/she must do so in writing.

Buyer has 24 hours from receipt of Seller's written acceptance to ratify it in writing. If Buyer fails to do so, Buyer's offer shall be deemed withdrawn and any contractual relationship between Buyer and Seller terminated.

18. Duration of Offer

This offer is submitted to Seller by Buyer on _____ , at _____ .M., Pacific Time, and will be considered revoked if not accepted by Seller in writing by _____ .M. on , _____ or, if prior to Seller's acceptance of this offer, Buyer revokes this offer in writing.

19. Other Terms and Conditions

_____

_____

_____

_____

_____

_____

_____

_____

_____

20. Risk of Damage to Property

If, before Buyer receives title to, or possession of, the property, it is substantially damaged by fire, flood, earthquake or other cause, Buyer shall be relieved of any obligation to buy the property and shall be refunded all deposits. When Buyer receives possession of the property, Buyer assumes sole responsibility for its physical condition. Seller shall maintain fire insurance on the property until the close of escrow.

21. Liquidated Damages

If Seller accepts this offer, and Buyer later defaults on the contract, Seller shall be released from Seller's obligations under this contract. By signing their initials here, Buyer (_____) and Seller (_____) agree that if Buyer defaults, Seller shall keep all deposits, up to three percent (3%) of the purchase price stated above.

22. Mediation of Disputes

If a dispute arises out of, or relates to, this agreement, Buyer and Seller ☐ agree ☐ do not agree to first try in good faith to settle the dispute by non-binding mediation before resorting to court action or binding arbitration. To invoke mediation, one party shall notify the other of his/her intention to proceed with mediation and shall provide the name of a chosen mediator. The other party shall have seven days to respond. If he/she disagrees with the first person's chosen mediator, the parties shall ask the escrow holder to choose the mediator or to recommend someone to choose the mediator. The mediator shall conduct the mediation session or sessions within the next three weeks. Costs of mediation shall be divided equally between Buyer and Seller.

Buyer _____   Seller _____

Buyer _____   Seller _____

23. Arbitration of Disputes*

Any dispute or claim in law or equity arising out of this agreement will be decided by neutral binding arbitration in accordance with the California Arbitration Act (C.C.P. § 1280 et seq.), and not by court action except as provided by California law for judicial review of arbitration proceedings. Judgment upon the award rendered by the arbitrator may be entered in any court having jurisdiction. The parties shall have the right to discovery in accordance with Code of Procedure § 1283.05. The parties agree that the following procedure will govern the making of the award by the arbitrator: (a) the Tentative Award will be made by the arbitrator within 30 days following submission of the matter to the arbitrator; (b) the Tentative Award will explain the factual and legal basis for the arbitrator's decision as to each of the principal controverted issues; (c) the Tentative Award will be in writing unless the parties agree otherwise; provided, however, that if the hearing is concluded within one day, the Tentative Award may be made orally at the hearing in the presence of the parties. Within 15 days after the Tentative Award has been served or announced, any party may serve objections to the Tentative Award. Upon objections being timely served, the arbitrator may call for additional evidence, oral or written argument or both. If no objections are filed, the Tentative award will become final without further action by the parties or arbitrator. Within 30 days after the filing of objections, the arbitrator will either make the Tentative Award final or modify or correct the Tentative Award, which will then become final as modified or corrected. The following matters are excluded from arbitration: (a) a judicial or non-judicial foreclosure or other action or proceeding to enforce a deed of trust, mortgage, or real property sales contract as defined in Civil Code § 2985; (b) an unlawful detainer action; (c) the filing or enforcement of a mechanic's lien; (d) any matter which is within the jurisdiction of a probate court, or small claims court; or (e) an action for bodily injury or wrongful death, or for latent or patent defects to which Code of Civil Procedure § 337.1 or § 337.15 applies. The filing of a judicial action to enable the recording of a notice of pending action, for order of attachment, receivership, injunction, or other provisional remedies, will not constitute a waiver of the right to arbitrate under this provision.

NOTICE: BY INITIALLING IN THE ["AGREE"] SPACE BELOW YOU ARE AGREEING TO HAVE ANY DISPUTE ARISING OUT OF THE MATTERS INCLUDED IN THE "ARBITRATION OF DISPUTES" PROVISION DECIDED BY NEUTRAL ARBITRATION AS PROVIDED BY CALIFORNIA LAW AND YOU ARE GIVING UP ANY RIGHTS YOU MIGHT POSSESS TO HAVE THE DISPUTE LITIGATED IN A COURT OR JURY TRIAL. BY INITIALLING IN THE ["AGREE"] SPACE BELOW YOU ARE GIVING UP YOUR JUDICIAL RIGHTS TO DISCOVERY AND APPEAL, UNLESS THOSE RIGHTS ARE SPECIFICALLY INCLUDED IN THE "ARBITRATION OF DISPUTES" PROVISION. IF YOU REFUSE TO SUBMIT TO ARBITRATION AFTER AGREEING TO THIS PROVISION, YOU MAY BE COMPELLED TO ARBITRATE UNDER THE AUTHORITY OF THE CALIFORNIA CODE OF CIVIL PROCEDURE. YOUR AGREEMENT TO THIS ARBITRATION PROVISION IS VOLUNTARY.

WE HAVE READ AND UNDERSTAND THE FOREGOING AND AGREE TO SUBMIT DISPUTES ARISING OUT OF THE MATTERS INCLUDED IN THE "ARBITRATION OF DISPUTES" PROVISION TO NEUTRAL ARBITRATION.

[_____] [_____] Buyer agrees   [_____] [_____] Buyer does not agree

[_____] [_____] Seller agrees   [_____] [_____] Seller does not agree

*This clause is based on a product of Professional Publishing, with permission. To find out more about Professional Publishing, its real estate products and its forms generator software *(Formulator)*, contact them at 365 Bel Marin Keys Blvd., Suite 100, Novato, CA 94949, at 415-884-2164.

24. Attorneys' Fees

If litigation or arbitration arises from this contract, the prevailing party shall be reimbursed by the other party for reasonable attorneys' fees and court or arbitration costs.

25. Entire Agreement

This document represents the entire agreement between Buyer and Seller. Any modifications or amendments to this contract shall be made in writing, signed and dated by both parties.

26. Time is of the Essence

Time is of the essence in this transaction.

27. Disclosures

_____ By initialling here, Buyer acknowledges that he/she has received a copy of the Real Estate Transfer Disclosure Statement, Lead-Based Paint and Lead-Based Paint Hazards Disclosure (for pre-1978 houses), the Natural Hazard Disclosure Statement, and documents concerning local ordinances for smoke detectors, energy and water conservation and conservation and inspection for hazardous waste (where applicable).

_____ By initialling here, Buyer acknowledges that he/she has received the following disclosure regarding a database of registered sex offenders: "Notice: The California Department of Justice, sheriff's departments, police departments serving jurisdictions of 200,000 or more and many other local law enforcement authorities maintain for public access a database of the locations of persons required to register pursuant to paragraph (1) of subdivision (a) of Section 290.4 of the Penal Code. The database is updated on a quarterly basis and a source of information about the presence of these individuals in any neighborhood. The Department of Justice also maintains a Sex Offender Identification Line through which inquiries about individuals may be made. This is a '900' telephone service. Callers must have specific information about individuals they are checking. Information regarding neighborhoods is not available through the '900' telephone service."

Buyer shall, within _____ days of acceptance of this offer, make further inquiries at the appropriate government agencies concerning the use of the property. If such inquiries disclose conditions or information unsatisfactory to Buyer, which Seller cannot or will not correct, Buyer may cancel this agreement and be refunded the deposit. If Buyer fails to notify Seller in writing of unsatisfactory conditions or information, Buyer shall be deemed to approve of the condition.

28. Buyer's Signature

This constitutes an offer to purchase the above listed property.

Broker _____   Buyer _____

by _____   Buyer _____

Address _____   Address _____

_____   _____

Telephone _____   Telephone _____

Date _____ Time _____ M.

29. Seller's Acceptance

Subject to: _____

Seller agrees to sell the property to Buyer in accordance to the terms and conditions specified above.

Broker _____   Seller _____

by _____   Seller _____

Address _____   Address _____

_____   _____

Telephone _____   Telephone _____

Date _____ Time _____ M.

ACCEPTANCE OF PURCHASE OFFER

_____

_____, the owner(s) of the

property at _____

_____ in the city of _____,

county of _____, California, hereby accept the offer to purchase the

property made on _____, by _____

_____.

_____   _____

Seller's signature   Date

_____   _____

Seller's signature   Date

COUNTEROFFER REVOCATION

_____

_____, the seller(s)

of the property at _____

_____ in the city of _____,

county of, _____ California, hereby revoke the counteroffer made on

_____, to _____

_____ buyer(s) and hereby authorize the escrow holders to return to buyer(s)

any deposit funds tendered by buyer(s).

_____   _____
Seller's signature   Date

_____   _____
Seller's signature   Date

Deposit received by:

_____   _____
Buyer's signature   Date

_____   _____
Buyer's signature   Date

SELLER'S DEMAND FOR REMOVAL OF CONTINGENCIES

Under the terms of the contract dated _____, between

_____ (Buyer) and

_____ (Seller) for

the purchase of the real property at _____

_____ (address), Seller

hereby demands that Buyer remove the following contingencies specified in Clause(s) _____ of the contract:

_____

_____

_____

_____

_____

_____

_____

_____

_____

_____

_____ within

☐ ninety-six (96) hours from receipt of this demand, if personally delivered.

☐ five (5) days from mailing this demand, if mailed by certified mail.

If Buyer does not remove this contingency within the time specified, the contract shall become void. Seller shall promptly return Buyer's deposit upon Buyer's execution of a release, releasing Buyer and Seller from all obligations under the contract.

_____   _____
Seller's signature   Date

_____   _____
Seller's signature   Date

Personally delivered on: _____

Mailed by certified mail on: _____

CONTINGENCY RELEASE

_____, (Buyer) of the

property at _____

_____ (address), hereby

removes the following contingency(ies) from the purchase contract dated _____:

_____

_____

_____

_____

_____

_____

_____

_____

_____

_____

_____

_____

_____

_____

If this release is based on accepting any inspection report, a copy of the report, signed by Buyer, is attached, and Buyer

releases Seller from liability for any physical defects disclosed by the attached report.

_____   _____
Buyer's signature   Date

_____   _____
Buyer's signature   Date

_____   _____
Seller's signature   Date

_____   _____
Seller's signature   Date

EXTENDING TIME TO MEET CONTINGENCIES

The material set out below is hereby made a part of the offer dated _____,

from _____ (Buyer) to

_____ (Seller) for

the purchase of the real property located at: _____

_____

The final date for Buyer's removal of all contingencies set out in Clause _____ of the contract, is hereby extended until

_____ (month, day and year), at _____ .M. (time).

_____   _____
Buyer's signature   Date

_____   _____
Buyer's signature   Date

_____   _____
Seller's signature   Date

_____   _____
Seller's signature   Date

RELEASE OF REAL ESTATE PURCHASE CONTRACT

_____ (Seller)

and _____ (Buyer)

hereby mutually release each other from any and all claims with respect to the real estate purchase contract dated

_____, for the property located at _____

_____.

It is the intent of this release to declare all rights and obligations arising out of the real estate purchase contract null and void.

☐ Buyer has received his/her deposit.

☐ Seller has directed the escrow holder to return Buyer's deposit.

_____   _____
Seller's signature   Date

_____   _____
Seller's signature   Date

_____   _____
Buyer's signature   Date

_____   _____
Buyer's signature   Date

LEASE-OPTION CONTRACT

Clause 1.   **Identification of Owner and Tenant**

This Agreement to create a Lease with Option to Purchase is made and entered into on _____,

between _____ (Owner or Lessor/Optionor) and

_____ (Tenant or Lessee/Optionee).

Clause 2.   **Identification of the Premises**

Subject to the terms and conditions below, Owner rents to Tenant, and Tenant rents from Owner, for residential purposes

only, the premises at _____

_____, California.

Clause 3.   **Defining the Term of the Tenancy**

The term of the rental shall begin on _____, and shall continue for a period of _____ months,

expiring on _____.

Should Tenant vacate before expiration of the term, Tenant shall be liable for the balance of the rent for the remainder of

the term, less any rent Owner collects or could have collected from a replacement tenant by reasonably attempting to re-

rent. Tenant who vacates before expiration of the term is also responsible for Owner's costs of advertising for a replace-

ment tenant.

Clause 4.   **Amount and Schedule for the Payment of Rent**

On signing this Agreement, Tenant shall pay to Owner the sum of \$_____ as rent, payable in advance, for the

period of _____, through _____. Thereafter, Tenant shall pay to Owner a

monthly rent of \$_____, payable in advance on the first day of each month, except when the first falls on a

weekend or legal holiday, in which case rent is due on the next business day. Rent shall be paid to

_____ at _____, California.

Clause 5.   **Late Fees**

If Tenant fails to pay the rent in full within five days after it is due, Tenant shall pay Owner a late charge of

\$_____ plus \$_____ for each additional day that the rent continues to be unpaid. The total late

charge for any one month shall not exceed \$_____. By this provision, Owner does not waive the right to insist

on payment of the rent in full on the day it is due.

Clause 6.   **Returned Check Charges**

In the event any check offered by Tenant to Owner in payment of rent or any other amount due under this Agreement is

returned for lack of sufficient funds, Tenant shall pay to Owner a returned check charge in the amount of

\$_____.

Clause 7.   Amount and Payment of Deposits

On signing this Agreement, Tenant shall pay to Owner the sum of $_____, which is equal to two months' rent, as and for security as that term is defined by Section 1950.5 of the California Civil Code, namely any payment, fee, deposit or charge to be used to compensate Owner for:

(a) Tenant's default in the payment of rent

(b) repair of damages to the premises, exclusive of ordinary wear and tear, or

(c) cleaning of the premises on termination of tenancy.

Tenant may not, without Owner's prior written consent, apply this security deposit to rent or to any other sum due under this Agreement.

Within three weeks after Tenant has vacated the premises, Owner shall furnish Tenant with an itemized written statement of the basis for, and the amount of, any of the security deposit retained by the Owner, including accounting for any interest required by local security deposit laws. Owner may withhold only that portion of Tenant's security deposit:

(a) to remedy any default by Tenant in the payment of rent

(b) to repair damages to the premises exclusive of ordinary wear and tear, or

(c) to clean the premises, if necessary.

Clause 8.   Utilities

Tenants shall be responsible for payment of all utility charges, except for the following, which shall be paid by Owner:

_____

_____

_____

_____ .

Clause 9.   Prohibition of Assignment and Subletting

Tenant shall not sublet any part of the premises or assign this lease without the prior written consent of Owner.

Clause 10. Condition of the Premises

Tenant acknowledges that (s)he has examined the premises, including appliances, fixtures, carpets, drapes and paint, and has found them to be in good, safe and clean condition and repair, except as otherwise noted on the written inventory of furniture and furnishings on the premises which Tenant has completed and given Owner, a copy of which Tenant acknowledges receipt of, and which is deemed to be incorporated into this Agreement by this reference.

Tenant agrees to:

(a) keep the premises in good order and repair and, upon termination of tenancy, to return the premises to Owner in a condition identical to that which existed when Tenant took occupancy, except for ordinary wear and tear

(b) immediately notify Owner of any defects or dangerous conditions in and about the premises of which (s)he becomes aware, and

(c) reimburse Owner, on demand by Owner or his or her agent, for the cost of any repairs to the premises damaged by Tenant or his or her guests or invitees.

The parties agree that the following appliances and fixtures will be included with the property:

☐ for sale if the option is exercised: _____

_____

☐ for rent only during the period of the lease: _____.

Clause 11. Possession of Premises

The failure of Tenant to take possession of the premises shall not relieve him or her of the obligation to pay rent. In the event Owner is unable to deliver possession of the premises to Tenant for any reason not within Owner's control, including but not limited to failure of prior occupants to vacate as agreed or required by law, or partial or complete destruction of the premises, Owner shall not be liable to Tenant, except for the return of all sums previously paid by Tenant to Owner, in the event Tenant chooses to terminate this Agreement because of Owner's inability to deliver possession.

Clause 12. Pets

No animal or other pet shall be kept on the premises without Owner's prior written consent, except: properly trained dogs needed by blind, deaf or physically disabled persons, and

☐ _____, under the following conditions:

_____

_____.

Clause 13. Owner's Access for Inspection and Emergency

Owner or Owner's agents may enter the premises in the event of an emergency, or to make repairs or improvements, supply agreed services, or exhibit the premises to prospective purchasers or tenants. Except in case of emergency, Owner shall give Tenant reasonable notice of intent to enter and shall enter only during regular business hours of Monday through Friday from 9:00 A.M. to 6:00 P.M. and Saturday from 9:00 A.M. to noon. In order to facilitate Owner's right of access, Tenant shall not, without Owner's prior written consent, alter or re-key any lock to the premises or install any burglar alarm system. At all times Owner or Owner's agent shall be provided with a key or keys capable of unlocking all such locks and gaining entry. Tenant further agrees to provide instructions on how to disarm any burglar alarm system should Owner so request.

Clause 14.   Prohibitions Against Violating Laws and Causing Disturbances

Tenant shall be entitled to quiet enjoyment of the premises. Tenant shall not use the premises in such a way as to violate any law or ordinance, including laws prohibiting the use, possession or sale of illegal drugs, commit waste or nuisance, or annoy, disturb, inconvenience or interfere with the quiet enjoyment of any other tenant or nearby resident.

Clause 15.   Repairs and Alterations

Except as provided by law or as authorized by the prior written consent of Owner, Tenant shall not make any repairs or alterations to the premises.

Clause 16.   Damage to Premises, Financial Responsibility and Renter's Insurance

In the event the premises are damaged by fire or other casualty covered by insurance, Owner shall have the option either to:

(a)   repair such damage and restore the premises, this Agreement continuing in full force and effect, or

(b)   give notice to Tenant at any time within thirty (30) days after such damage terminating this Agreement as of a date to be specified in such notice. In the event of the giving of such notice, this Agreement shall expire and all rights of Tenant pursuant to this Agreement shall terminate.

Owner shall not be required to make any repair or replacement of any property brought onto the premises by Tenant.

Tenant agrees to accept financial responsibility for any damage to the premises from fire or casualty caused by Tenant's negligence. Tenant shall carry a standard renter's insurance policy from a recognized insurance firm, or, as an alternative, warrant that (s)he will be financially responsible for losses not covered by Owner's fire and extended coverage insurance policy. Repair of damage or plumbing stoppages caused by Tenant's negligence or misuse will be paid for by Tenant.

Clause 17.   Option Terms

Tenant shall have the option to purchase the property for the sum of _____ and no/100 dollars ($_____), providing the Tenant exercises this option by giving written notice of that exercise to Owner at the above address, not later than _____, and completes the purchase not later than ninety (90) days from the above notice. The purchase shall be completed according to the terms of a purchase contract and escrow instructions mutually executed by the parties within thirty (30) days of Tenant's notice to Owner that Tenant intends to exercise the option.

Clause 18.   Right to Record Option

This option may be recorded in favor of Tenant (Optionee) and for that purpose Owner (Optionor) agrees to sign this Agreement in the presence of a notary.

Clause 19. Right to Assign or Sell Option

This option may be assigned or sold by Tenant to another party. For this right, Tenant agrees to:

a. ☐ pay Owner, with this agreement, the sum of _____ and no/100 dollars

($_____), which is not refundable to Tenant under any circumstance, even if Tenant does not exercise this

option.

b. ☐ pay Owner, in addition to monthly rent stated above, the sum of _____ and no/100 dollars

($_____), each month, beginning on _____ and ending on _____.

This sum is not to be considered as rent but is to be in consideration of the right of option, and is not refundable to the Tenant

under any circumstance, even if Tenant does not exercise the option.

The parties agree that any sums paid by Tenant to Owner under Clause 21 below, shall be credited against the purchase

price in the event Tenant exercises the option to buy.

Clause 20. Costs of Exercising Option

The parties agree that general financing and transaction costs at the time the option is exercised cannot be estimated in

advance, and are therefore not contingencies of this contract. However, the parties agree that at the time this option is

exercised:

- Expenses of owning the property (real estate taxes, insurance and special assessments) shall be prorated or divided between the parties as to the date of close of escrow.

- Tenant shall order a title search on the property and pay for title insurance satisfactory to Tenant and any lenders involved in the purchase transaction, and will pay for any necessary escrow, notary and recording fees. Tenant shall have ten days from the exercise of the option in which to report in writing any objections to the condition of title, and Owner shall make every effort in good faith to remove such exceptions to clear title within ten days thereafter, or else this contract may be cancelled at the option of either party.

- Tenant may, at any time prior to the exercise of this option, have the property inspected at his or her own expense by a licensed general contractor, pest control operator or any other professional deemed necessary to advise Tenant concerning the physical condition of the property. If Tenant notifies Owner in writing, on or before the above date for exercise of the option, of objections on the part of Tenant concerning the condition of the property, and the parties cannot reach an agreement concerning these objections, the Tenant need not exercise this option.

Clause 21. Summary of Funds Received From Tenant by Owner

Nonrefundable option fee	$_____
Refundable security deposit	$_____
Nonrefundable rent	$_____
TOTAL	$_____

Clause 22. Time

Time shall be of the essence of this agreement.

Clause 23. Entire Agreement

This document constitutes the entire Agreement between the parties, and no promises or representations, other than those contained here and implied in law, have been made by Owner or Tenant.

Clause 24. Additional Provisions

_____

_____

_____

_____

_____

_____

_____

_____

_____

_____

_____

_____

_____

_____

_____

_____

_____

_____

_____   _____
Owner or Lessor/Optionee Date   Date

_____   _____
Owner or Lessor/Optionee Date   Date

_____   _____
Tenant or Lessee/Optionee   Date

_____   _____
Tenant or Lessee/Optionee   Date

Index

CATALOG

...more from Nolo Press

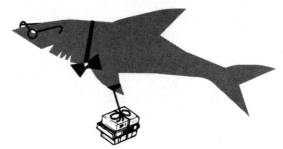

⊡ Book with disk

⊙ Book with CD-ROM

CALL 800-992-6656 OR USE THE ORDER FORM IN THE BACK OF THE BOOK

	PRICE	CODE

ESTATE PLANNING & PROBATE

	PRICE	CODE
8 Ways to Avoid Probate (Quick & Legal Series)	$15.95	PRO8
9 Ways to Avoid Estate Taxes (Quick & Legal Series)	$22.95	ESTX
How to Probate an Estate (California Edition)	$39.95	PAE
Make Your Own Living Trust	$24.95	LITR
Nolo's Law Form Kit: Wills	$14.95	KWL
Nolo's Will Book (Book w/Disk—PC)	$29.95	SWIL
Plan Your Estate	$24.95	NEST
Quick & Legal Will Book (Quick & Legal Series)	$15.95	QUIC

FAMILY MATTERS

	PRICE	CODE
Child Custody: Building Parenting Agreements That Work	$26.95	CUST
The Complete IEP Guide	$24.95	IEP
Divorce & Money: How to Make the Best Financial Decisions During Divorce	$26.95	DIMO
Do Your Own Divorce in Oregon	$19.95	ODIV
Get a Life: You Don't Need a Million to Retire Well	$18.95	LIFE
The Guardianship Book (California Edition)	$39.95	GB
How to Adopt Your Stepchild in California	$34.95	ADOP
How to Raise or Lower Child Support in California (Quick & Legal Series)	$19.95	CHLD
A Legal Guide for Lesbian and Gay Couples	$25.95	LG
The Living Together Kit	$29.95	LTK
Nolo's Pocket Guide to Family Law	$14.95	FLD
Using Divorce Mediation: Save Your Money & Your Sanity	$21.95	UDMD

GOING TO COURT

	PRICE	CODE
Beta Your Ticket: Go To Court and Win! (National Edition)	$19.95	BEYT
Collect Your Court Judgment (California Edition)	$29.95	JUDG
The Criminal Law Handbook: Know Your Rights, Survive the System	$24.95	KYR
Everybody's Guide to Small Claims Court (National Edition)	$18.95	NSCC
Everybody's Guide to Small Claims Court in California	$18.95	CSCC
Fight Your Ticket ... and Win! (California Edition)	$19.95	FYT
How to Change Your Name in California	$34.95	NAME
How to Mediate Your Dispute	$18.95	MEDI
How to Seal Your Juvenile & Criminal Records (California Edition)	$24.95	CRIM
How to Sue For Up to $25,000...and Win!	$29.95	MUNI
Mad at Your Lawyer	$21.95	MAD
Represent Yourself in Court: How to Prepare & Try a Winning Case	$29.95	RYC

HOMEOWNERS, LANDLORDS & TENANTS

	PRICE	CODE
Contractors' and Homeowners' Guide to Mechanics' Liens (Book w/Disk—PC)	$39.95	MIEN
The Deeds Book (California Edition)	$24.95	DEED
Dog Law	$14.95	DOG
Every Landlord's Legal Guide (National Edition, Book w/Disk—PC)	$34.95	ELLI
Every Tenant's Legal Guide	$26.95	EVTEN
For Sale by Owner in California	$24.95	FSBO
How to Buy a House in California	$24.95	BHCA
The Landlord's Law Book, Vol. 1: Rights & Responsibilities (California Edition)	$34.95	LBRT
The Landlord's Law Book, Vol. 2: Evictions (California Edition)	$34.95	LBEV
Leases & Rental Agreements (Quick & Legal Series)	$18.95	LEAR
Neighbor Law: Fences, Trees, Boundaries & Noise	$17.95	NEI
Renters' Rights (National Edition—Quick & Legal Series))	$15.95	RENT
Stop Foreclosure Now in California	$29.95	CLOS
Tenants' Rights (California Edition)	$21.95	CTEN

HUMOR

	PRICE	CODE
29 Reasons Not to Go to Law School	$9.95	29R
Poetic Justice	$9.95	PJ

⌑ Book with disk

◉ Book with CD-ROM

		PRICE	CODE

IMMIGRATION

	PRICE	CODE
How to Get a Green Card: Legal Ways to Stay in the U.S.A.	$24.95	GRN
U.S. Immigration Made Easy	$44.95	IMEZ

MONEY MATTERS

		PRICE	CODE
▣	101 Law Forms for Personal Use (Quick & Legal Series, Book w/disk—PC)	$24.95	SPOT
	Bankruptcy: Is It the Right Solution to Your Debt Problems? (Quick & Legal Series)	$15.95	BRS
	Chapter 13 Bankruptcy: Repay Your Debts	$29.95	CH13
	Credit Repair (Quick & Legal Series)	$15.95	CREP
▣	The Financial Power of Attorney Workbook (Book w/disk—PC)	$24.95	FINPOA
	How to File for Chapter 7 Bankruptcy	$26.95	HFB
	IRAs, 401(k)s & Other Retirement Plans: Taking Your Money Out	$21.95	RET
	Money Troubles: Legal Strategies to Cope With Your Debts	$19.95	MT
	Nolo's Law Form Kit: Personal Bankruptcy	$16.95	KBNK
	Stand Up to the IRS	$24.95	SIRS
	Take Control of Your Student Loans	$19.95	SLOAN

PATENTS AND COPYRIGHTS

		PRICE	CODE
▣	The Copyright Handbook: How to Protect and Use Written Works (Book w/disk—PC)	$29.95	COHA
	Copyright Your Software	$24.95	CYS
	How to Make Patent Drawings Yourself	$29.95	DRAW
	The Inventor's Notebook	$19.95	INOT
▣	License Your Invention (Book w/Disk—PC)	$39.95	LICE
	Patent, Copyright & Trademark	$24.95	PCTM
	Patent It Yourself	$46.95	PAT
	Patent Searching Made Easy	$24.95	PATSE
◉	Software Development: A Legal Guide (Book with CD-ROM)	$44.95	SFT

RESEARCH & REFERENCE

		PRICE	CODE
◉	Government on the Net (Book w/CD-ROM—Windows/Macintosh)	$39.95	GONE
◉	Law on the Net (Book w/CD-ROM—Windows/Macintosh)	$39.95	LAWN
	Legal Research: How to Find & Understand the Law	$24.95	LRES
	Legal Research Made Easy (Video)	$89.95	LRME
	Legal Research Online & in the Library (Book w/CD-ROM—Windows/Macintosh)	$39.95	LRO

SENIORS

	PRICE	CODE
Beat the Nursing Home Trap	$21.95	ELD
The Conservatorship Book (California Edition)	$44.95	CNSV
Social Security, Medicare & Pensions	$21.95	SOA

SOFTWARE

Call or check our website at www.nolo.com for special discounts on Software!

		PRICE	CODE
◉	LeaseWriter CD—Windows/Macintosh	$99.95	LWD1
◉	Living Trust Maker CD—Windows/Macintosh	$79.95	LTD2
◉	Small Business Legal Pro 3 CD—Windows/Macintosh	$79.95	SBCD3
◉	Personal RecordKeeper 5.0 CD—Windows/Macintosh	$59.95	RKD5
◉	Patent It Yourself CD—Windows	$229.95	PPC12
◉	WillMaker 7.0 CD—Windows/Macintosh	$69.95	WMD7

Special Upgrade Offer
Get 25% off the latest edition of your Nolo book

It's important to have the most current legal information. Because laws and legal procedures change often, we update our books regularly. To help keep you up-to-date we are extending this special upgrade offer. Cut out and mail the title portion of the cover of your old Nolo book and we'll give you 25% off the retail price of the NEW EDITION of that book when you purchase directly from us. For more information call us at 1-800-992-6656. This offer is to individuals only.

▣   Book with disk

◉   Book with CD-ROM

ORDER FORM

Code	Quantity	Title	Unit price	Total
		Subtotal		
		California residents add Sales Tax		
		Basic Shipping ($6.50)		
		UPS RUSH delivery $8.00–any size order*		
		TOTAL		

Name

Address

(UPS to street address, Priority Mail to P.O. boxes)   * Delivered in 3 business days from receipt of order.
S.F. Bay Area use regular shipping.

FOR FASTER SERVICE, USE YOUR CREDIT CARD AND OUR TOLL-FREE NUMBERS

Order 24 hours a day	1-800-992-6656
Fax your order	1-800-645-0895
Online	www.nolo.com

METHOD OF PAYMENT

☐ Check enclosed
☐ VISA   ☐ MasterCard   ☐ Discover Card   ☐ American Express

Account #   Expiration Date

Authorizing Signature

Daytime Phone

PRICES SUBJECT TO CHANGE.

VISIT OUR OUTLET STORES!   VISIT US ONLINE!

You'll find our complete line of books and software, all at a discount.

BERKELEY
950 Parker Street
Berkeley, CA 94710
1-510-704-2248

on the Internet
www.nolo.com

NOLO PRESS 950 PARKER ST., BERKELEY, CA 94710

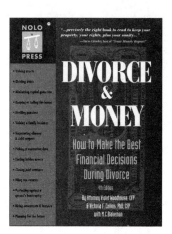

Take 2 Minutes
& Give Us Your 2 cents

Your comments make a big difference in the development and revision of Nolo books and software. Please take a few minutes and register your Nolo product—and your comments—with us. Not only will your input make a difference, you'll receive special offers available only to registered owners of Nolo products on our newest books and software. Register now by:

PHONE
1-800-992-6656

FAX
1-800-645-0895

EMAIL
cs@nolo.com

or **MAIL** us
this registration card

REMEMBER:
Little publishers have big ears. We really listen to you.

fold here

 NOLO

REGISTRATION CARD

PRESS

NAME	DATE
ADDRESS	
CITY	STATE ZIP
PHONE	E-MAIL

WHERE DID YOU HEAR ABOUT THIS PRODUCT?

WHERE DID YOU PURCHASE THIS PRODUCT?

DID YOU CONSULT A LAWYER? (PLEASE CIRCLE ONE)   YES   NO   NOT APPLICABLE

DID YOU FIND THIS BOOK HELPFUL?   (VERY)   5   4   3   2   1   (NOT AT ALL)

COMMENTS

WAS IT EASY TO USE?   (VERY EASY)   5   4   3   2   1   (VERY DIFFICULT)

DO YOU OWN A COMPUTER? IF SO, WHICH FORMAT? (PLEASE CIRCLE ONE)   WINDOWS   DOS   MAC

☐ If you do not wish to receive mailings from these companies, please check this box.
☐ You can quote me in future Nolo Press promotional materials. Daytime phone number _____.

FSBO 4.0

NOLO IN THE NEWS

"Nolo helps lay people perform legal tasks without the aid—or fees—of lawyers."
—USA TODAY

Nolo books are ..."written in plain language, free of legal mumbo jumbo, and spiced with witty personal observations."
—ASSOCIATED PRESS

"...Nolo publications...guide people simply through the how, when, where and why of law."
—WASHINGTON POST

"Increasingly, people who are not lawyers are performing tasks usually regarded as legal work... And consumers, using books like Nolo's, do routine legal work themselves."
—NEW YORK TIMES

"...All of [Nolo's] books are easy-to-understand, are updated regularly, provide pull-out forms...and are often quite moving in their sense of compassion for the struggles of the lay reader."
—SAN FRANCISCO CHRONICLE

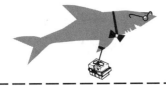

fold here

NOLO

PRESS

NOLO PRESS
950 Parker Street
Berkeley, CA 94710-9867

Attn: FSBO 4.0